Elizabeth Barrett Browning's *Aurora Leigh*

Reading Guides to Long Poems

Published:

John Milton's Paradise Lost: *A Reading Guide*
Noam Reisner
Hbk: 978 0 7486 3999 1
Pbk: 978 0 7486 4000 3

Edmund Spenser's The Faerie Queene: *A Reading Guide*
Andrew Zurcher
Hbk: 978 0 7486 3956 4
Pbk: 978 0 7486 3957 1

Homer's Odyssey: *A Reading Guide*
Henry Power
Hbk: 978 0 7486 4110 9
Pbk: 978 0 7486 4109 3

Alfred Lord Tennyson's In Memoriam: *A Reading Guide*
Anna Barton
Hbk: 978 0 7486 4135 2
Pbk: 978 0 7486 4134 5

Elizabeth Barrett Browning's Aurora Leigh: *A Reading Guide*
Michele C. Martinez
Hbk: 978 0 7486 3971 7
Pbk: 978 0 7486 3972 4

Visit the Reading Guides to Long Poems website at
www.euppublishing.com/series/rglp

Elizabeth Barrett Browning's
Aurora Leigh
A Reading Guide

Michele C. Martinez

EDINBURGH
University Press

© Michele C. Martinez, 2012

Edinburgh University Press Ltd
22 George Square, Edinburgh

www.euppublishing.com

Typeset in 10.5/13 Sabon
by Servis Filmsetting Ltd, Stockport, Cheshire, and
printed and bound in the United States of America
by Edwards Brothers Malloy

A CIP record for this book is available from the British Library

ISBN 978 0 7486 3971 7 (hardback)
ISBN 978 0 7486 3972 4 (paperback)
ISBN 978 0 7486 5441 3 (webready PDF)
ISBN 978 0 7486 5443 7 (epub)
ISBN 978 0 7486 5442 0 (Amazon ebook)

Contents

List of Illustrations

Acknowledgements

This book has benefited greatly from the advice, encouragement and patience of Sally Bushell, to whom I am very grateful. The generosity of Harvard's Fuerbringer Summer Faculty Grant made the completion of the manuscript possible, and I wish to thank Tom Jehn, the Harvard College Writing Program Director, for his warm support.

Ohio University Press kindly granted permission for the generous excerpts from *Aurora Leigh* in the *Guide*. The Browning Settlement courteously gave permission for the portrait illustration by Matilda Carter.

I owe deep thanks to Amanda Mooers, for her assiduous transcription and invaluable personal assistance. This book is affectionately dedicated to my children, Madeline and Jeremy, and my husband, Peter Nohrnberg.

Series Editors' Preface

The form of the long poem has been of fundamental importance to Literary Studies from the time of Homer onwards. The *Reading Guides to Long Poems Series* seek to celebrate and explore this form in all its diversity across a range of authors and periods. Major poetic works – *The Odyssey, The Faerie Queene, Paradise Lost, The Prelude, In Memoriam, The Waste Land* – emerge as defining expressions of the culture which produced them. One of the main aims of the series is to make contemporary readers aware of the importance of the long poem for our literary and national heritage.

How 'long' is a long poem? In 'The Philosophy of Composition' Edgar Allan Poe asserted that there is 'a distinct limit, as regards length, to all works of literary art – the limit of a single sitting'. Defined against this, a long poem must be one which *exceeds* the limit of a single sitting, requiring sustained attention over a considerable period of time for its full appreciation. However, the concept of poetic length is not simply concerned with the number of lines in a poem, or the time it takes to read it. In 'From Poe to Valéry' T. S. Eliot defends poetic length on the grounds that 'it is only in a poem of some length that a variety of moods can be expressed . . . These parts can form a whole more than the sum of the parts; a whole such that the pleasure we derive from the reading of any part is enhanced by our grasp of the whole.' Along with Eliot, the Series Editors believe that poetic length creates a unique space for a varied play of meaning and tone, action and reflection, which results in particular kinds of reading and interpretation not possible for shorter works. The *Reading Guides* are therefore concerned with communicating the pleasure and enjoyment of engaging with the form in a range of ways – focusing on particular episodes, tracing out patterns of poetic imagery, exploring form, reading and re-reading the text – in order to allow the reader to experience the multiple interpretative layers that the long poem holds within it. We also believe that a self-awareness about *how* we read the long poem may help to provide the modern reader with a necessary fresh perspective upon the genre.

The *Reading Guides to Long Poems Series* will engage with major works in new and innovative ways in order to revitalise the form of the long poem for a new generation. The series will present shorter 'long poems' in their entirety, while the longest are represented by a careful selection of essential parts. Long poems have often been read aloud, imitated, or even translated in excerpts, so there is good precedent for appreciating them through selective reading. Nevertheless, it is to be hoped that readers will use the *Guides* alongside an appreciation of the work in its entirety or, if they have not previously done so, go on to read the whole poem.

Ultimately, the *Edinburgh Reading Guides to Long Poems Series* seeks to be of lasting value to the discipline of Literary Studies by revitalising a form which is in danger of being marginalised by the current curriculum but is central to our understanding of our own literature, history and culture.

Sally Bushell with Isobel Armstrong and Colin Burrow

Chapter 1

Mapping and Making the Long Poem: *Aurora Leigh* in its Biographical and Literary Contexts

What form is best for poems? Let me think
Of forms less, and the external. Trust the spirit,
As sovran nature does, to make the form;
For otherwise we only imprison spirit
And not embody.

Aurora Leigh, Book V, lines 223–7

Form and spirit are the essential components of Elizabeth Barrett Browning's poetry, and it is in her masterpiece *Aurora Leigh* that she chose the traditional form of the English epic – blank verse – to embody the modern spirit of the Victorian Age. The pentameter line and freedom from end-rhymes echo the oratorical and conversational cadences of Milton, Wordsworth, Shelley and Tennyson, who are, for EBB,[1] important antecedents. Novelists, such as George Sand, Elizabeth Gaskell and Charlotte Brontë, also inspired *Aurora Leigh*'s exploration of artistic ambition, sexual transgression and spiritual passion. But, before EBB, no poet had put blank verse to work in quite the same way as she: for while *Aurora Leigh* sings in the classical and Miltonic sense of being divinely inspired, the poem also offers a multiplicity of contemporary voices debating and protesting, reporting and reflecting, coveting and desiring. Challenging any attempt to categorise it simply, *Aurora Leigh* has a plot and cast of characters that resemble a novel's or a play's, and a narrative voice that is intensely lyrical and visionary. In its narrative complexity and energy, *Aurora Leigh* is a long poem of enduring fascination to twenty-first-century readers.

During its composition, EBB adopted the term 'novel-poem'[2] to encompass its variety of literary modes and subgenres, as well as its range of subject matter. While primarily an autobiographical memoir, or *Künstlerroman* ('artist-novel'), it also contains elements of epistolary fiction, epic quest, reform essay, *ars poetica*, topographical poem, amatory verse and devotional lyric. The variety that characterises *Aurora Leigh*'s form might suggest confusion, yet its narrator – the title character – speaks in a clear, passionate and often humorous voice expressing ideas and feelings still relevant to today's readers. The central questions of the poem are: how does one become an artist? Is art purely a vehicle for personal or philosophical expression? Can it be part of a social mission, bridging the gap between rich and poor? Can art help victims of abuse, injustice and stigma? Is it necessary to repudiate domesticity and marriage in the pursuit of a higher calling? To answer these questions, *Aurora Leigh* stages serious arguments, which, as its narrator matures, are revised and modified. While learning some hard lessons from her life experiences, Aurora never loses her conviction that poetry is vitally relevant to society.

Whether it was EBB's breakthrough success in the mid-1840s that sparked her interest in writing a long poem or her lifelong admiration of Homer (*Iliad* and *Odyssey*) and later writers of epic-length poems, such as Dante (*The Divine Comedy*), Milton (*Paradise Lost*) and Byron (*Don Juan*), she expressed a desire to write:

> a poem of a new class, in a measure—a Don Juan, without the mockery & impurity, . . under one aspect,—& having unity, as a work of art,—& admitting of as much philosophical dreaming & digression (which is in fact a characteristic of the age) as I like to use.[3]

What EBB describes is the conception of her great long poem, *Aurora Leigh*, which she would compose over the next eleven years and finally publish in November 1856. Transforming the character of Byron's 1820s errant womaniser–traveller (though not losing completely his satirical edge), EBB creates an Anglo-Italian female protagonist, who recounts the story of her life up to the moment she becomes a critically successful poet and finds amatory fulfilment. While quasi-autobiographical in its story of a woman's self-made path to authorship, the first-person narrator's 'philosophical dreaming and digression' into social questions is polemical. There is a sense that the protagonist is 'rushing into drawing rooms and the like, "where angels fear to tread"; and so, meeting face to face and without mask the Humanity of the age'.[4] EBB not only invests her title protagonist with all the narrative gusto she herself possessed but also confronts specific social problems that were the subjects of her ballads and lyrics: urban poverty, sexual exploitation and women's work. Motherhood is a central topic and trope in the text as well, reflecting EBB's own experience (after three miscarriages) in successfully bearing a son, Robert Wiedemann Barrett Browning, known fondly as

'Pen'. But as much as Aurora is a novelistic commentator on her own life and time, she is, above all, a visionary poet seeking to 'keep up open roads / Betwixt the seen and unseen [. . .] to prove what lies beyond / Both speech and imagination'.[5] Thus, in addition to being a work of fictional autobiography and social criticism, *Aurora Leigh* explores the mind's capacity for aesthetic apprehension and spiritual contemplation: modes of perception and thought that illuminate beauty and offer hope to readers dejected or damaged by the harshness of everyday life.

In the context of the Victorian triple-decker novel and other contemporary long poems, *Aurora Leigh*'s length may not seem unusual. But with approximately 11,000 lines divided into nine books, Barrett Browning's magnum opus is 2,000 lines longer than Milton's *Paradise Lost*, 4,000 lines longer than Wordsworth's *The Prelude* (1850) and 9,000 lines longer than Tennyson's *In Memoriam* (1850). Even Victorian readers were surprised by the length and girth of the poem and alternately delighted or repulsed by its conversational tone, prodigious learning and edgy subject matter. Critics, such as the novelist George Eliot, felt that the poem itself lived and breathed like a person: 'its melody, fancy, imagination—what we may call its poetical *body*—is everywhere informed by a *soul*, namely by genuine thought and feeling'.[6] The fact that the poetical body is female and rather frank about her mind and heart disturbed the Scottish critic W. E. Aytoun: 'The extreme independence of Aurora detracts from the feminine charm, and mars the interest which we otherwise might have felt in so intellectual a heroine.'[7] In contrast, John Ruskin, the great Victorian art theorist, educator and collector, thought the poem was brilliant: 'I like it *all*, familiar parts and unfamiliar, passionate and satirical, evil telling and good telling, philosophical and dramatic—all.'[8] That a woman – largely self-educated and often in poor health – produced a poem as powerfully embodied and voiced as those by the Poet Laureate Tennyson prompts most readers to wonder just how she did it.

Biographical Account

First-time readers of *Aurora Leigh* frequently want to know how much of the narrative is based on the author's life and how much is fiction. Is there a correlation between poet and protagonist such as there is between EBB and the passionate speaker of *Sonnets from the Portuguese* (1850), which were penned for Robert Browning but not published until after their marriage? Elizabeth Barrett Moulton Barrett (1806–61) was born in County Durham to Mary Graham Clarke and Edward

Moulton-Barrett and spent her childhood at a residence adorned with turrets and minarets, called Hope End, near Ledbury, Herefordshire.[9] She was the eldest child in a family of eleven, whose upbringing reflected the prosperity of her parents' Jamaican plantation holdings.[10] Exempt from the domestic cares that might be expected of an eldest daughter, EBB was, by the time she was nine years old, regarded as the '*Poet Laureat of Hope-End*', an epithet her adoring father bestowed for 'some lines on virtue'.[11] At this tender age, she had also begun reading Greek history, English and Scottish poetry, Shakespeare's plays and Pope's translation of Homer's *Iliad*. In two autobiographical reminiscences, 'Glimpses into My Own Life and Literary Character' (c. 1820–1) and an untitled essay (c. 1840), EBB declares that, by the time she was eleven, 'she wished to be considered an authoress' and 'the feminine of Homer'.[12] The comments reflect the burgeoning poet's unusually capacious education, which her parents encouraged, as they also oversaw the formal schooling of their second child and eldest son, Edward, whom EBB affectionately called 'Bro'. The account of Aurora Leigh's upbringing in Books I and II rehearses the paternal encouragement to read the classics, as well as EBB's own self-motivated learning.

Separated in age by only fifteen months and bound by strong affections, Bro and 'Ba' (as she was known to him and her other siblings) shared complementary temperaments and a mutual love of learning. So involved were their lives that between 1817 and 1820 the two shared a classics tutor, Daniel McSwiney, until Bro was sent to Charterhouse for formal schooling. Despite her brother's departure, EBB kept up her Latin and Greek studies through letters with him and McSwiney, developing a deep passion for the latter language. EBB's love of Greek may have been inspired by her affection for Byron's poetry, and she carried the torch of his nationalist cause into later life.[13] Yet her passion for reading, translating and composing was tempered by physical afflictions that began in the first year of Bro's absence. She suffered from severe headaches and muscular convulsions, an ailment that baffled her doctors and for which she was prescribed opium for the first time in 1821.[14] EBB's fragile health persisted throughout her life, and it came to be that opiate drugs were a source of great relief and (during her child-bearing years) profound sorrow.

Illness may have slowed EBB's productivity at times but not enough to prevent her from composing short plays and prose compositions, as well as lyric and narrative poetry. In 1820 her father privately printed *The Battle of Marathon*, four books of heroic couplets that dramatically recount the military triumph of Athens over Persian invasion in the fifth century BC. This historical narrative is followed by the first poems EBB published in a periodical – *The New Monthly Magazine* of 1821 – which were on the subject of modern-day Greek liberty. But EBB did not limit her studies to Greece alone and in 1824 began work on a poem that demonstrated the wide range of her reading and learning: *An Essay on Mind, with Other Poems*, published in London in 1826. Written in the heroic couplet style of the verse essay, the poem contemplates the operations of the mind, drawing on eighteenth-century metaphysics, and then turns to the mind's inventions, particularly philosophy, historiography and poetry. While *The Battle of Marathon* and *An Essay on Mind* reflect EBB's substantial reading in history and philosophy, the contents of the 1826 volume also display EBB's gifts as a lyric and dramatic poet. Composed in a variety of English stanza forms, most of the poems commemorate individuals whose lives or work impressed her, including her father, Edward Moulton-Barrett, her brothers Bro, Septimus and 'Stormy', Lord Byron, the Spanish widow–patriot, Teresa del Riego, and the Greek poet–patriot, Rigas Feraios.

EBB's range of verse forms and subject matter is reflected in Aurora Leigh's own résumé, of which she is both proud and critical. She enumerates her lyric and narrative experiments – both successful and not – in Book I, lines 942 to 1002; Book III, lines 204 to 250, 306 to 343; and Book V, lines 84 to 134. Her success with a long poem comes in Book VII, lines 551 to 564. We never learn the subject of the poem, except that the author claims to 'have written truth' (line 749). As noted above, EBB began her career translating Greek poetry and then turned to didactic poetry, as well as popular ballads and romances. She did not achieve her first major transatlantic success until she was thirty-eight, with *Poems* (1844). At the time of writing her verse memoir and achieving her first major critical success, Aurora Leigh is supposed to be twenty-six or twenty-seven. Compressing her protagonist's career into a shorter time frame, EBB deflects an exact correspondence between their writing lives.

Unlike her author, Aurora has no siblings. For EBB, Bro's departure for school was a traumatic separation. Yet his absence also led to wider intellectual cultivation and poetic development. Confident in her knowledge of the classics, yet yearning for more regular intellectual commerce, EBB was delighted to receive praise on *An Essay on Mind* by the classics scholar and landscape theorist Uvedale Price, with whom she began a lively correspondence on the subject of Greek pronunciation. In the next two decades EBB maintained several (mainly epistolary) friendships that fostered her knowledge of ancient Greek and broadened her fame as a poet. The first was with another Greek scholar, a neighbour of the

Barrett family named Hugh Stuart Boyd, who, like Mr Price, cultivated EBB's acquaintance after reading and admiring *An Essay on Mind*.

Despite the fact that the two did not meet for over a year (EBB thought that her visiting his home might not be deemed appropriate), Boyd's epistolary friendship expanded EBB's taste for Greek drama and poetry. When EBB finally did visit him at home, he introduced her to the Greek Christian poets, particularly his translations of Gregory of Nazianzus and Synesius of Cyrene. For years, EBB read and discussed Boyd's works with him, and in 1841 *The Athenaeum* offered her the chance to publish four essays on his beloved subject. With great authority, enthusiasm and wit, EBB published in 1842 her critical discussions of Gregory, Synesius and eighteen others – collectively titled 'Some Account of the Greek Christian Poets'. While expressing some regret that these 'meek heroic Christians' cannot 'be crowned with a true complete poet's name', she finds their humility, vehemence and eloquence worth conveying to a modern audience (*Works* IV. 369).

As EBB looked to Boyd for comfort and distraction from many personal trials – the death of her mother in 1828 and her grandmother in 1829, and the sale of Hope End in 1832 due to financial losses in Jamaica – she also began publishing ballads in literary magazines and annuals and her first poetry collection *Prometheus Bound Translated from the Greek of Aeschylus, and Miscellaneous Poems* (1833) and *The Seraphim, and Other Poems* (1838). The Barrett family moved permanently away from Herefordshire in 1832 for financial reasons and EBB's health, but physical distance did not diminish her and Boyd's epistolary connection. With the wider publication of her poetry, however, EBB also acquired new correspondents and intimates, especially her cousin, John Kenyon (to whom *Aurora Leigh* is warmly dedicated), Mary Russell Mitford, Benjamin Robert Haydon, Anna Brownell Jameson, Richard Hengist Horne, and finally Robert Browning. These and siblings who dared to marry and move away (much to Edward Moulton-Barrett's disapproval) displaced Boyd as interlocutors in EBB's emotional and intellectual life.

While modern poets and novelists were as important as ancient authors to EBB, she expressed her gratitude to and rivalry with Boyd – as a translator and ostensibly Homeric poet – in the sonnet sequence 'To Hugh Stuart Boyd' and the occasional poem 'The Wine of Cyprus'. These poems foreground her friend's blindness from ophthalmia in his early thirties and represent his disability as a source of divine insight. Boyd was an important influence on *Aurora Leigh*; their warm, erudite correspondence is a source of the poem's more obscure classical references, and Boyd's blindness most certainly influenced the fate of Romney Leigh as much as Brontë's Rochester did. Both Boyd and Romney's blindness is integral to the two poets' roles as 'seers' in both the literal and oracular sense.[15]

The 1830s and 1840s were a time of unsettling personal transition and startling literary productivity for EBB. Several life-altering events steered a new course for the poet and contributed to the making of her transatlantic literary celebrity. In July 1840 EBB received news that her beloved Bro had drowned while sailing with a friend in Tor Bay. The shock of his death coincided with a precipitous decline in her health, which was quite serious for the rest of the year. In an attempt to lift her spirits, EBB's intimate correspondent, Mary Russell Mitford, gave her a spaniel puppy, Flush, who would become the poet's close companion (and in England the object of dog-napping) for the next thirteen years. EBB met Mitford, who was a prose fiction writer and periodical editor, in 1836 through her cousin and unofficial literary agent, John Kenyon, the man who introduced EBB to important members of London's literary establishment and eventually to her suitor, Robert Browning.

The years leading up to Bro's tragic death were immensely productive and saw the beginnings of EBB's literary celebrity. Her lyric drama on angels who witnessed Christ's sacrifice, called *The Seraphim*, received wide critical acknowledgement, and her ballads and occasional verse – contributed mainly to literary annuals and periodicals – appealed greatly to popular and erudite readers alike. Although EBB's illness and withdrawal in this period stoked the public perception of her as a bookish angel with a pen, her poetry engaged with social and political concerns of the day. Until 21 September 1846, the day EBB's marriage to Robert Browning was announced in *The Times* and other newspapers, her literary promoters and even her family had perpetuated the iconic image of an ethereal, seraphic EBB.

The other significant life-altering event of these decades was EBB's introduction to fellow poet Robert Browning in January 1845. Their secretive eighteen-month courtship, staged mostly in letters and occasional visits, resulted in a private marriage ceremony and the removal of their new household from England to Florence, Italy. The southern destination was chosen for its salutary weather, expatriate Anglophone artist circles and distance from the wrath of EBB's father, who irrationally disapproved of marriage for any of his offspring. Defying patriarchal injunction, braving continental travel as a semi-invalid and leaving behind her beloved siblings and familiar London, EBB embarked upon this adventure, with the assistance of the art writer and social critic

Anna Brownell Jameson, who herself knew the perils and joys of continental travel from her excursions to Europe's great art cities. Virtually overnight, the nature of EBB's celebrity shifted from hermit-like poetess to romantic, visionary heroine, and her poetry in this and the last full decade of her life only supported that shift in her public persona.

While the 1840s were, for EBB, a mixture of psychic turmoil (as an estranged daughter, bereft sister and thwarted mother) and womanly fulfilment (as a wife, poet and, with the birth of her son in 1849, a mother), her poetry was galvanised by Anglo-American reform movements and European revolutionary foment. To periodicals and magazines, EBB contributed protest poems on the subject of factory and child labour ('The Cry of the Human' [1842], 'The Cry of the Children' [1844]) and abolitionism ('The Runaway Slave at Pilgrim's Point' [1848]). Over several years she composed a verse narrative about witnessing the cause of Italian liberty unfold on the streets of Florence outside her house (*Casa Guidi Windows* [1851]). In 1844 the eminent publisher Edward Moxon published a two-volume edition of her collected verse entitled *Poems*, which sealed her reputation as a major literary figure and included the verse play, *A Drama of Exile*, in which Eve is a powerfully voluble figure of grief and redemption. *A Drama of Exile* reflects EBB's feminist belief, which was advocated by many of her female associates of the time, including Anna Jameson, that women's voices deserve to be heard and female suffering and self-sacrifice should not be either taken for granted or deemed socially acceptable. In 1850 Chapman and Hall reissued the 1844 collection along with a host of new ballads and lyrics, which had previously appeared in periodicals, as well as the lyric sequence *Sonnets from the Portuguese*, and revised versions of *The Seraphim* and *Prometheus Bound*. Upon the death of Wordsworth in April 1850, the critic Henry Chorley in *The Athenaeum* nominated EBB to be his successor as the Poet Laureate. Although Alfred Tennyson earned that honour a few months later, Chorley was the first critic ever to suggest publicly a female candidate.

It would seem that EBB had reached the pinnacle of her fame and might be satisfied with her success in the 1840s. Yet during that decade she tirelessly composed and vastly expanded her novel-poem *Aurora Leigh*. EBB's life as an expatriate artist in Italy informs the poem's setting: Aurora's Tuscany is EBB's, although she omits much of her own sociability from Aurora's character. Also, missing from Aurora's narrative is the seething political turmoil surrounding Italian unification, a movement to which EBB was passionately committed. Instead, the Arno Valley with its sublime sunsets, Tuscany's Edenic flora and fauna, the pious, gossiping *donne* – these scenic details pervade the latter books of *Aurora Leigh*, capturing the region's bounty, colour and charm. Like many an English expatriate, EBB regarded Italy as a 'motherland', welcoming to a middle-class, Protestant woman and her eclectic circle of friends and eliding national differences among them.[16]

While she spent some years correcting and revising *Aurora Leigh* following its initial publication in December 1856, EBB continued to publish poetry in periodicals and produced one more volume during her lifetime, *Poems Before Congress* (1860), and a collected volume, *Last Poems* (1862), which was issued the year after her death. *Poems Before Congress* is her most overtly political collection, containing a preface that attacks Britain for 'non-intervention' in the fate of a 'neighbour' struggling to become an independent republic. The book title refers to an eagerly anticipated transnational congress on Italy, which failed to take place in January 1860, and the cause of Italian liberation preoccupies the volume. EBB's most scathing indictment of American slavery, 'A Curse for a Nation', closes the collection, a jeremiad that incited previously favourable critics to accuse her of meddling in affairs where women should not.

Last Poems offers a window into the range of EBB's lyric interests (as well as some of her translations of Greek and Latin literature) and extends the strain of vehement feeling about Italian politics to other topics (to cite Dorothy Mermin's concise list): 'maternity, femininity, sexuality, and death'.[17] With considerable self-possession and outspoken bitterness, the poems portray, among other speakers, an abandoned mother ('Void in Law'), an aristocratic adulteress ('Lord Walter's Wife') and a bereft Italian patriot–mother ('Mother and Poet'). The much-anthologised 'A Musical Instrument' exposes the sexual violence suppressed in retellings of a myth – Ovid's Pan and Syrinx from *Metamorphoses* – commonly used to represent poetic creativity. One of the most painful lyrics is 'De Profundis,' which was written in the wake of Bro's death in 1840 but possessed new meaning for EBB in 1860 to 1861 with the deaths of her dear friend Anna Jameson (March 1860), her beloved sister Henrietta (November 1860) and the Piedmontese minister, Camillo di Cavour (June 1861), whom EBB viewed as critical in achieving Italy's independence from Austria. The poem expresses world-weariness and despondency, but the speaker ultimately finds consolation in the parallel between her own trial-of-days-on-end and that of Christ's. The concluding simile is both wistful and profound, reflecting with childlike wonder on the mystery of death: 'as a child drops his pebble small / Down some deep well, and hears it fall / Smiling—so

I [...].'[18] Only two weeks after Cavour passed away, EBB suffered a major decline in her health and, 'cradled in [her husband's] arms', died from burst abscesses in her lungs.[19]

EBB is buried in the Protestant Cemetery, Florence, amid a constellation of English poets who died in exile: Shelley, Keats, Clough and Landor among them. In honour of his friend and compatriot, the English artist Frederic Leighton designed a significant grave marker: a marble sarcophagus, raised on six columns and adorned on each side with a bas-relief medallion, depicting a laurelled woman (Poetry), a celestial harp (devotional verse), an ancient lyre (classical verse) and an Italian lute (political poetry). The tomb's elevated, monumental design is reminiscent of Petrarch's in Arquà. In addition to the grave monument, EBB's former home, Casa Guidi, functions as a small museum devoted to the life and work of the Brownings, as well as a *pensione* to visitors. It is fitting that the neoclassical monument and modern guesthouse should represent two sides of EBB's character: the devoted classicist and hostess to friends of many nations.

Aurora Leigh's Genesis and Major Influences

As letters to John Kenyon and Mary Russell Mitford attest, the genesis of *Aurora Leigh* seems to have taken place in the autumn and winter of 1844. To both her cousin and her friend, she expresses the desire to write 'a poem comprehending the aspect and manners of modern life and flinching at nothing of the conventional' and 'a sort of novel-poem [...] not too complex, and admitting of high application'.[20] When Mitford suggests Napoleon as a possible subject for such a work, EBB responds with a fuller account of what she means:

> No—I am afraid of Napoleon for a subject: & also it w^d. not I fancy, suit me [...] I don't want to have to do with masses of men, I sh^d. make dull work of it so. A few characters—a simple story—& plenty of room for passion & thought—that is what I want .. & am not likely to find easily .. without your inspiration. [...] I want to write a poem of a new class, in a measure—a Don Juan, without the mockery and impurity ... under one aspect, —& having unity, as a work of art, —& admitting of as much philosophical dreaming & digression (which is in fact a characteristic of the age) as I like use. Might it not be done, even if I could not do it? & think of trying at any rate.[21]

Mitford seems to sense the epic nature of EBB's ambition and, based on her knowledge of EBB's passionate feelings about the larger-than-life Napoleon Bonaparte, the latter seems to be a suitable topic. On the question of the French Emperor's character, EBB was in some agreement with Thomas Carlyle, who, in *On Heroes, Hero-Worship, and the Heroic in History* (1841), represents Napoleon as a vain, power-hungry man but also a charismatic, inspiring leader.[22] He sees the General's suppression of anarchy in the Revolution's first phase as a triumph and believes that he deserved the admiration of his men. But Carlyle also perceives a 'charlatan-element' in Napoleon's character and argues that it got the better of him once he crowned himself Emperor of France.[23] Mitford might have thought the self-contradictions of this not-so-distant historical figure worth exploring in a major poem, especially since EBB had published a powerful verse reflection on imperial ambition called 'Napoleon's Return' (later retitled 'Crowned and Buried') in *The Athenaeum* of 4 July 1840.

The occasion of transferring Napoleon's ashes from St Helena to Paris had prompted EBB's verse overview of the Emperor's stunning military victories, his compromised republican ideals and the consequences of his 1814 abdication, which restored royal power to France's other newly proclaimed republics. The poem might have stopped there, but its epic interest emerges in the fate and significance of Napoleon's ashes, which were interred on the British-ruled isle of St Helena from the time of his death in 1821 until 1840. As in Homer's *Iliad* and Sophocles' *Electra*, EBB's narrator thinks that the remains of a military leader are owed the respect of repatriation and burial, according to his nation's custom, and funerary rites serve as a form of peacemaking. In a dialogue between France and England, the latter declares that where Napoleon is buried, so should be 'all former strifes twixt thee and me'.[24] She sympathetically imagines Paris to be a tearful Electra welcoming the funeral urn of her brother, and the arrival of Napoleon's ashes in Paris to be a kind of last triumphal march. Yet while EBB vehemently condemns Napoleonic despotism in the poem, she also seems to admire the Emperor's 'genius to be loved'.[25] 'Crowned and Buried' recognises Napoleon's epic heroism, his *kleos*, but the narrator ultimately leaves it to the 'angels' to discern 'whether / The crowned Napoleon or the buried clay / Be worthier'.[26]

In rejecting a world-famous military figure as the subject of her novel-poem, EBB turned to what she knew: her own life story and those of other women. While not strictly autobiographical in the poem's plot, *Aurora Leigh*'s intellectual and emotional life draws heavily on the author's, particularly her classical education, aesthetic and political views, reclusive, passionate temperament and epistolary sociability. Critics have noted Aurora's resemblance to other female poets of the period and argued that aspects of her narrative echo the stories of other women artists.[27] In other words, EBB displaced Napoleon's rise to power with a woman's journey from ordinary life to literary fame. Such a substitution can also be seen in Charlotte Brontë's *Villette* (1853), which focuses not on the Napoleonic Monsieur Paul but on the aspiring teacher–performer Lucy Snowe.

Although EBB never formally called *Aurora Leigh* an epic, critics have enumerated and scrutinised its relationship to classical, Romantic and Victorian forms of that genre.[28] The poem's prodigious line-length, division into symmetrical books, central protagonist who journeys and struggles towards a goal, and use of epic conventions such as the catalogue, invocation, simile, mythological allusion, prophecy and *in medias res* beginning all point to EBB's engagement with epic predecessors. The literary scholar Herbert Tucker has identified the protagonist's intensity of feeling and the presence of 'fluent imagery' to be a form of 'somatic epic machinery connecting sensation to purpose, "flesh" to the "sacrament of souls" (5.15–16), "physics" to a "larger metaphysics" (6.206–7)'.[29] He argues that *Aurora Leigh* is the pinnacle production of a 'spasmodic' development in epic, which took place in the first half of the nineteenth century and which EBB associates with female physicality and desire.[30] Tucker's analysis dovetails with an earlier feminist essay, which had identified EBB's redefinition of the 'heroic' in 'female terms'.[31] The fact that her protagonist is a modern rather than mythological woman and a poet rather than a wife does not diminish EBB's engagement with Homer, particularly the *Odyssey*, which features a homesick protagonist on an eventful journey from Troy to Ithaca, seeking his family after a ten-year exile. Aurora's origins in and return to Italy suggest a similar kind of *nostos*, or 'homecoming'. Furthermore, as the orphan protagonist finds herself struggling to stay afloat amid life's currents, the poem is awash in metaphors of swimming and being shipwrecked, as well as allusions to Odysseus' homecoming.[32]

To make an epic hero out of an orphaned Anglo-Italian girl is to suggest a plot perhaps more novelistic than epic.[33] *Aurora Leigh*'s resemblance to other *Bildungs-* and *Künstlerromane*, such as Germaine de Staël's *Corinne, or Italy*, Charlotte Brontë's *Jane Eyre*, Charles Kingsley's *Alton Locke* and Elizabeth Gaskell's *Ruth* is certainly no accident. EBB read novels voraciously, and the writer she admired over all others was George Sand, for whom she wrote two dedicatory sonnets and who may have inspired the name of her protagonist.[34] The fact that EBB preferred the hybrid term 'novel-poem' for *Aurora Leigh* suggests the extent to which prose fiction influenced her work. In identifying the connection between the novel and epic, Marjorie Stone has argued that *Aurora Leigh* is:

> a particularly striking example of what Bakhtin terms the 'novelized' epic. [. . .] When the epic is novelized, the world is brought into a 'zone of maximal contact with the present'; its style becomes 'dialogized', reflecting a 'multilanguaged consciousness' that disrupts epic stylization with parody and self-parody; and reverence for a valorized, past world of national heroes is replaced by familiarization and laughter.[35]

As a form of 'novelized epic', *Aurora Leigh* unapologetically takes contemporary life as its subject and creates a dialogue between epic and the novel. Classical, Christian and Romantic epic poetry was strongly associated with masculine spheres of action, be it martial (Homer, Virgil), theological (Dante, Milton) or philosophical (Wordsworth). EBB takes care to demonstrate the capacity of her feminine subject, the Victorian woman artist, not only to engage with these purportedly masculine disciplines but also to incorporate the domestic and social spheres, which were typically the subject of novels by women and other reform-minded writers. Epic style is recognisable in *Aurora Leigh*'s form, conventions and allusions, and is less a parody than a pastiche.[36] However, when it comes to reverence for the 'national heroes' of past epics, Aurora explicitly rejects that stance: 'All actual heroes are essential men, / And all men possible heroes.'[37] By virtue of her role as narrator and protagonist, Aurora implicitly extends that claim to heroines as well.

Education, courtship, labour, poverty and authorship constitute the life stories of Aurora Leigh and her counterpart, Marian Erle, yet, like Wordsworth in *The Prelude* (1850), Aurora relates these incidents with an eye to the disposition of her own mind and soul, her intellectual and moral development. As Chris Vanden Bossche has noted, *The Prelude* possesses epic's circular journey from exile to home but relocates the journey from an Edenic setting strongly associated with childhood to a New Jerusalem accessed by the poet through artistic vision and endeavour. Both Aurora's and Wordsworth's versions of Eden are characterised by a close identification with nature (in Italy's Tuscan hills and England's Lake District, respectively) and exile, a result of education and socialisation.[38] Both narrators experience personal crises amid the failure of a social revolution (for Aurora Christian socialism, for Wordsworth the French Revolution) and both overcome their crises through the achievement of 'transcendent vision'.[39]

The parallels to and echoes of *The Prelude* are pervasive in *Aurora Leigh*, and of the poets of his generation, EBB regarded Wordsworth as a great poet 'in the proper sense of greatness, the profounder thinker, the nearer to the poetic secrets of nature, more universal, more elevated, more full & consistent in his own poetic individuality—& more influential for good upon the literature of his country and age' than his younger contemporary George Gordon, Lord Byron.[40] But in citing Byron's *Don Juan* (1819–24) as a model for *Aurora Leigh* in her 1844 letter to Mary Russell Mitford, EBB expresses her preference for a different kind of poet. Certainly, both writers created cosmopolitan subjects, capable of traveling between private and public spheres and commenting on events transpiring in both.[41]

In an 1842 letter to Hugh Stuart Boyd, EBB expressed her admiration for Byron's poetic innovation and modernity: 'he was a great and wonderful poet—passionate—eloquent—witty—with all powers of swift allusion and sarcasm and satire—full and rapid in the mechanical resources of his art, and capable of a sufficient and brilliant conveyance of philosophic thought and argument'.[42] Like Byron's conversational narrator, EBB preferred a freewheeling mode of discursive poetry capable of switching the gears of philosophical and imaginative thought to realistic description, lyric flights, classical allusion and satirical observation,[43] although in a later letter she claims to disavow Byron's 'mockery and impurity', thinking (perhaps) of many an English periodical reviewer's response to the Don's scathing wit, political invective and illicit sexuality.[44] Yet *Aurora Leigh* possesses elements of all three: the poem contains many instances of social satire, aimed like *Don Juan* at the pretension and prejudice of the privileged classes, and a sympathetic subplot involving a so-called fallen woman and her child.[45] On political matters Aurora abides by a Whig, reformist platform but in a self-determined rather than collective capacity. Her narration offers a vehement critique of what EBB perceives to be the limits of socialism, particularly the repression of individual action and will to the demands of a homogenised group.[46]

The genesis of the first draft of *Aurora Leigh* has been traced to a notebook dated 1853, but Margaret Reynolds surmises that EBB began writing in it prior to that year, possibly as early as 1846.[47] According to Reynolds, serious commitment to the text, however, did not begin until 'early in 1853, after the Brownings' return from an extended journey to England and France, which had lasted from May 1851 to November 1852'.[48] There is a draft manuscript of the poem (Wellesley), as well as numerous manuscript scraps, dispersed upon the death of EBB's son, which show further work on the poem. The scrap-work, according to Reynolds, comprised a form of pre-writing and manuscript checking, which allowed EBB to consolidate what she wrote in the draft. The poet's productive summer with the manuscript is reflected in a July 1853 letter to her brother George: 'my poem is growing heavy on my hands—& will be considerably longer than the "Princess" when finished. I mean it to be beyond all question my best work—only intention does not always act itself out in evidence.'[49] Keeping Tennyson's satirical long poem on women's education, *The Princess* (1847), in mind as a benchmark, EBB thinks she is close to finishing the manuscript. However, she continued to work on *Aurora Leigh* for the next three years, charting assiduously the line length of her poem in her correspondence.

Why should EBB care to compete with Tennyson's *The Princess*, which was subtitled 'A Medley' and, in a serio-comic spirit, addressed the controversial topic of women's university education? For one thing, *The Princess* is a long poem that explores several contemporary issues that EBB was developing in the manuscript of her yet-to-be-named novel-poem: women's intellectual autonomy, gynocentric community, the compatibility of love and learning, the interplay between lyric song and epic narrative, and the relationship between romance and realist modes. Second, EBB recognised the poem's mixed gender politics, which seem to advocate equality between the sexes and undermine that idea in subtle ways. So, for example, while the university plot, which takes place in a medieval setting, lies at the heart of Tennyson's poem, its modern telling by a group of male undergraduates, celebrating a festival day on an ancient Victorian estate, results in a kind of mock-epic account, complete with similes, catalogues and other conventions. And although the proto-feminist Lilia, a sister of one of the storytellers, incites her brother and his friends to recount the 'poetess' Princess Ida's short-lived establishment of a women's college, the poem undercuts Lilia's ideal by according narrative authority to the men and the occasional lyric moments to the women.[50] In *Aurora Leigh*, EBB reverses Tennyson's gendered narrative structure, giving Aurora complete authorial control over her story. As the narrator, she chooses the target of mock-heroic sentiment and composes the numerous instances of lyric in her text, which she deploys as a mode not of feminine but of spiritual expression.

Thus, while the two poems seem to possess a different gender politics of genre, they do share an ideal of male-female partnership in love and social reform. Princess Ida and Prince Ralph do not abandon Ida's university project, only her restrictive no-men-on-campus policy.[51] And Lilia, who appears to be merely a listener for much of the storytelling, adorns a 'broken statue' of Prince Ralph with 'a scarf of orange' and 'a rosy silk', putting forth a vision of her ancestor as a cross-dressed hero.[52] *Aurora Leigh* reaches a similar denouement: the protagonist and her suitor Romney pledge to be married partners in the service of God and Art, and Aurora takes charge of Romney's care, for he has been blinded in a fire that destroyed the Leigh ancestral home. As Romney basks in the warm glow of Aurora's affections, he, like the statue of Ralph, appears to be a broken man dependent on his female partner's vision.

In December 1855, EBB began transcribing the parts of the poem she considered finished into fair copy (Harvard), and her husband Robert began reading it. He had already arranged for an English publisher, Chapman and Hall, and finalised an agreement with an American one, C. S. Francis. Through the first few months of 1856, Browning encouraged EBB to continue transcribing and expanding the poem. Adding to her workload was Chapman and Hall's suggestion that a new, three-volume edition of EBB's *Poems* should be brought out, including a revised version of *Casa Guidi Windows*. EBB managed to complete these revisions, as well as compose the final sections of *Aurora Leigh*, which stretched out to nine books by June 1856. In August the fair copy was sent to the typesetter for proofs, and while the Brownings visited London and spent time with EBB's ailing cousin John Kenyon on the Isle of Wight, they worked arduously on revisions and corrections. By October proofs of the poem were nearly finished, and EBB wrote the title-page dedication to John Kenyon, who died just over a year later in 1857.[53] She and Robert returned to Florence by the end of that month, after an absence of nearly a year. On 1 November, Chapman and Hall published the fourth edition of *Poems* in two volumes, and on the 15th *Aurora Leigh* appeared simultaneously in England and America with the post-date of 1857. The poem sold so well that Chapman and Hall issued a second of impression at the end of January.

Aurora Leigh went through five editions during EBB's lifetime, the fourth being the last one she corrected and revised herself. According to Reynolds, EBB was not entirely satisfied with the fourth edition, published in June 1859, and had left behind a list of unincorporated corrections.[54] Although EBB was uneasy about the text, she recognised the public's desire for another edition of *Aurora Leigh* and more biographical details about the author. The 1859 edition is unusual for its inclusion of an engraved frontispiece portrait, depicting a three-quarter-length view of EBB standing sideways before a writing table. Framed by her long, black curls, EBB's face looks out at the reader with a mixed expression of modesty and directness. The engraving, which was overseen by Dante Gabriel Rossetti, is based on an 1858 photograph taken in Le Havre, France, and certainly offers an improved likeness, eliding all signs of EBB's current age and recent illness. Most importantly, the portrait captures the youth, determination and intelligence of EBB's protagonist, whose quest for artistic perfection, like the author's, was ongoing even at the height of her fame.[55]

Summary of the Poem

Although *Aurora Leigh* is written in blank verse, a form typically associated with the martial deeds of epic, the philosophical observations of the verse essay or the chattiness of the familiar epistle, its central subject is the life of a woman writer. Prior to *Aurora Leigh*, Wordsworth's *The Prelude* had used the form in an autobiographical manner, but EBB's innovation was to fictionalise her account. Aurora should not be confused with EBB, even if aspects of her history are strikingly similar. Critics have noted Aurora's resemblance to fictional heroines as well as real-life acquaintances and observed that it is Marian who possesses EBB's heavy, dark locks and not the golden-curled Aurora.[56]

Book I

The narrator Aurora begins with a short justification of her project ('I who have written much in prose and verse / For others' uses, will write now for mine') and then commences with her history, starting with early childhood.[57] She remembers (as best she can) her Italian mother, who dies when she is scarcely four years old, and her father, 'an austere Englishman', who raises the child in the Tuscan hills. Their loyal servant Assunta keeps domestic order for the bereaved family and adores her small charge. Of her childhood, Aurora recounts her filial attachment to nature and her father's mournful but affectionate disposition, as he educated her 'out of books'.[58] We learn that, before his death when Aurora is thirteen, Mr Leigh passes on his melancholy disposition to his daughter in addition to an intense faith in love.

With the death of both parents, the adolescent Aurora is forced to leave Italy (painfully separated from Assunta) and travel alone to England, where her father's sister awaits her at a country estate. The contrast between Italian and English manners could not be greater, as Aurora finds her aunt to be a bitter, unloving woman, resentful of her brother's marriage choice and constrained by rigid ideals of domestic order and femininity. She educates Aurora accordingly, emphasising drawing-room accomplishments, superficial knowledge and religious pieties – qualities that ostensibly prepare Aurora for courtship and eventually motherhood. About midway through Book I, Aurora meets her cousin, Romney Leigh, a reform-minded young man and the master of nearby Leigh Hall, who seeks her company for friendship. While Aurora values the Edenic solitude of her aunt's estate, continuing to educate herself out of the books of her father's library and initiating her vocation as a poet, she also enjoys conversation-filled walks with Romney and his friend, the painter Vincent Carrington. Book I ends in a mode of pastoral lyricism and hymn-like thanks, as Aurora sets aside Romney's worldly concerns by placing her faith in God.

Book II

Aurora continues to recount her life in England, as Book II begins with the auspicious occasion of Aurora's twentieth birthday. The narrator looks back to that June morning when, alone in her aunt's garden, she decides to confirm her poetic vocation. In a pastiche of Staël's Corinne crowning herself at the Roman Capitol, Aurora makes herself a wreath of ivy. While securing it around her forehead, Romney Leigh catches her in the act and causes her to blush. Romney, too, feels awkward, although for a different reason: he has come to propose marriage. However, before the proposal can be uttered, Aurora's suitor inadvertently insults her with the comment that writing poetry suits neither a modern woman nor her time. The two cousins launch into a lengthy debate about what constitutes proper work; for the privileged, educated Romney, work is a labour that improves society, especially the material needs of the poor, whom he claims do not need art but shelter, food and employment. As part of his social mission, Romney seeks Aurora as a wife and 'helpmate' (Book II, line 402). Romney's smug righteousness infuriates Aurora, who argues that the needs of the soul are as important as those of the body and that poetry speaks to and elevates the soul. She further declares that it is her right as an individual – not merely as a woman – to pursue poetry as a vocation.

Aurora's vehemence silences Romney, who reluctantly retreats from the discussion, and outrages her aunt, who angrily reveals not only Romney's intended proposal but also the Leigh fathers' plan that the cousins should one day marry and consolidate the family fortune. Despite the fact that Aurora has feelings for Romney, she firmly rejects all forms of patriarchal constraint: 'My soul is not a pauper; I can live / At least my soul's life, without alms from men' (Book II, lines 681–2).

But Aurora's aunt recognises the young woman's conflicted feelings and, after accusing her of being a lovelorn fool, leaves the poet blushing and tearful in the garden. Six weeks later, Aurora finds her aunt dead and learns that she has left her an income of £300 plus another substantial sum of £30,000. Suspicious of the extra largesse, Aurora queries Romney about its origins, only to discover that he wishes to gift his cousin with Leigh family money he feels is owed to her. Aurora views the inheritance as a form of coercion and tears up the remunerative document. The action results in a final parting of the two cousins: she for literary work in London and he for philanthropic management on his estate and in London.

Book III

Book III begins three years later with Aurora's reflections on the challenging life she had chosen for herself.[59] After a long day of writing, she continues '[b]eyond the stroke of midnight' reading letters from fans, critics and her friend Vincent Carrington (Book III, line 27). The letters suggest Aurora's popular success but limited critical acclaim. Carrington's letter, which Aurora renders in full, offers a brief glimpse into Romney's reform work and establishes the painter's own aesthetic rapport with the poet. Aurora appreciates the support of Carrington but is frustrated with herself; the erotically charged fire of creation is strong within her. But her poetry, she judges, lacks vitality. Moreover, she cannot devote herself to her art in the way she would like and must earn a living writing reviews and tales. She takes some heart in the idea that her experiences contribute to the growth of her soul, which will strike out in a poetic flame when the time is right.

The sudden arrival of an 'English dame' to her rooms interrupts Aurora's thoughts (Book III, line 345) and introduces a new complexity to the poet's work-driven life. Lady Waldemar seeks help from Aurora, as she pursues the love of Romney Leigh. Lady Waldemar treats Aurora as a bluestocking – intellectual and passionless – someone disinterested in the heart. Of course, she knows nothing of Aurora and Romney's past and is more concerned with another obstacle: a beautiful young drover's daughter named Marian Erle, whom Romney (ostensibly out of charity) has asked to be his wife. Lady Waldemar wants Aurora to intervene in the relationship, a request that, despite her hurt feelings, the poet rejects outright. Lady Waldemar promptly leaves Aurora but not without telling her where Marian resides and delivering some condescending remarks about being a lady poet. Aurora is so disturbed by the visit that she goes out into the streets of London, specifically the impoverished St Margaret's Court, to find Marian Erle.

Aurora successfully locates Marian, who mistakes Aurora's entrance for Romney's and warmly greets her once she knows the relation. Aurora retells Marian's history: her abusive parents, solace in nature, pauper's education and itinerant upbringing. She eventually became a seamstress to earn her keep, but to earn more cash her mother handed her over to a man 'with beast's eyes' (Book III, lines 1050). Marian ran frantically away from the man into the countryside and passed out in a ditch. She wound up in a hospital where she lay in fever for many weeks. It is here that Romney Leigh discovered Marian and took her into his care. He found her respectable work as a seamstress in London and a safe place to live. Book III ends with Marian and Romney parting, and she imagining their meeting after death.

Book IV

Book IV continues with Aurora's narration of Marian's story. Having found a new position in another London shop, Marian briefly recounts her friendship with an ailing fellow seamstress, Lucy Gresham. After many weeks of Marian attempting to nurse Lucy back to health, the latter dies in Marian's arms. So distraught is her friend that she will not let the corpse be retrieved. Marian is brought back to her senses, however, by Romney Leigh, whose voice she has not heard for a year. Romney is tender towards Marian and, after some time being reacquainted with her, proposes marriage. Aurora's narration lapses into a dense configuration of metaphors at this point, representing Marian as a frightened bird and an array of benign animals.[60] Aurora's description of Marian struggling to articulate her feelings conveys not her poor education but rather the young woman's deep discomfort with Romney's offer and her gracious thought that Romney's love might be a gift from God. Neither woman sees Romney's gift as the result of erotic passion. Aurora recognises the patronising social motive behind it, and Marian feels (as Aurora did) more like a 'handmaid' than a lover. Neither woman is willing to confront him about his actions – that is, until Romney himself appears in Marian's room.[61]

Romney's arrival precipitates another debate between the cousins about what the marriage proposal means. It becomes quickly clear to Romney that Aurora is fond of Marian, so he tries to present their engagement as a kind of cousinly gift. In response, Aurora suggests that Romney express his passionate love for Marian and imagine her among the portraits of his ancestors. Aurora's answer takes him aback, and after a pause, he suggests that the love she describes does not exist in the current age. Marian remains silent through the exchange, and while we do not know her thoughts, her actions on her wedding day only confirm her discomfort with the match.

One month after the awkward conversation in Marian's room, she and Romney's nuptial is scheduled to take place in a Hampstead Heath church. Aurora's description of those attending the service suggests an infection of the masses, as Romney's lower-class charges mingle with his upper-class peers. Charged with metaphors of disease and suppuration, her language conveys anxiety about the urban poor.[62] But even as Aurora recoils from them, she also sharply observes the upper-class men's gossip as they await the bride's arrival. She also more sympathetically introduces the character of Lord Howe, a liberal aristocrat and patron of the arts. When Romney appears, it is clear that something is wrong; Marian has disappeared. The announcement causes the crowd to riot, as they think he has tricked the bride. Aurora escapes the mêlée and, via Lord Howe, reads the letter that Marian left behind for Romney. The epistle is an eloquent apology and explanation of her departure. It seems that Lady Waldemar has intervened, convincing Marian that she could never be good enough for Romney and sending her far away. Aurora is appalled by the news but not surprised. She never told Romney about Lady Waldemar's designs. So, when he becomes suspicious of Marian's story, Aurora defends her. Exhausted, disappointed and disillusioned, Romney and Aurora go their separate ways once more at the end of Book IV.

Book V

Book V is the centrepiece of the nine-book poem and divides between Aurora's reflections on her poetry and a social gathering at the home of Lord Howe, Aurora's patron. While *Aurora Leigh* contains many lyrical and conversational verse paragraphs about art amid the romance plot, Book V is the only one that focuses solely on Aurora's aesthetic ideals and her problems executing them. Thus, in light of such intense self-scrutiny, the opening sentence is an injunction to self: 'Aurora Leigh, be humble'. Yet the poet cannot seem to exercise restraint and a lyrical effusion follows the command. In a series of natural and erotic analogies Aurora asks: can her poetry harness the creative energies that make beauty in the world and, in doing so, harmonise man and nature? While the teeming catalogue suggests that the answer to her questions is 'yes',

Aurora claims to have reached the opposite conclusion: 'I must fail, / Who fail at the beginning to hold and move / One man, – and he my cousin [. . .]' (Book V, lines 30–2). The startling answer demonstrates not only a division in the poet between artist and critic but also woman and artist.

However, we learn quickly that the answer is a feint; Aurora's statement simply mimics a modern view that a woman's artistic fulfilment depends on personal happiness. The syllogism goes that because Aurora is alone in the world, she cannot succeed as a poet. But Aurora rejects it outright and launches into a critical assessment of her literary accomplishments and ambition. First, she boldly overturns contemporary notions that epics have died out and argues that classical authors treated past heroes, such as Hector and Arthur, as men and not gods. Likewise, Aurora seeks to write a long poem that represents her age: to create 'a living art, / Which thus presents and thus records true life' (lines 221–2). *Aurora Leigh* is certainly the culmination of such an ideal, but the narrator of the poem at this point in her history thinks she has yet to achieve it.

Second, Aurora is sad about art and love, but not in the way most critics think. She has not yet handed over a great poem to her public; therefore, she has not received the kind of love associated with poetic fame. In a separate issue, Aurora's orphanhood is a source of sadness, especially since she has no other family ties except her cousin Romney, whom she has not seen for two years. In order to combat feeling low, Aurora forces herself to socialise with 'the lights and talkers at Lord Howe's' (line 581).

In the second half of Book V, Aurora's point of view moves from internal thought to external observation. Moreover, as her teary eyes dry out, her observations tend towards caricature. Lady Waldemar's snaky presence fuels Aurora's bitter descriptions, as does the gossip of three men: an undergraduate with socialist sympathies, a pious aesthete, Sir Blaise Delorme, and a 'bilious' critic, Grimwald (line 657). Aurora overhears their exchange about Romney Leigh's love affairs and reform agenda, learning that he is engaged to Lady Waldemar, a match the men find as absurd as his prior engagement to a working-class woman. Lord Howe interrupts their conversation by drawing attention to a quietly seething Aurora sitting on a nearby sofa. Lord Howe tells Aurora that he has defended her from eager fans, seeking autographs or advice on poetry, and brings her a letter from a lovelorn suitor. It is clear from this interaction that Aurora enjoys the adoration of her readers. But Lord Howe perceives that Aurora suffers from a lack of intimacy and suggests she should temporarily cease working to pursue a relationship. Aurora's indignation ends their conversation and is compounded by the arrival of Lady Waldemar, who parades her closeness with Romney before Aurora.

Escaping the party as fast as possible, Aurora returns home to consider her feelings about Romney's engagement. She decides that, for him, marriage is only a form of 'self-aggrandisement' and wonders whether he could truly love anyone.[63] Her thoughts offer some comfort, and after penning a congratulatory note to Lady Waldemar, Aurora settles on leaving England. The destination is her birthplace, Italy, so she must think about financing her journey and new life. In this meditation we learn that Aurora has written a 'long poem' that remains in manuscript but may provide some future source of income.[64] She also decides to sell her father's books and leave the haggling over the manuscript to Vincent Carrington, the painter who also acts as her literary agent. Aurora's final lines in Book V are an apostrophe to Italy, whom she addresses as a nursing mother and in (a Miltonic negative simile) a sublime landscape.

Book VI

Book VI begins with Aurora's reflections on the French, which her traversal through Paris inspires as she journeys southwards. She admires French idealism, which, even if practically untenable in the case of Fourierism, still has the admirable goal of social equity. She finds Louis Napoleon, a democratically elected monarch, to be a happy paradox and loves the raffish beauty of 'fair fantastic Paris': a blend of nature and architecture, commerce and art, republic and empire. Amid the street crowds, Aurora finds herself repelled by ugliness and imperfection but tries to maintain a humanitarian interest in people's souls.[65] She wonders if poetry could improve the lives of the disenfranchised by elevating their thoughts above necessity. In the middle of her rumination, Aurora thinks she has spied the face of Marian Erle, and her narrative abruptly shifts gears as the poet frantically attempts to find her. Failing in this first attempt, Aurora returns to her inn, haunted by Marian's face. Although Italy calls to her, Aurora puts off her departure for several weeks. Her search ends when, one morning in the Quai aux Fleurs, she finds the frightened seamstress, who tries to flee from her. Aurora manages to arrest Marian's flight by calling out Romney's name.

A resigned Marian leads Aurora to her room, and there reveals a surprise: a dimpled, curly-haired, one-year-old boy. It takes Aurora some time to register both Marian's beatific absorption in the child and the possible illicit reason for his existence. At first, Aurora judges Marian harshly, accusing her of stealing the child and then of being 'seduced', upon learning that the child is hers (line 766). Marian strongly reproaches Aurora's word choice, explaining that beasts do not seduce their prey. Aurora immediately understands that her friend has been raped and weeps with regret over her wrong, hurtful conclusions. She begs that Marian tell her story, which Marian does as though she were recounting someone else's life: 'And she, I said, was murdered; Marian's dead' (line 813). However, it is as a mother that some aspect of Marian survives and (in the eyes of both women) regains innocence.

Marian's story replicates the terrible events from her childhood: an older woman, this time Lady Waldemar, sent her away, and a man attacked her, this time raping her. Moreover, Aurora learns that it was Lady Waldemar who convinced Marian to jilt Romney at the altar and who offered to find her work with a friend in Australia. But Lady Waldemar did not see that the person leading Marian to her new life was a procuress in the white slave trade. After being secured on a ship against her will, Marian was drugged and then violated. The attack so traumatised her that she became catatonic, and her captors released her. Marian wandered the French countryside for miles until sympathetic field-workers gave her a place to sleep. Book VI ends with Marian's account of living the 'old tramp-life' again, feeling fearful and 'undone' (line 1270).

Book VII

Book VII resumes Marian's story: she attempts to fathom Lady Waldemar's motives (but gives up) and explains how she was taken in by a miller's wife, who finds her work as a servant in Paris. But when the young mistress perceives that Marian is pregnant, she accuses her of being untruthful and unchaste and dismisses her. Marian is shocked about her condition, not realising it herself until that moment. Aurora interrupts Marian to express her horror about the mistreatment and declares that she would rather be with prostitutes than such a perfidious woman. Marian receives sympathy from a fellow seamstress, who takes her in and lets her work with baby in tow. Aurora is so moved by Marian's courage and honesty that she invites her to Italy, offering to work for and defend the little family.

With Marian and her baby asleep in an adjoining room, Aurora reexamines her feelings about Romney's engagement to Lady Waldemar and wonders if she should tell him about Marian. Deciding that such a disclosure would only make him unhappy, Aurora ends up blaming herself for the catastrophe: for, in not accepting Romney's marriage proposal years earlier, she has created the conditions for Marian Erle's victimisation. To right the wrong she has caused, Aurora becomes Marian and her baby's guardian and sets forth her plan to care for the two in a letter to Lord Howe. In a separate letter to Lady Waldemar, she pens a searing indictment of her actions and a threat of exposure, should she in any way make her future spouse Romney unhappy.

With her plans in order, Aurora, Marian and the baby set out on a transcontinental train ride for Italy. Aurora vigilantly registers the changing landscapes and eagerly anticipates their arrival. She finds a house outside Florence with a spectacular view of the Arno valley and the Vallombrosan mountains. The three live there for many weeks before a letter arrives from Vincent Carrington. The news is good, though mitigated somewhat by news of Romney. First, Aurora's long poem has been reviewed positively; her sex has not impeded its success. Second, Carrington has married his beautiful model, Kate Ward, whose love for Aurora's poetry has mediated their courtship. Finally, he shares the news that Lady Waldemar has nursed a feverish Romney through a recent illness. Aurora receives these tidings somberly. She assumes Romney has married Lady Waldemar and that idea casts a shadow over everything. Even the notice of her poem inspires but a modest reflection: 'The book has some truth in it, I believe' (line 744). Aurora goes on to explain what she means by 'truth', in an extended Swedenborgian meditation: Art is a lens for perceiving God and magnifying a kind of 'larger life' (line 890). Aurora wonders, however, if Art might be limited in what it can show of Love.

Aurora turns away from these thoughts to describe the heat of the Tuscan sun, her peaceful life with Marian and the baby, and her sadness over the loss of Romney to another woman: 'Tenderly / And mournfully I lived' (lines 1052–3). Her mind also returns to the memory of her father and her distant childhood. She does not visit her parents' graves because she feels as though she were a ghost among them. While such feelings might suggest chronic melancholy, Aurora enjoys the anonymity of living in what she now considers to be a foreign land, being a *flâneuse* on the streets of Florence and observing the natives. On one of her jaunts, she spies a familiar figure, Sir Blaise Delorme, from whose sight she ducks away. Book VII ends with Aurora's thoughts of dissolving into the Italian evening, never to be found again.

Book VIII

But if Aurora seems overcome by the night at the end of Book VII, we find her, on another evening, sitting on the terrace of her house at the opening of Book VIII. Looking from her tower high above Bellosguardo, Aurora watches Marian in the garden, feeding a fig to her baby in a kind of Edenic paradise. Aurora's high position suggests her elevated thoughts, which turn to heaven, God and the Tuscan landscape, as well as her distance from earthly pleasure. Suddenly, Aurora's imaginative flight is interrupted by the arrival of Romney Leigh. Aurora at first thinks that he has brought Lady Waldemar with him. But he quickly denies it, claiming he has a letter from her instead. Aurora begs him to sit with her to look at the stars, and Romney mutters, 'then you do not know' (line 93). Aurora thinks he refers to his marriage and says she got the news from Vincent Carrington. Romney then wonders if she means Carrington's marriage to Kate Ward, which Aurora confirms. Then, Romney presses her further: did she not receive a letter from Lord Howe? Aurora answers no and blames Sir Blaise for not delivering it. Irritated with the formality, Aurora accuses Romney of being supercilious, sending a letter ahead of him. But thinking she might know something of his situation, Romney wishes Aurora might learn to pity what he has become. Still deluded that he is married to Lady Waldemar, Aurora expresses no sympathy for him. Romney decides to change the subject and enquire about Marian. Aurora's curt reply explains that she is well and occupied.

Romney's next declaration startles his cousin: 'I have read your book, / Aurora' (lines 260–1); her response is to acknowledge and move on from that topic. But Romney persists in describing how it 'lives in [him]' (line 266), to which Aurora replies that the poem lived in her first and she finds it 'foolish, feeble, and afraid' (line 274). Romney insists that the book has raised him up and changed his mind about what a poem can do. In response, Aurora recalls their far-off June conversation, which took their lives in different directions, and thinks it is sad that he could not have believed in her then. Romney readily acknowledges his error and passionately expresses his regret. Moreover, he claims that he has sought Aurora – 'My Italy of women' (line 358) – for her ability to comfort his soul, which has been sorely tried and humbled by God.

Aurora becomes more receptive to Romney's conversation after hearing him speak of humility, and he begins the story of his recent catastrophe. He admits that his socialist experiment could not prevent the crimes that poverty in his community had created and relates how those he tried to help turned against him. Interrupting him to say that she too has failed in her ambitions, Aurora regrets her youthful arrogance. But Romney objects once more to her claim of failure, for her long poem has shown him 'truths not yours, indeed / But set within my reach by means of you' (lines 610–11). The truths he has most taken to heart are the ruinous nature of materialism and the need to revive God's word in men's hearts. Turning away from collectivist social ideals, Romney has come to embrace individualist Christian principles. In light of his speech, Aurora intuits that the phalanstery[66] at Leigh Hall has failed; as Romney tells it, not only did the inhabitants turn against their beneficent sponsor through vandalism and threats, but they also burned the building to the ground. On that terrible day, Romney managed to save one portrait from the Leigh family's collection. All that remains of the estate is a 'great charred circle' (line 1032). The experience left Romney gravely ill, as well as full of humility and regret.

While Aurora expresses sympathy for his plight, she distances herself emotionally from what he has suffered. The spectre of Lady Waldemar looms before her, and her next speech emphasises the impossibility of their being more than just friends. Once Romney catches her drift, he is quick to correct her error. And the last gesture of Book VIII is Romney's handing over of Lady Waldemar's letter, which Aurora grabs in order to '[tear] the meaning out' (line 1253).

Book IX

Book IX begins with the letter in full: a response to Aurora's harsh missive sent after discovering Marian in Paris. While frank about her failure to win Romney's heart, Lady Waldemar denies knowledge of Marian's victimisation and is sardonic about Aurora's status as a successful poet and Romney's unrequited lover. The epistle concludes with a vehement curse. Feeling the heat of Lady Waldemar's ire, Aurora realises her mistake about Romney's affections and then expects he has come to claim her heart. But her assumption is wrong; Romney has come to seek Marian for a wife once more. As Aurora pauses in stunned silence, the saint-like Marian enters the conversation. Aurora describes Marian's 'proud, pathetic voice', which gratefully acknowledges Romney's acceptance of her and her illegitimate child but observes that they would only tarnish his reputation (lines 196, 206). Marian asks Aurora to support this idea, but the poet does no such thing, advocating the marriage wholeheartedly. Marian is so grateful for the endorsement that she falls to the ground in tears, kissing Romney's foot, and then rises to speak again. Her speech relinquishes Romney from any obligation to her, admitting that she never loved him (because she has always regarded him high above love) and proclaiming that she loves no one except her child and God.

After Marian withdraws from the room, Romney turns to Aurora for forgiveness. He sees the audacity of his proposal to the seamstress and openly acknowledges his love for Aurora. Towards the end of his speech, he blurts out that he cannot see; his blindness is the result of being hit with a beam by Marian Erle's father in the conflagration that destroyed Leigh Hall (line 547). Aurora weeps over the revelation, but Romney assures her that he has not lost hope. Romney's confession incites Aurora to declare her love for him and to proclaim that 'Art is much, but love is more' (line 656). What she means is that, in loving Romney, she fulfills God's will: 'Art symbolizes heaven, but Love is God / And makes heaven' (lines 658–9). Aurora's declaration prompts a passionate, tearful kiss, and here the narrative becomes detached from the scene, as Aurora meditates on the origins and progress of their romance. She also apostrophises the night and darkness. The narrative returns to the two lovers' conversation as Romney proclaims Aurora to be his 'dearest light of souls' (line 831) and the two improvise commitment vows. In the final speech of the poem, Romney exhorts Aurora to 'shine out for two' (line 910) and make 'Art a service' (line 915). His psalm-like conclusion places their faith in God, and in Book IX's last verse paragraph, Aurora describes the horizon line of the Italian landscape fading into a vision of the New Jerusalem.

Aurora Leigh at a Glance

The text in **bold** represents material from the poem given in extracts and discussed in Chapter 2.

Written in England:

Book I. **Opening simile between the poem and portraiture; Aurora's description of her parents and meditation on her mother's portrait;** the orphaned Aurora goes to live with her **unloving aunt in England; landscape description of her aunt's estate and her perception of nature from her room; Aurora's call to be a poet and first poems; her reflection in a looking-glass;** describes her cousin Romney Leigh and painter Vincent Carrington as friends.

Book II. **Aurora's self-coronation on her twentieth birthday; Romney Leigh's arrival and debate with Aurora about women poets and social reform; his marriage proposal and Aurora's rejection.**

Book III. Aurora living as a commercial writer in London; **letter from Vincent Carrington, a painter;** introduction of **Lady Waldemar and her news that Romney is engaged to a seamstress, Marian Erle;** Aurora visits Marian, who recounts her life of abuse and hardship until meeting Romney, who helps her escape it.

Book IV. Marian sees Romney as a saviour and confirms that he has proposed marriage; Romney arrives during the conversation with Aurora, who is sceptical that he loves her; **the two cousins converse about issues of the day;** the wedding day arrives; **Aurora's description of the guests; Marian** fails to show up at the altar and **leaves a letter for her fiancé.**

Book V. A pivotal book: **Aurora begins with her thoughts on art, particularly epic poetry;** Lord Howe's party and **three gossipy young men; Aurora's decision to leave England for Italy.**

Written in Paris and Italy:

Book VI. Aurora's discovery of Marian in Paris; Aurora finds out that **Marian has a baby;** Aurora's harsh judgement of Marian and then reversal of opinion on hearing her story; Marian explains Lady Waldemar's betrayal, as well as **her own abduction, rape and abandonment.**

Book VII. Marian discovers that she is pregnant and, after difficulty finding a sympathetic employer, finds work with a seamstress; **Aurora expresses horror about her experience and offers to take her and the baby to Italy;** the journey to and arrival in Tuscany; letters to Lord Howe and Lady Waldemar.

Book VIII. Romney's arrives at Aurora's home a changed man; Aurora remains distant, as she thinks he has married Lady Waldemar; **Romney comments on Aurora's book and his new social vision;** he recounts the destruction of Leigh Hall and produces a letter from Lady Waldemar.

Book IX. Lady Waldemar's defensive letter; Romney proposes to Marian once more, and she refuses out of devotion to her child; after apologising to Aurora, Romney professes his true love for her; **he also admits to having been blinded in the Leigh Hall riot; Aurora confesses her true love for him; their physical passion expresses higher spiritual communion;**

Romney calls for Aurora to put her poetry in service of God; Aurora's last words comprise a sonnet that envisions the New Jerusalem.

Notes

1. The initials were the poet's choice of signature, and I retain them throughout the *Guide*.
2. Letter to Mary Russell Mitford, 24 December 1844, *Brownings' Correspondence*, vol. 9, p. 293.
3. Letter to Mary Russell Mitford, 30 December 1844, *Brownings' Correspondence*, vol. 9, p. 304.
4. Letter to Robert Browning, 27 February 1845, *Brownings' Correspondence*, vol. 10, pp. 102–3.
5. *Aurora Leigh*, Book II, lines 468–9, 472–3.
6. Eliot, p. 307.
7. Aytoun, p. 33.
8. Ruskin to Robert Browning, 27 November 1856, *The Letters of John Ruskin*, vol. I, p. 247.
9. The repetition of the name Barrett reflects EBB's intricate family history. 'Barrett' was EBB's middle name and 'Moulton' the surname. But her father adopted 'Moulton-Barrett' in order to come to terms with his father and uncle's wills (Barrett, p. x). EBB dropped the hyphen from her full name and the 'M' for Moulton in her initials.
10. EBB was not proud of her family's involvement in slavery and strongly supported abolitionism.
11. *Brownings' Correspondence*, vol. 1, p. 350.
12. For 'Glimpses', see ibid. pp. 348–56. For the untitled essay featuring an autobiographical character called 'Beth', see ibid. 360–2. For the quotations, see ibid. p. 360.
13. EBB translated Byron's dream of a Greek republic into a vision of an Italian one. Her correspondence and poetry document the triumphs and failures of the *Risorgimento*, Italy's unification movement that flourished 1815 to 1870. EBB witnessed the revolutions of 1848 to 1849 and died before seeing the successful ousting of Austria by Garibaldi and others in 1861.
14. Based on EBB's medical records, personal correspondence and painted portraits, D. A. B. Young concludes that the poet suffered from poliomyelitis, or, as we know the disease, polio. The initial illness, which seems to have resulted in a spinal curvature and deformation of the ribcage, created the conditions for EBB's later pulmonary disorders.
15. See Rodas, pp. 112–15, on the dynamic between sight and blindness. See also Carpenter, pp. 52–68; Jones, pp. 21–35; and Flint, pp. 64–92.
16. See Keirstead, pp. 65–89; Taylor, 'People Diplomacy', pp. 59–83; and Gilbert, p. 198, on EBB's cosmopolitanism. Chapman argues that, in EBB's correspondence and poetry, Florence is represented as 'hallucinatory, ineffable, unrepresentable' and 'a version of the woman artist striving to fuse aesthetics with politics' (pp. 131, 137).
17. Mermin, p. 236.
18. *Works*, vol. V, p. 56, lines 118–20.
19. Stone and Taylor, p. 41.
20. Letter to Kenyon, 8 October 1844, *Brownings' Correspondence*, vol. 9, p. 177; letter to Mitford, *Brownings' Correspondence*, vol. 9, p. 293.

21. Letter to Mitford, 30 December 1844, *Brownings' Correspondence*, vol. 9, p. 304.
22. On EBB and Carlyle, see Hayter, p. 128.
23. See *On Heroes*, p. 390.
24. *Works*, vol. II, p. 11, line 94.
25. Ibid. p. 13, line 161.
26. Ibid. p. 14, lines 166–8. *Kleos* is Greek for glory achieved in battle.
27. See Peterson, pp. 109–45; and Martinez, 'Sister Arts', pp. 214–26.
28. See Moers, p. 40; Friedman, pp. 217–23; Stone, 'Genre Subversion', pp. 101–27; Mermin, pp. 183–4; Laird, pp. 353–70; Bailey, pp. 117–37; and Tucker, pp. 377–84.
29. Tucker, p. 378.
30. Ibid. pp. 379–81. 'Spasmodicism' is a literary movement that springs from the tenets of Romanticism. Its adherents advocate the principle that the poet's mind is a sensorium and poetry the mode of expressing intense physical sensations and currents of feeling, emotion and thought.
31. Friedman, p. 217.
32. *Aurora Leigh*, Book I, lines 235–50, 378–80; Book II, lines 67–8, 1242–7; Book V, lines 952–4; Book VII, lines 470–2; and Book VIII, lines 507–13, 849–50, 1207. Allusions to the *Odyssey* are more specific as the poem progresses.
33. On the influence of novels on *Aurora Leigh*, see Kaplan, pp. 16–35; Taplin, pp. xiii–xviii; Mermin, 'Genre and Gender', pp. 7–11. On EBB's subversive use of epic conventions within a novelistic narrative, see Tucker, 'Epic Solutions', pp. 62–85.
34. 'George Sand' is the pseudonym of Amandine Aurore Lucile Dupin (1804–76), French author of reviews, novels and memoirs. EBB was delighted to meet her in February 1852.
35. Stone, 'Genre Subversion', p. 126.
36. Parody typically mocks the conventions and features of a genre; pastiche imitates and honours them.
37. *Aurora Leigh*, Book V, lines 151–2.
38. Vanden Bossche, p. 30. Kathleen Blake argues that, unlike that of Wordsworth's narrator, Aurora's achievement of poetic success conflicts with her need for love (pp. 387–98).
39. Vanden Bossche, pp. 31–2. Linda Peterson argues that, in the opening lines of the second verse stanza of *Aurora Leigh*, the protagonist 'claims partnership with an undebased Romantic tradition [that is Wordsworthian rather than Byronic] and a masculine form of autobiography', p. 120. She also demonstrates how EBB 'question[s] and modifies[s]' the 'Wordsworthian paradigm' (Peterson, pp. 127–45).
40. *Brownings' Correspondence*, vol. 6, p. 171.
41. Byron's *Don Juan* (1819–24) was considered scandalous and inappropriate for ladies. Barrett Browning was not allowed to read it while in her father's household. See Stone, 'Versions', pp. 123–41; Mermin, *Origins*, p. 184.
42. *Brownings' Correspondence*, vol. 6, p. 171.
43. Jeffrey chronicles Byron's engagement with Homer throughout *Don Juan*, which, although a mock-epic, does not parody Homer's poetry (pp. 188–92).
44. Letter to Mitford, 30 December 1844, *Brownings' Correspondence*, vol. 9, p. 304. For a summary of responses EBB might have known, see Stone, 'Versions of Byron', p. 131.
45. Marian Erle's story prompted EBB's brother George, who looked over proof sheets in 1856, to perceive a disturbing parallel between *Aurora Leigh* and *Don Juan*. In a letter to her sister Arabel, EBB defends her poem from the charge:

'No, George, not "worse than Don Juan" by any manner of means, because the intention is *not* licentious—There's a great difference. I admit, it's [Marian's rape and illegitimate child] a horrible situation—but I wanted a horrible situation to prove a beautiful verity.' Letter to Arabel, 4 October 1856, Lewis, vol. 2, p. 257. See also Lewis, p. 258, n. 6.

46. See especially Book II, lines 473–81.

47. Reynolds, p. 79.

48. Ibid. p. 80.

49. Landis, p. 200.

50. Friedman, pp. 204–5, offers the best account of the gendered tension between lyric and epic poetry. On Tennyson and EBB's subversion of the gendered norms Friedman identifies, see Stone, 'Genre Subversion', pp. 101–27. For a historicised interpretation of gender and genre in the two poems, see Taylor, '"School-Miss Alfred"', p. 8. Taylor discusses Victorian medical discourse that attributed women's biological and maternal impediments to rigorous intellectual application and persuasively argues that Tennyson refutes such claims in *The Princess*.

51. Taylor, '"School-Miss Alfred"', pp. 14–15. Taylor argues that both *The Princess* and *Aurora Leigh* advance a controversial idea: namely, that women need not sacrifice sexual and maternal fulfilment in order to succeed as intellectuals and artists.

52. *The Princess*, lines 102, 103. In the final lines of the poem, Lilia 'disrobe[s]' the statue in an act that restores gender order on the Vivian estate and seems to please the male narrator.

53. Kenyon's will apportioned to EBB and Robert a combined sum of £11,000, giving them much-needed financial security.

54. Reynolds, 'Editorial Introduction', p. 103.

55. For more on EBB and portraiture, see Martinez, 'Perils'.

56. See Moers, p.188; Kaplan, pp. 22–34; Peterson, pp. 109–45; and Martinez, 'Sister Arts', pp. 214–26.

57. *Aurora Leigh*, Book I, lines 2–3.

58. Ibid. Book I, line 189.

59. On the economic and legal perils of women's authorship, see Hoeckley, pp. 135–61.

60. Book IV, lines 133–6, 156–67.

61. Book IV, lines 227, 228.

62. On sources for the language of contagion in London, see Walsh, pp. 171–7; and Karlin, pp. 119–22.

63. Book V, line 1088.

64. Book V, line 1213.

65. Book VI, line 81.

66. 'A cooperative community based on the egalitarian principles of French socialist Charles Fourier (1772–1837) and having shared property, possessions and so on; a building or set of buildings occupied by such a community' (*Oxford English Dictionary* [OED] 1).

Chapter 2

Interpreting *Aurora Leigh*: Text, Commentary, Analysis

Poetic Vision: Book I, lines 1–173, 324–39, 568–709, 971–1066

Aurora Leigh is a poem about the life of a poet and her poetry and moves between autobiography and aesthetics in equal measure. Uniting the two subjects is the narrator Aurora's emphasis on *seeing*, which she deems integral to the development of selfhood and literary art. John Ruskin's pronouncement from volume III (1856) of *Modern Painters* effectively describes Aurora's outlook: 'the greatest thing a human soul ever does in this world is to *see* something, and tell what it *saw* in a plain way [. . .] to see clearly is poetry, prophecy, and religion' (V. 333).

The following excerpts from Book I illustrate the poem's interest in portraits, natural description and the gaze (that of the poet and other characters). It is important to notice when Aurora invites the reader to participate in her vision (addressing a 'you') or uses an analogy, metaphor or mythological allusion in order to describe what she sees. Visual description is rich and complicated in the text and not a topic limited to Book I.

The opening three verse paragraphs of the poem move from a painter-poet analogy to the importance of the gaze as a means of divine revelation. For EBB and her contemporaries, seeing and being seen constituted important modes of self-analysis as well as a means of representing one's relationship with nature, society and God. This is not to say that EBB, like Ruskin, regards painting as a higher mode of understanding than writing. Rather, Aurora's analogy between portrait and poem suggests not only the powerful memorial function of both arts but also poetry's power to convey the vitality of what Aurora calls the 'soul'.

Of writing many books there is no end;*
And I who have written much in prose and verse
For others' uses, will write now for mine, –
Will write my story for my better self
As when you paint your portrait for a friend,   5
Who keeps it in a drawer and looks at it
Long after he has ceased to love you, just
To hold together what he was and is.*

I, writing thus, am still what men call young;
I have not so far left the coasts of life   10
To travel inland, that I cannot hear
That murmur of the outer Infinite*
Which unweaned babies smile at in their sleep
When wondered at for smiling; not so far,
But still I catch my mother at her post   15
Beside the nursery-door, with finger up,
'Hush, hush – here's too much noise!' while her sweet eyes
Leap forward, taking part against her word
In the child's riot. Still I sit and feel
My father's slow hand, when she had left us both,   20
Stroke out my childish curls across his knee,
And hear Assunta's daily jest (she knew
He liked it better than a better jest)
Inquire how many golden scudi went
To make such ringlets.* O my father's hand,   25

Line 1. In the opening sentence of the poem, Aurora joins two declarative statements: a slightly altered quotation from Ecclesiastes 12.12 ('Of making many books there is no end [. . .]') and an explanation of why the author is writing. While the Biblical allusion proclaims that writing is bad for you (the quotation continues: 'and much study is a weariness of the flesh'), the second extended statement suggests that writing is a necessary evil: a way of 'hold[ing] together' one's identity.

Lines 5–8. What makes *Aurora Leigh*'s opening so striking is the narrator's analogy of portrait painting to describe not only the act of self-representation but also the desire (gendered male) to keep one's identity intact. As Gregory Giles has observed, 'the tenor of this simile indicates the poem Aurora writes, [which acts] as a kind of time capsule that will remind her who she has been and how it stands in comparison to who she is now' (125).

Line 12. Echoing language from Wordsworth's *Ode: Intimations on Immortality from Recollections of Early Childhood* (1807), which describes an infant's intuitive connection to 'that immortal sea / Which brought us hither' (line 163–4), Aurora characterises herself as a version of Wordsworth's 'Babe' who 'leaps up on his Mother's arm' and grows into Nature's 'Foster-Child' and 'Priest' (lines 49, 82, 72). Aurora revises the ode's assertion that childhood becomes a 'prison-house' (*Intimations* ode, line 67), suggesting that her mother encouraged the kind of joy that Wordsworth's poem values.

Lines 24–5. Reynolds notes that the association between gold and hair was typical of fairytales and Pre-Raphaelite poetry, and the reference to Italian currency alerts us that Aurora's birthplace is Italy (p. 6, n. 6). Aurora's association of her father's hand with materialism and her mother's eyes with play suggests the division between adulthood and childhood, as well as the secular and divine. These dichotomies assume national associations as well when we learn that Aurora's father is English and her mother 'a Florentine'.

Stroke heavily, heavily the poor hair down,
Draw, press the child's head closer to thy knee!
I'm still too young, too young, to sit alone.

I write. My mother was a Florentine,
Whose rare blue eyes were shut from seeing me   30
When scarcely I was four years old, my life
A poor spark snatched up from a failing lamp
Which went out therefore. She was weak and frail;
She could not bear the joy of giving life,
The mother's rapture slew her. If her kiss   35
Had left a longer weight upon my lips
It might have steadied the uneasy breath,
And reconciled and fraternized my soul
With the new order. As it was, indeed,
I felt a mother-want about the world,   40
And still went seeking, like a bleating lamb
Left out at night in shutting up the fold, –
As restless as a nest-deserted bird
Grown chill through something being away, though what
It knows not. I, Aurora Leigh, was born   45
To make my father sadder, and myself
Not overjoyous, truly. Women know
The way to rear up children, (to be just)
They know a simple, merry, tender knack
Of tying sashes, fitting baby-shoes,   50
And stringing pretty words that make no sense,
And kissing full sense into empty words,
Which things are corals to cut life upon,
Although such trifles: children learn by such,
Love's holy earnest in a pretty play   55
And get not over-early solemnised,
But seeing, as in a rose-bush, Love's Divine
Which burns and hurts not, – not a single bloom, –
Become aware and unafraid of Love.*
Such good do mothers. Fathers love well   60
– Mine did, I know, – but still with heavier brains,
And wills more consciously responsible,
And not as wisely, since less foolishly;
So mother's have God's licence to be missed.

My father was an austere Englishman,   65
Who, after a dry life-time spent at home

Line 59. Aurora compares maternal love to the evidence of 'Love's Divine' that Moses discovers
in Exodus 3:2. Mothers are like the angel who reveals the 'rose-bush' (line 57).

In college-learning, law, and parish talk,
Was flooded with a passion unaware,
His whole provisioned and complacent past
Drowned out from him that moment. As he stood   70
In Florence, where he had come to spend a month
And note the secret of Da Vinci's drains,
He musing somewhat absently perhaps
Some English question . . whether men should pay
The unpopular but necessary tax   75
With left or right hand* – in the alien sun
In that great square of the Santissima,*
There drifted past him (scarcely marked enough
To move his comfortable island-scorn,)
A train of priestly banners, cross and psalm,   80
The white-veiled rose-crowned maidens holding up
Tall tapers, weighty for such wrists, aslant
To the blue luminous tremor of the air,
And letting drop the white wax as they went
To eat the bishop's wafer at the church;*   85
From which long trail of chanting priests and girls,
A face flashed like a cymbal on his face,
And shook with silent clangour brain and heart,
Transfiguring him to music. Thus, even thus,
He too received his sacramental gift   90
With eucharistic meanings;* for he loved.

And thus beloved, she died. I've heard it said
That but to see him in the first surprise
Of widower and father, nursing me,
Unmothered little child of four years old,   95
His large man's hands afraid to touch my curls,
As if the gold would tarnish, – his grave lips
Contriving such a miserable smile,
As if he knew needs must, or I should die,
And yet 'twas hard, – would almost make the stones   100

Line 76. An allusion to Matthew 6:3: 'But when thou doest alms, let not thy left hand know what thy right hand doeth.'

Line 77. The Piazza Santissima Annunziata.

Lines 78–85. The procession is likely the celebration of the nativity of the Virgin on 8 September. The church of the Santissima Annunziata belongs to the Servite order, which has a special symbol: the image of the Virgin stabbed with seven swords. See lines 160–1 below.

Line 91. These lines create a parallel between Aurora's mother receiving communion in celebration of the Eucharist and Aurora's father falling in love with her at first sight. Aurora attributes a sacramental quality to amatory vision. The metaphor of clanging cymbals to describe her father's gaze recalls the percussion played to celebrate God in 1 Chronicles 13 and 15.

Cry out for pity.* There's a verse he set
In Santa Croce* to her memory, –
'Weep for an infant too young to weep much
When death removed this mother' – stops the mirth
To-day, on women's faces when they walk   105
With rosy children hanging on their gowns,
Under the cloister, to escape the sun
That scorches in the piazza. After which,
He left our Florence, and made haste to hide
Himself, his prattling child, and silent grief,   110
Among the mountains above Pelago;
Because unmothered babes, he thought, had need
Of mother nature more than others use,
And Pan's white goats,* with udders warm and full
Of mystic contemplations, come to feed   115
Poor milkless lips of orphans like his own –
Such scholar-scraps he talked, I've heard from friends,
For even prosaic men, who wear grief long,
Will get to wear it as a hat aside
With a flower stuck in't. Father, then, and child,   120
We lived among the mountains many years,
God's silence on the outside of the house,
And we, who did not speak too loud, within;
And old Assunta to make up the fire,
Crossing herself whene'er a sudden flame   125
Which lightened from the firewood, made alive
That picture of my mother on the wall.
The painter drew it after she was dead;
And when the face was finished, throat and hands,
Her cameriera carried him, in hate   130
Of the English-fashioned shroud, the last brocade
She dressed in at the Pitti; 'he should paint
No sadder thing than that,' she swore, 'to wrong
Her poor signora.' Therefore, very strange
The effect was.   135

Much of Book I focuses on Aurora's upbringing by her widower father and their housekeeper Assunta, yet her mind returns often to the memory of her mother. In a passage that has become a nexus for

Line 101. See Luke 19:40.
Line 102. Florence's famous church, where many of the city's most eminent citizens lie buried.
Lines 114–15. The god Pan inhabits the forests of Arcadia, tending his flocks, pursuing innocent nymphs and making music on his pipes. Aurora's classically educated father likes to think that Mother Nature, represented as Pan's she-goats, might help nurture a motherless child. There is also a sense that the classics will foster the growing girl.

modern critics of the poem, Aurora describes looking at her mother's portrait, which was painted soon after she died. While the opening lines of *Aurora Leigh* suggest that a portrait might be used 'to hold together what [a viewer] is and was', Mrs Leigh's portrait does not offer such an object lesson for her daughter. Critics have argued that the portrait 'mirrors [Aurora's] ambivalence toward femininity' (Gelpi, p. 40; Yook, pp. 181–208) and, through a plethora of literary allusions, emphasises 'maternal inaccessibility and loss' and 'the muddled images of women available to Aurora' (Christ, p. 149; Cooper, p. 156). The onslaught of images is also reminiscent of a phantasmagoria show, which (as Terry Castle argues about post-Enlightenment discourse) had shifted in meaning from strictly a form of public entertainment to a private expression or trope of psychological haunting.

> I, a little child, would crouch 135
> For hours upon the floor with knees drawn up,
> And gaze across them, half in terror, half
> In adoration, at the picture there, –
> That swan-like supernatural white life
> Just sailing upward from the red stiff silk* 140
> Which seemed to have no part in it nor power
> To keep it from quite breaking out of bounds.
> For hours I sate and stared. Assunta's awe
> And my poor father's melancholy eyes
> Still pointed that way. That way went my thoughts 145
> When wandering beyond sight. And as I grew
> In years, I mixed, confused, unconsciously,
> Whatever I last read or heard or dreamed,
> Abhorrent, admirable, beautiful,
> Pathetical, or ghastly, or grotesque, 150
> With still that face ... which did not therefore change,
> But kept the mystic level of all forms
> Hates, fears, and admirations, was by turns
> Ghost, fiend, and angel, fairy, witch, and sprite,
> A dauntless Muse who eyes a dreadful Fate, 155
> A loving Psyche who loses sight of Love,
> A still Medusa with mild milky brows
> All curdled and all clothed upon with snakes
> Whose slime falls fast as sweat will; or anon
> Our Lady of the Passion, stabbed with swords 160

Line 140. The metaphor conveys an idea of the mother's Madonna- (or possibly Leda-)like assumption to heaven and her leaving behind an empty shroud. Mrs Leigh's 'white life' has escaped the confines of the silk, the painting and, in the course of the description, Aurora's vision.

Where the Babe sucked; or Lamia in her first
Moonlighted pallor, ere she shrunk and blinked
And shuddering wriggled down to the unclean;*
Or my own mother, leaving her last smile
In her last kiss upon the baby-mouth   165
My father pushed down on the bed for that, –
Or my dead mother, without smile or kiss,
Buried in Florence. All which images,
Concentred on the picture, glassed themselves
Before my meditative childhood, as   170
The incoherencies of change and death
Are represented fully, mixed and merged,*
In the smooth fair mystery of perpetual Life.

On the death of Aurora's father, which occurs when she is thirteen, the orphan is sent to the English home of her closest living relative. In this passage, Aurora's aunt wordlessly, but violently, conveys her resentment towards her new charge.[1] Her anger towards Aurora stems both from a xenophobic hatred of her mother, who took Mr Leigh away from his family, and from bitterness about having to disrupt her 'cage-bird life' (line 305). When Aurora sees her father's sister for the first time (after a long sea journey), she clings to her, yearning for affection and security. The aunt responds with a wrenching rebuff and penetrating examination; throughout Book I her basilisk-like gaze keeps a check on Aurora's happiness:

                   There, with some strange spasm
Of pain and passion, she wrung loose my hands   325
Imperiously, and held me at arm's length,
And with two grey steel naked-bladed eyes
Searched through my face, – ay, stabbed it through and through,
Through brows and cheeks and chin, as if to find
A wicked murderer in my innocent face,   330
If not here, there perhaps. Then, drawing breath,
She struggled for her ordinary calm

Lines 146–63. The mixture of benign and malignant characters reflects the poet's range of reading in the classics, folklore and the New Testament. In Greek mythology, nine Muses preside over the arts, and the Fates determine a mortal's lifespan. Psyche is the bride of Aphrodite's son Eros, who, due to his wife's disobedience, subjects her to various trials. Medusa is a beautiful Gorgon, who incurs the wrath of Athena and is transformed into a snake-haired monster. Our Lady of the Passion is based on Luke 2:33–5. An icon of the Servite order, the image evolved from one into seven swords, symbolising the sorrows suffered by Christ's mother. In Greek legend Lamia was the mistress of Zeus, whose wife Hera discovered the affair and killed several of their children. Lamia avenged the loss by preying on the children of others.
Line 172. See EBB's 'The Picture Gallery at Penshurst', in which the portrait of Waller's Saccharissa is 'in death laid by, / As any blotted scroll' (*Works*, vol. 4, p. 240, lines 39–40).

And missed it rather, – told me not to shrink,
As if she had told me not to lie or swear, –
'She loved my father and would love me too   335
As long as I deserved it.' Very kind.

I understood her meaning afterward;
She thought to find my mother in my face,
And questioned it for that.

Even as Aurora writhes under the affliction of her aunt's domestic
tyranny, she creates an alternative world in which her mind's eye exer-
cises its power to perceive beauty and sublimity in the landscape. The
verse description of the environs surrounding Aurora's room in her
aunt's house rehearses many *topoi* of English loco-descriptive poetry
and, according to Reynolds, recalls the pastoral landscape of the Malvern
Hills where EBB spent her childhood.[2] Aurora's chamber is an inner
sanctum that replicates in domestic decor the green world outside, but it
is not an occult place. Rather, the poet apostrophises 'you', the reader,
to imagine standing inside, pushing one's 'head out' the window and
being 'baptised into the grace / And privilege of seeing . . .'. The ellipses
are Aurora's and signal an important change of register in the text. Once
the verse moves from inside to outside, the poet introduces 'seeing' as a
theme and characterises it as a sacrament bestowed by nature:

I had a little chamber in the house,
As green as any privet-hedge a bird
Might choose to build in, though the nest itself
Could show but dead-brown sticks and straws; the walls   570
Were green, the carpet was pure green, the straight
Small bed was curtained greenly, and the folds
Hung green about the window which let in
The out-door world with all its greenery.
You could not push your head out and escape   575
A dash of dawn-dew from the honeysuckle,
But so you were baptized in the grace
And privilege of seeing . . .
                    First, the lime,*
(I had enough there, of the lime, to be sure, –
My morning-dream was often hummed away   580
By the bees in it;) past the lime, the lawn,
Which, after sweeping broadly round the house,
Went trickling through the shrubberies in a stream

Line 578. While a typical tree of English gardens, the lime was most famously celebrated in
Coleridge's 'This Lime-Tree Bower My Prison'.

Of tender turf, and wore and lost itself
Among the acacias, over which you saw   585
The irregular line of elms by the deep lane
Which stopped the grounds and dammed the overflow
Of arbutus and laurel. Out of sight
The lane was; sunk so deep, no foreign tramp
Nor drover of wild ponies out of Wales   590
Could guess if lady's hall or tenant's lodge
Dispensed such odours, – though his stick well-crooked
Might reach the lowest trail of blossoming briar
Which dipped upon the wall.* Behind the elms,
And through their tops, you saw the folded hills   595
Striped up and down with hedges, (burly oaks
Projecting from the line to show themselves)
Through which my cousin Romney's chimneys smoked
As still as when a silent mouth in frost
Breathes, showing where the woodlands hid Leigh Hall;   600
While, far above, a jut of table-land,
A promontory without water, stretched, –
You could not catch it if the days were thick,
Or took it for a cloud; but, otherwise,
The vigorous sun would catch it up at eve   605
And use it for an anvil till he had filled
The shelves of heaven with burning thunderbolts,*
Protesting against night and darkness: – then,
When all his setting trouble was resolved
To a trance of passive glory, you might see   610
In apparition on the golden sky
(Alas, my Giotto's background!)* the sheep run
Along the fine clear outline, small as mice
That run along a witch's scarlet thread.

Not a grand nature. Not my chestnut-woods   615
Of Vallombrosa,* cleaving by the spurs

Line 578–94. Aurora's description of her aunt's property constitutes a picturesque landscape. The wandering lawn and 'irregular line of elms' are typical features of the picturesque, an aesthetic that values nature's ruggedness within carefully constructed views. The obscurity of the lane suggests the divide between the landowner and tenants (or outsiders, as Aurora notes), who were not entitled to enjoy the views. EBB's friend, Sir Uvedale Price, had written a treatise on the class conflict created by English estates landscaped in the picturesque manner. See his *Thoughts on the Defence of Property* (1797).

Line 607. In contrast to the picturesque, the sublime inspires awe and fear in the viewer; an angry sky suggests the wrath of a higher power, whether nature or God. Aurora uses the 'vigorous sun', setting at dusk, as a source of sublime effects on the promontory.

Line 612. Giotto di Bondone (b. 1267–75, d. 1337), Italian artist of the late Middle Ages, who, according to Leonardo, rendered nature as he saw it rather than stylised it (*Grove Art Online*).

Lines 615–26. The mention of Vallombrosa evokes a tradition of epic simile that Milton

To the precipices. Not my headlong leaps
Of waters, that cry out for joy or fear
In leaping through the palpitating pines,
Like a white soul tossed out to eternity   620
With thrills of time upon it. Not indeed
My multitudinous mountains, sitting in
The magic circle, with the mutual touch
Electric, panting from their full deep hearts
Beneath the influent* heavens, and waiting for   625
Communion and commission. Italy
Is one thing, England one.

                    On English ground
You understand the letter, – ere the fall,
How Adam lived in a garden.* All the fields
Are tied up fast with hedges, nosegay-like;   630
The hills are crumpled plains, the plains, parterres,
The trees, round, woolly, ready to be clipped;
And if you seek for any wilderness
You find, at best, a park. A nature tamed
And grown domestic like a barn-door fowl,   635
Which does not awe you with its claws and beak,
Nor tempt you to an eyrie too high up,
But which, in cackling, sets you thinking of
Your eggs to-morrow at breakfast, in the pause
Of finer meditation.
                 Rather say   640
A sweet familiar nature, stealing in
As a dog might, or child, to touch your hand
Or pluck your gown, and humbly mind you so
Of presence and affection, excellent
For inner uses, from the things without.   645

I could not be unthankful, I who was
Entreated thus and holpen.* In the room
I speak of, ere the house was well awake,
And also after it was well asleep,
I sat alone, and drew the blessing in   650

---

introduces to English poetry in *Paradise Lost*, Book 1, line 300 ff. Aurora's list of negative similes to describe the English landscape – by means of an Italian one – is also a rhetorical feature found in *Paradise Lost*.

    Line 625. Exercising celestial or astral influence or occult power (*OED*).

    Lines 627–9. Aurora conflates two Biblical allusions. The first comes from 2 Corinthians 3:6: 'The letter killeth, but the spirit giveth life.' The description of Adam in the Garden of Eden appears in Genesis 2:15.

    Line 647. Helped.

Of all that nature. With a gradual step,
A stir among the leaves, a breath, a ray,
It came in softly, while the angels made
A place for it beside me. The moon came,
And swept my chamber clean of foolish thoughts   655
The sun came, saying, 'Shall I lift this light
Against the lime-tree, and you will not look?
I make the birds sing – listen! but, for you,
God never hears your voice, excepting when
You lie upon the bed at nights and weep.'   660

Then, something moved me. Then, I wakened up
More slowly than I verily write now,
But wholly, at last, I wakened, opened wide
The window and my soul, and let the airs
And out-door sights sweep gradual gospels in,   665
Regenerating what I was.* O Life,
How oft we throw it off and think, – 'Enough,
Enough of life in so much! – here's a cause
For rupture; herein we must break with Life,
Or be ourselves unworthy; here we are wronged,   670
Maimed, spoiled for aspiration; farewell Life!'
And so, as froward* babes, we hide our eyes
And think all ended. – Then, Life calls to us,
In some transformed, apocalyptic, new voice,
Above us, or below us, or around: 675
Perhaps we name it Nature's voice, or Love's,
Tricking ourselves, because we are more ashamed
So own our compensations than our griefs:
Still, Life's voice! – still, we make our peace with Life.

And I, so young then, was not sullen.   680
Soon I used to get up early, just to sit
And watch the morning quicken in the grey,

Line 661–6. Compare to Ruskin in *Modern Painters*, vol. 3, part 4, p. 306:

> And if we now take final and full view of the matter we shall find that the love of nature,
> wherever it has existed, has been a faithful and sacred element of human feeling; that is to
> say, supposing all circumstances otherwise the same with respect to two individuals, the
> one who loves nature most will be *always* found to have more *faith in God* than the other.
> [. . .] I boldly assert the result is constantly the same: the nature worship will be found to
> bring with it such a sense of the presence and power of a Great Spirit as no mere reasoning
> can either induce or controvert; and where that nature worship is innocently pursued, i.e.
> with due respect to other claims on time, feeling, and exertion, and associated with the
> higher principles of religion,—it becomes the channel of certain sacred truths, which by no
> other means can be conveyed.

Line 672. Forward, precocious.

And hear the silence open like a flower,
Leaf after leaf, – and stroke with listless hand
The woodbine through the window, till at last   685
I came to do it with a sort of love,
At foolish unaware: whereat I smiled,
A melancholy smile, to catch myself
Smiling for joy.*
                         Capacity for joy
Admits temptation. It seemed, next, worth while   690
To dodge the sharp sword set against my life;
To slip down stairs through all the sleepy house,
As mute as any dream there, and escape
As a soul from the body, out of doors,
Glide through the shrubberies, drop into the lane,   695
And wander on the hills an hour or two,
Then back again before the house should stir.

Or else I sate on in my chamber green,
And lived my life, and thought my thoughts, and prayed
My prayers without the vicar; read my books,   700
Without considering whether they were fit
To do me good. Mark, there. We get no good
By being ungenerous, even to a book,
And calculating profits, – so much help
By so much rending. It is rather when   705
We gloriously forget ourselves, and plunge
Soul-forward, headlong, into a book's profound,
Impassioned for its beauty and salt of truth –
'Tis then we get the right good from a book.

It is in her idyllic room where she can 'draw in' nature and study her books that Aurora begins her work as a poet. While her aunt has attempted to teach her niece select domestic arts and give her a smattering of learning, Aurora absorbs what she can from her father's books and attempts to extend her short-lived classical education. Her self-designed syllabus is audacious and ambitious, as she tackles Greek and Latin literature, as well as early Christian poetry. She describes the difficulty of her labour and her knowledge that success is not easily achieved.

Lines 680–9. See Ruskin on Wordsworth's lines:

> 'In such high hour / Of visitation from the living God / *Thought* was not' [*The Excursion*, Book I, lines 211–13; Ruskin's emphasis]. And [Wordsworth] refers to the intense delight which he himself felt, and which he supposes other men feel, in nature, during their thoughtless youth, as an intimation of their immortality, and a joy which indicates their having come fresh from the hand of God. (*Modern Painters*, vol. 3, part 4, pp. 313–14).

Critical of her early verse, which she thinks is artificial and imitative, she, nonetheless, feels the poetic calling, as though she were one of God's prophets. Her monastic life and soldier-like determination is reflected in her appearance, which she describes in a verbal self-portrait:

> And so, like most young poets, in a flush
> Of individual life, I poured myself
> Along the veins of others, and achieved
> Mere lifeless imitations of live verse,*
> And made the living answer for the dead,   975
> Profaning nature. 'Touch not, do not taste,
> Nor handle,'* – we're too legal, who write young:
> We beat the phorminx* till we hurt our thumbs,
> As if still ignorant of counterpoint;
> We call the Muse, – 'O Muse, benignant Muse,' –   980
> As if we had seen her purple-braided head,*
> With the eyes in it, start between the boughs
> As often as a stag's. What make-believe,
> With so much earnest! what effete results,
> From virile efforts! what cold wire-drawn* odes   985
> From such white heats! - bucolics,* where the cows
> Would scare the writer if they splashed the mud
> In lashing off the flies, – didactics, driven
> Against the heels of what the master said;
> And counterfeiting epics, shrill with trumps   990
> A babe might blow between two straining cheeks
> Of bubbled rose, to make his mother laugh;
> And elegiac griefs, and songs of love,
> Like cast-off nosegays picked up on the road,
> The worse for being warm: all these things, writ   995
> On happy mornings, with a morning heart,
> That leaps for love, is active for resolve,
> Weak for art only. Oft, the ancient forms
> Will thrill, indeed, in carrying the young blood.
> The wine-skins, now and then, a little warped,   1000

Line 974. Compare these thoughts to EBB's description of English poetry before Wordsworth in the extract 'William Wordsworth' in Chapter 3 of this *Guide*.

Lines 976–7. Colossians 2:21.

Line 978. An ancient Greek musical instrument, having (usually) seven strings and resembling a cithara or lyre (*OED*).

Line 981. 'The epithet "violet-tressed" or "violet haired" is borrowed from Pindar. See *Pythian Odes* 1.3 and *Isthnian Odes* 7.23' (Reynolds, p. 33, n. 2).

Line 985. 'Lacking in intensity; weak, thin' (*OED*).

Line 986. A pastoral form of poetry, considered low in a classical hierarchy of verse, the highest being epic.

Will crack even, as the new wine gurgles in.
Spare the old bottles! – spill not the new wine.*

By Keats's soul, the man who never stepped
In gradual progress like another man,
But, turning grandly on his central self,   1005
Ensphered himself in twenty perfect years*
And died, not young, (the life of a long life,
Distilled to a mere drop, falling like a tear
Upon the world's cold cheek to make it burn
For ever;) by that strong excepted soul,   1010
I count it strange, and hard to understand,
That nearly all young poets should write old;
That Pope was sexagenarian at sixteen,*
And beardless Byron academical,*
And so with others. It may be, perhaps,   1015
Such have not settled long and deep enough
In trance, to attain to clairvoyance, – and still
The memory mixes with the vision, spoils,
And works it turbid.
              Or perhaps, again,
In order to discover the Muse-Sphinx,*   1020
The melancholy desert must sweep round,
Behind you, as before. –
              For me, I wrote
False poems, like the rest, and thought them true.
Because myself was true in writing them.
I, peradventure, have writ true ones since   1025
With less complacence.
              But I could not hide
My quickening inner life from those at watch.
They saw a light at a window now and then,
They had not set there. Who had set it there?
My father's sister started when she caught   1030

Lines 998–1002. See Matthew 9:17 and Luke 5:37.

Lines 1003–6. The name John Keats (1795–1821) had, by the mid-nineteenth century, become nearly synonymous with Romantic genius. His youth and working-class origins seemed to belie the sophistication and passion of his verse.

Line 1013. Alexander Pope (1688–1744), an Augustan poet of precocious ability, who claimed to have composed his *Pastorals* (1709) when he was sixteen.

Line 1014. George Gordon, Lord Byron (1788–1824), typified another version of Romantic precocity. Like Pope's, his earliest verse, which he claims to have written at age fourteen, revitalised classical forms.

Line 1020. Aurora imagines a hybrid creature that might inspire her poetry and impart some of the occult knowledge possessed by her preternaturally gifted predecessors. She jokingly suggests that adopting the stereotypical mood of melancholy might help.

My soul agaze in my eyes. She could not say
I had no business with a sort of soul,
But plainly she objected, – and demurred,
That souls were dangerous things to carry straight
Through all the spilt saltpetre of the world.   1035
She said sometimes, 'Aurora, have you done
Your task this morning? have you read that book?
And are you ready for the crochet here?' –
As if she said, 'I know there's something wrong,
I know I have not ground you down enough   1040
To flatten and bake you to a wholesome crust
For household uses and proprieties,
Before the rain has got into my barn
And set the grains a-sprouting. What, you're green
With out-door impudence? you almost grow?'   1045
To which I answered, 'Would she hear my task,
And verify my abstract of the book?
And should I sit down to the crochet work?
Was such her pleasure?' Then I sate and teased
The patient needle till it spilt the thread,   1050
Which oozed off from it in meandering lace
From hour to hour. I was not, therefore, sad;
My soul was singing at a work apart
Behind the wall of sense, as safe from harm
As sings the lark when sucked up out of sight,   1055
In vortices of glory and blue air.*
And so, through forced work and spontaneous work,
The inner life informed the outer life,
Reduced the irregular blood to a settled rhythm,
Made cool the forehead with fresh-sprinkling dreams,   1060
And, rounding to the spheric soul the thin,
Pined body, struck a colour up the cheeks
Though somewhat faint. I clenched my brows across
My blue eyes greatening in the looking-glass,
And said, 'We'll live, Aurora! we'll be strong.   1065
The dogs are on us – but we will not die.'

Love and Poetry: Book II, lines 1–225, 333–541

The opening verses of Book II establish an important theme in *Aurora
Leigh*: the ostensible conflict between a woman's poetic calling and her

---

Lines 1055–6. In 'To a Skylark' (1827), Wordsworth apostrophises a bird that in flight
possesses a 'privacy of glorious light' (line 8).

desire for amatory fulfilment. Keeping in mind that this narrative is retrospective, we note that while the older Aurora recognises her dual identity – 'Woman and artist, – either incomplete' – the younger Aurora focuses solely on becoming a poet. But the young woman's 'fancies' do not 'fly' for long, as the 'eyes' of her cousin and suitor, Romney Leigh, create a caesura in line 60, and a new verse paragraph begins in which Aurora is brought back to earth 'fixed'. Comparing her crowning gesture to that of a caryatid, an ancient Greek architectural column used to uphold a temple roof, Aurora suggests feelings of obsolescence, helplessness and self-mockery, which she betrays with a blush. Aurora's pairing of two similes – one that freezes and the other that vivifies – transforms Romney's gaze into an unwitting source of Pygmalion-like power. For, as we soon learn, young, idealistic, chauvinist Romney loves his cousin and hopes that Aurora's 'dreaming of the stone and bronze' (that is, poetic fame) will melt in his adoring hands.

In the following excerpt Romney turns out to be a giant obstacle in Aurora's path to poetic glory. First, he does not believe women can be poets; second, he does not think poetry matters in a nation of want; and, third, a woman could never have made a sacrifice as important as Christ's. Romney's shocking words stay with Aurora until their reconciliation in Book VIII. There, Romney and Aurora revisit their Book II debate and revise their answers to these important questions: can a woman be a legitimate poet? Does poetry matter in a materialistic society? Is Romney's philanthropic enterprise a worthwhile cause? Is love possible for individuals committed to higher ideals? As Helen Cooper has observed, 'Books [I–IV] are repeated in reverse order in Books [VI–IX],' making Books II and VIII symmetrical to one another.[3] The symmetry shows Aurora's 'transformation from being the object of Romney's gaze to being the subject of her own vision'.[4] Cooper notes that all the books hinge on Book V, in which Aurora meditates on the progress and nature of her art. Governing her self-criticism in that book, however, is Romney's and other male critics' scepticism toward women artists. Aurora is smart enough to know that she has an achievable goal, so long as she stays committed to poetry, but loneliness and self-doubt shadow the sun in that June-born woman.

> Times followed one another. Came a morn
> I stood upon the brink of twenty years,
> And looked before and after, as I stood
> Woman and artist, – either incomplete,
> Both credulous of completion. There I held   5
> The whole creation in my little cup,

And smiled with thirsty lips before I drank,
'Good health to you and me, sweet neighbour mine,
And all these peoples.'
                    I was glad, that day;
The June was in me, with its multitudes   10
Of nightingales all singing in the dark,
And rosebuds reddening where the calyx* split.
I felt so young, so strong, so sure of God!
So glad, I could not choose be very wise!
And, old at twenty, was inclined to pull   15
My childhood backward in a childish jest
To see the face of't once more, and farewell!
In which fantastic mood I bounded forth
At early morning, – would not wait so long
As even to snatch my bonnet by the strings,   20
But, brushing a green trail across the lawn
With my gown in the dew, took will and way
Among the acacias of the shrubberies,
To fly my fancies in the open air
And keep my birthday, till my aunt awoke   25
To stop good dreams. Meanwhile I murmured on,
As honeyed bees keep humming to themselves,
'The worthiest poets have remained uncrowned
Till death has bleached their foreheads to the bone,
And so with me it must be, unless I prove   30
Unworthy of the grand adversity,
And certainly I would not fail so much.
What, therefore, if I crown myself to-day
In sport, not pride, to learn the feel of it,
Before my brows be numb as Dante's own   35
To all the tender pricking of such leaves?
Such leaves! what leaves?'
                    I pulled the branches down
To choose from.
                    'Not the bay! I choose no bay,
(The fates deny us if we are overbold)
Nor myrtle – which means chiefly love; and love   40
Is something awful which one dare not touch
So early o' mornings. This verbena strains
The point of passionate fragrance; and hard by,

Line 12. 'The whorl of leaves (sepals), either separate or grown together, and usually green, forming the outer envelope in which the flower is enclosed while yet in the bud' (*OED* 1.a).

This guelder-rose, at far too slight a beck
Of the wind, will toss about her flower-apples.   45
Ah – there's my choice, – that ivy on the wall,
That headlong ivy!* not a leaf will grow
But thinking of a wreath. Large leaves, smooth leaves,
Serrated like my vines, and half as green.
I like such ivy, bold to leap a height   50
'Twas strong to climb; as good to grow on graves
As twist about a thyrsus*; pretty too,
(And that's not ill) when twisted round a comb.'
Thus speaking to myself, half singing it,
Because some thoughts are fashioned like a bell   55
To ring with once being touched, I drew a wreath
Drenched, blinding me with dew, across my brow,
And fastening it behind so, turning faced
. . My public! – cousin Romney – with a mouth
Twice graver than his eyes.
                                     I stood there fixed, –   60
My arms up, like the caryatid, sole
Of some abolished temple, helplessly
Persistent in a gesture which derides
A former purpose. Yet my blush was flame,
As if from flax, not stone.
                                     'Aurora Leigh,   65
The earliest of Aurora's!'
                                     Hand stretched out
I clasped, as shipwrecked men will clasp a hand,
Indifferent to the sort of palm. The tide
Had caught me at my pastime, writing down
My foolish name too near upon the sea   70
Which drowned me with a blush as foolish. 'You,
My cousin!'
                     The smile died out in his eyes
And dropped upon his lips, a cold dead weight,
For just a moment, 'Here's a book, I found!
No name writ on it – poems, by the form;   75
Some Greek upon the margin, – lady's Greek,
Without the accents.* Read it? Not a word.

Lines 46–7. Rejecting the usual bay (associated with the god of poetry, Apollo) and myrtle (associated with the goddess of love, Venus), as well as the 'passionate' verbena and easily buffeted guelder-rose, Aurora decides that ivy, a hardy climbing plant associated with the votaries of Dionysius (the god of pleasure), is best.

Line 52. Thyrsus: carried by Dionysius (Bacchus) and his votaries during their revels, it is a staff adorned with ivy or vines.

Lines 76–7. Based on historical evidence, EBB and other scholars argued against the use of

I saw at once the thing had witchcraft in't,
Whereof the reading calls up dangerous spirits;
I rather bring it to the witch.'
                      'My book!   80
You found it' . .
               'In the hollow by the stream,
That beech leans down into – of which you said,
The Oread in it has a Naiad's heart*
And pines for waters.'
                 'Thank you.'
                      'Thanks to *you*.
My cousin! that I have seen you not too much   85
A witch, a poet, scholar, and the rest,
To be a woman also.'
                     With a glance
The smile rose in his eyes again, and touched
The ivy on my forehead, light as air.
I answered gravely, 'Poets needs must be   90
Or men or women – more's the pity.'
                        'Ah,
But men, and still less women, happily,
Scarce need be poets. Keep to the green wreath,
Since even dreaming of the stone and bronze
Brings headaches, pretty cousin, and defiles   95
The clean white morning dresses.'*
                   'So you judge!
Because I love the beautiful I must
Love pleasure chiefly, and be overcharged
For ease and whiteness! well, you know the world,
And only miss your cousin, 'tis not much.   100
But learn this; I would rather take my part
With God's Dead, who afford to walk in white
Yet spread His glory, than keep quiet here,
And gather up my feet from even a step,
For fear to soil my gown in so much dust.*   105
I choose to walk at all risks. – Here, if heads
That hold a rhythmic thought, must ache perforce,

accents in writing Greek. Here, Romney suggests that the lack of accents is not rigorous and reflects a 'lady's' limited capacity to learn the classics.

   Line 83. An oread inhabits hills, mountains or grottos; a naiad is a water spirit, inhabiting various bodies of water.

   Lines 93–6. The association between poetic fame and sculptural representation is famously codified in Alexander Pope's *The Temple of Fame* (1715).

   Lines 101–5. See Revelation 3:4. 'Thou hast a few names even in Sardis which have not defiled their garments; and they shall walk with me in white: for they are worthy.'

For my part, I choose headaches – and to-day's
My birthday.'
    'Dear Aurora, choose instead
To cure such. You have balsams.'*
      'I perceive!   110
The headache is too noble for my sex.
You think the heartache would sound decenter,*
Since that's the woman's special, proper ache,
And altogether tolerable, except
To a woman.'
    Saying which, I loosed my wreath,   115
And, swinging it beside me as I walked,
Half petulant, half playful, as we walked,
I sent a sidelong look to find his thought, –
As falcon set on falconer's finger may,
With sidelong head, and startled, braving eye,   120
Which means, 'You'll see – you'll see! I'll soon take flight,
You shall not hinder.' He, as shaking out
His hand and answering 'Fly then,' did not speak,
Except by such a gesture. Silently
We paced, until, just coming into sight   125
Of the house-windows, he abruptly caught
At one end of the swinging wreath, and said
'Aurora!' There I stopped short, breath and all.

'Aurora, let's be serious, and throw by
This game of head and heart. Life means, be sure,   130
Both heart and head, – both active, both complete,
And both in earnest. Men and women make
The world, as head and heart make human life.
Work man, work woman, since there's work to do
In this beleaguered earth, for head and heart,   135
And thought can never do the work of love!
But work for ends, I mean for uses, not
For such sleek fringes (do you call them ends?
Still less God's glory?) as we sew ourselves
Upon the velvet of those baldaquins*   140
Held 'twixt us and the sun. That book of yours,

Line 110. 'An aromatic oily or resinous medicinal preparation, usually for external application, for healing wounds or soothing pain' (*OED*).

Lines 111–12. Aurora catches Romney's gendered head and heart dichotomy typical of their era.

Line 140. A 'baldaquin' is a canopy of rich, embroidered brocade suspended above an altar or pulpit. The word 'fringes' in line 138 refers to the loose ends of such a fabric and implies that Aurora's writing is merely ornamental.

I have not read a page of; but I toss
A rose up – it falls calyx down, you see!
The chances are that, being a woman, young,
And pure, with such a pair of large, calm eyes,   145
You write as well . . and ill . . upon the whole,
As other women. If as well, what then?
If even a little better, . . still what then?
We want the Best in art now, or no art.
The time is done for facile settings up   150
Of minnow gods, nymphs here, and tritons there;*
The polytheists have gone out in God,*
That unity of Bests. No best, no God!
And so with art, we say. Give art's divine,
Direct, indubitable, real as grief,   155
Or leave us to the grief we grow ourselves
Divine by overcoming with mere hope
And most prosaic patience. You, you are young
As Eve* with nature's daybreak on her face,
But this same world you are come to, dearest coz,   160
Has done with keeping birthdays, saves her wreaths
To hang upon her ruins, – and forgets
To rhyme the cry with which she still beats back
Those savage, hungry dogs that hunt her down
To the empty grave of Christ.* The world's hard pressed;   165
The sweat of labour in the early curse
Has (turning acrid in six thousand years)*
Become the sweat of torture. Who has time,
An hour's time . . think! . . to sit upon a bank
And hear the cymbal tinkle in white hands!   170
When Egypt's slain, I say, let Miriam sing! –
Before – where's Moses?'*
                'Ah – exactly that
Where's Moses? – is a Moses to be found?
You'll sink him vainly in the bulrushes,

Line 151. Minor deities: nymphs inhabit the earth, rivers and streams; tritons the sea.

Line 152. Those who believe in multiple gods rather than the single god of Judeo-Christian or Islamic belief.

Line 159. Drawing on Genesis 2:18–23, Romney implies Eve's youth and subservience to Adam.

Line 165. See Matthew 27 and 28. Christ's body disappears from the tomb of Joseph of Arimathea, where it was laid after the crucifixion. Romney uses the reference to suggest that a world desperate with persecution and want does not care about poetry.

Line 167. In the nineteenth century, events from Genesis were thought to have taken place around 4000 BC.

Line 172. See Exodus 15:19–21. Miriam leads the children of Israel in song after Moses has defeated Pharaoh and his army.

While I in vain touch cymbals.* Yet, concede,   175
Such sounding brass* has done some actual good,
(The application in a woman's hand,
If that were credible, being scarcely spoilt,)
In colonising beehives.'
               'There it is! –
You play beside a death-bed like a child,   180
Yet measure to yourself a prophet's place
To teach the living. None of all these things,
Can women understand. You generalize
Oh, nothing, – not even grief! Your quick-breathed hearts,
So sympathetic to the personal pang,   185
Close on each separate knife-stroke, yielding up
A whole life at each wound; incapable
Of deepening, widening a large lap of life
To hold the world-full woe. The human race
To you means, such a child, or such a man,   190
You saw one morning waiting in the cold,
Beside that gate, perhaps. You gather up
A few such cases, and, when strong, sometimes
Will write of factories and of slaves,* as if
Your father were a negro, and your son   195
A spinner in the mills. All's yours and you,
All, coloured with your blood, or otherwise
Just nothing to you. Why, I call you hard
To general suffering. Here's the world half blind
With intellectual light, half brutalised   200
With civilization, having caught the plague
In silks from Tarsus,* shrieking east and west
Along a thousand railroads, mad with pain
And sin too! . . does one woman of you all,
(You who weep easily) grow pale to see   205
This tiger shake his cage? – does one of you
Stand still from dancing, stop from stringing pearls
And pine and die, because of the great sum

Line 175. Cymbals appear in lines 170 and 175, and are associated with the singer and prophet David; Miriam plays the timbrel in Exodus 15. The origins of Moses as a foundling among bulrushes appears in Exodus 2:3; significantly, Miriam is often credited with his discovery (Scheinberg, p. 71, n. 14).

Line 176. See 1 Corinthians 13:1.

Lines 192–4. Romney refers to protest poems like those EBB had written. See 'The Cry of the Children' (1843) and 'The Runaway Slave at Pilgrim's Point' (1847). His accusation captures a conservative view of women writers in the 1840s: namely, that their causes are personal and not humanitarian. The allusion is a sly nod to EBB's readers, who, aware of her success as a poet, would have recognised the hollowness of Romney's statement.

Line 202. A city in southern Turkey and an ancient crossroads for land and sea trade routes.

Of universal anguish? – Show me a tear
Wet as Cordelia's,* in eyes bright as yours,   210
Because the world is mad. You cannot count,
That you should weep for this account, not you!
You weep for what you know. A red-haired child
Sick in a fever, if you touch him once,
Though but so little as with a finger-tip,   215
Will set you weeping! but a million sick . .
You could as soon weep for the rule of three,*
Or compound fractions. Therefore, this same world
Uncomprehended by you must remain
Uninfluenced by you. – Women as you are,   220
Mere women, personal and passionate,
You give us doating mothers, and perfect wives.
Sublime Madonnas, and enduring saints!
We get no Christ from you, – and verily
We shall not get a poet, in my mind.'   225

     * * *

     There he glowed on me
With all his face and eyes. 'No other help?'
Said he – 'no more than so?'
      'What help?' I asked.   345
'You'd scorn my help, – as Nature's self, you say,
Has scorned to put her music in my mouth,
Because a woman's. Do you now turn round
And ask for what a woman cannot give?'

'For what she only can, I turn and ask,'   350
He answered, catching up my hands in his,
And dropping on me from his high-eaved brow
The full weight of his soul, – 'I ask for love,
And that, she can; for life in fellowship
Through bitter duties – that, I know she can;   355
For wifehood – will she?'
      'Now,' I said, 'may God
Be witness 'twixt us two!' and with the word,
Meseemed I floated into a sudden light
Above his stature, – 'am I proved too weak
To stand alone, yet strong enough to bear   360
Such leaners on my shoulder? poor to think,
Yet rich enough to sympathise with thought?

Line 210. See *King Lear* IV, vii, 71.
Line 217. The golden ratio, or rule of proportion.

Incompetent to sing, as blackbirds can,
Yet competent to love, like HIM?'*
                                    I paused:
Perhaps I darkened, as the light-house will   365
That turns upon the sea. 'It's always so!
Anything does for a wife.'
                          'Aurora, dear,
And dearly honoured' – he pressed in at once
With eager utterance, – 'you translate me ill.
I do not contradict my thought of you   370
Which is most reverent, with another thought
Found less so. If your sex is weak for art,
(And I who said so, did but honour you
By using truth in courtship) it is strong
For life and duty. Place your fecund heart   375
In mine, and let us blossom for the world
That wants love's colour in the grey of time.
My talk, meanwhile, is arid to you, ay,
Since all my talk can only set you where
You look down coldly on the arena-heaps   380
Of headless bodies, shapeless, indistinct!
The Judgment-Angel* scarce would find his way
Through such a heap of generalised distress,
To the individual man with lips and eyes,
Much less Aurora. Ah, my sweet, come down,   385
And, hand in hand, we'll go where yours shall touch
These victims, one by one! till, one by one,
The formless, nameless trunk of every man
Shall seem to wear a head, with hair you know,
And every woman catch your mother's face   390
To melt you into passion.'
                          'I am a girl,'
I answered slowly; 'you do well to name
My mother's face. Though far too early, alas,
God's hand did interpose 'twixt it and me,
I know so much of love, as used to shine   395
In that face and another. Just so much;
No more indeed at all. I have not seen
So much love since, I pray you pardon me,
As answers even to make a marriage with,
In this cold land of England. What you love,   400

Line 364. Ostensibly, Christ.
Line 382. See Revelation 20:4.

Is not a woman, Romney, but a cause:
You want a helpmate, not a mistress, sir,
A wife to help your ends, – in her no end!
Your cause is noble, your ends excellent,
But I, being most unworthy of these and that,   405
Do otherwise conceive of love. Farewell.'

'Farewell, Aurora, you reject me thus?'
He said.
              'Sir, you were married long ago.
You have a wife already whom you love,
Your social theory. Bless you both, I say.   410
For my part, I am scarcely meek enough
To be the handmaid of a lawful spouse.
Do I look a Hagar*, think you?'
                                'So, you jest!'

'Nay so, I speak in earnest,' I replied.
'You treat of marriage too much like, at least,   415
A chief apostle; you would bear with you
A wife . . a sister* . . shall we speak it out?
A sister of charity.'
                      'Then, must it be
Indeed farewell? And was I so far wrong
In hope and in illusion, when I took   420
The woman to be nobler than the man,*
Yourself the noblest woman, in the use
And comprehension of what love is, – love,
That generates the likeness of itself
Through all heroic duties? so far wrong   425
In saying bluntly, venturing truth on love,
'Come, human creature, love and work with me,' –
Instead of, 'Lady, thou art wondrous fair,
'And, where the Graces walk before, the Muse
'Will follow at the lighting of the eyes,   430
'And where the Muse walks, lovers need to creep
'Turn round and love me, or I die of love.''

Line 413. See Genesis 16. Hagar was the handmaid of Sarah, wife of Abraham. Too old to bear a child, Sarah suggested that Abraham take Hagar as his mistress, which he did. Although Hagar bore a son called Ishmael, she never became a true wife.
Lines 416–17. See 1 Corinthians 9:5. The 'chief apostle' is St Paul. Aurora takes Paul's exhortation to 'lead about a sister, a wife' to mean that marriage can be used as a resource for furthering Christ's mission.
Line 421. A commonplace Victorian notion. See the excerpt from Ellis's *The Women of England* (1838) in this *Guide*.

With quiet indignation I broke in.
'You misconceive the question like a man,
Who sees a woman as the complement   435
Of his sex merely.* You forget too much
That every creature, female as the male,
Stands single in responsible act and thought
As also in birth and death. Whoever says
To a loyal woman, 'Love and work with me,'   440
Will get fair answers, if the work and love
Being good themselves, are good for her – the best
She was born for. Women of a softer mood,
Surprised by men when scarcely awake to life,
Will sometimes only hear the first word, love,   445
And catch up with it any kind of work,
Indifferent, so that dear love go with it:
I do not blame such women, though, for love,
They pick much oakum*; earth's fanatics make
Too frequently heaven's saints. But *me*, your work   450
Is not the best for, – nor your love the best,
Nor able to commend the kind of work
For love's sake merely. Ah, you force me, sir,
To be over-bold in speaking of myself:
I, too, have my vocation, – work to do,   455
The heavens and earth have set me, since I changed
My father's face for theirs, and though your world
Were twice as wretched as you represent
Most serious work, most necessary work,
As any of the economists'. Reform,   460
Make trade a Christian possibility,
And individual right no general wrong;
Wipe out earth's furrows of the Thine and Mine,
And leave one green, for men to play at bowls;
With innings for them all! . . what th[e]n, indeed,   465
If mortals were not greater by the head
Than any of their prosperities? what then,
Unless the artist keep up open roads
Betwixt the seen and unseen, – bursting through
The best of your conventions with his best   470
The speakable, imaginable best

Lines 434–6. Reynolds believes the remark to be a reply to Tennyson's *The Princess* (1847), Part 7, lines 283–6: 'either sex alone / Is half itself, and in true marriage lies / Nor equal, nor unequal: each fulfils / Defect in each' (p. 51, n. 7).

Line 449. Pulling apart old rope used in caulking the seams of ships; convicts and workhouse inmates typically picked oakum.

God bids him speak, to prove what lies beyond
Both speech and imagination? A starved man
Exceeds a fat beast: we'll not barter, sir,
The beautiful for barley. – And, even so,   475
I hold you will not compass your poor ends
Of barley-feeding and material ease,
Without a poet's individualism
To work your universal. It takes a soul,
To move a body: it takes a high-souled man,   480
To move the masses*, even to a cleaner stye:
It takes the ideal, to blow a hair's breadth off
The dust of the actual. – Ah, your Fouriers* failed,
Because not poets enough to understand
That life develops from within. – For me,   485
Perhaps I am not worthy, as you say,
Of work like this: perhaps a woman's soul
Aspires, and not creates! yet we aspire,
And yet I'll try out your perhapses, sir;
And if I fail . . why, burn me up my straw   490
Like other false works – I'll not ask for grace,
Your scorn is better, cousin Romney. I
Who love my art, would never wish it lower
To suit my stature. I may love my art,
You'll grant that even a woman may love art,   495
Seeing that to waste true love on anything,
Is womanly, past question.'
                              I retain
The very last word which I said, that day,
As you the creaking of the door, years past,
Which let upon you such disabling news   500
You ever after have been graver. He,
His eyes, the motions in his silent mouth,
Were fiery points on which my words were caught,

Line 481. Reynolds (p. 52, n. 9) cites EBB's letter to Isa Blagden, Sunday [no date], 1850:

> in every advancement of the work hitherto, the individual has led the masses . . . Now in these new theories [Christian socialism, Fourierism], the individual is ground down into the multitude, and society must be 'moving all together' if it moves at all;—restricting the very possibility of progress by the use of the lights of genius. Genius is always *individual*. (*Letters of EBB* 1. 467)

Thomas Carlyle expresses the same sentiment in *On Heroes, Hero-Worship, and the Heroic in History* (1841).

Line 483. Charles François-Marie Fourier (1772–1837), a social theorist who promoted the reconstruction of society through the formation of communal associations of producers called *phalanges* (or phalanxes). His major works were *Théorie des quatre mouvements et des destinées générales* (1808) [*The Social Destiny of Man and Theory of the Four Movements* (1857)] and *Le Nouveau Monde industriel* [*The New Industrial World* (1829–30)].

Transfixed for ever in my memory
For his sake, not their own. And yet I know   505
I did not love him* .. nor he me .. that's sure ..
And what I said, is unrepented of,
As truth is always. Yet .. a princely man! –
If hard to me, heroic for himself!
He bears down on me through the slanting years,   510
The stronger for the distance. If he had loved,
Ay, loved me, with that retributive face, ..
I might have been a common woman now,
And happier, less known and less left alone;
Perhaps a better woman after all,   515
With chubby children hanging on my neck
To keep me low and wise. Ah me, the vines
That bear such fruit are proud to stoop with it.
The palm stands upright in a realm of sand.
And I, who spoke the truth then, stand upright,   520
Still worthy of having spoken out the truth,
By being content I spoke it, though it set
Him there, me here. – O woman's vile remorse,
To hanker after a mere name, a show,
A supposition, a potential love!   525
Does every man who names love in our lives,
Become a power for that? is love's true thing
So much best to us, that what personates love
Is next best? A potential love, forsooth!
We are not so vile. No, no – he cleaves, I think,   530
This man, this image, – chiefly for the wrong
And shock he gave my life, in finding me
Precisely where the devil of my youth
Had set me, on those mountain-peaks of hope
All glittering with the dawn-dew, all erect   535
And famished for the noon,* – exclaiming, while
I looked for empire and much tribute,
'Come, I have some worthy work for thee below.
Come, sweep my barns, and keep my hospitals,
And I will pay thee with a current coin   540
Which men give women.'

Line 506. It is important to remember that Aurora is looking back on this day seven years later (Book II, line 1238). See Morgan, pp. 124–35, on the poem's complex temporality.

Lines 533–6. The allusion to the 'devil' at dawn suggests Satan on the morning of Eve's temptation in *Paradise Lost*, Book IX, lines 192–6. Being 'famished for the noon' implies Aurora's vocation, since Apollo is god of the sun and poetry. Aurora is likely mocking her own pretension, while still expressing dismay over Romney's mundane alternative proposition.

Epistolary Fiction: Book III, lines 41–143, 344–538; Book IV, lines 393–437, 553–601, 885–985

Books III and IV take place seven years after Aurora and Romney have parted ways and recount important developments in the life of the protagonist. For one, she lives in a room of her own, making a living as a writer and pursuing her dream of becoming a great poet. Her reflections on the urban writer's life are alternately beleaguered, satirical and impassioned, as she describes her relations with critics, publishers, fans and a painter friend, Vincent Carrington. Second, both Books III and IV are written after an unfortunate event that takes place in Book IV: a failed marriage ceremony between the gentleman reformer, Romney Leigh, and a drover's daughter, Marian Erle. In Book III Aurora traces the origins of the relationship, which she learns about from a conniving aristocrat named Lady Waldemar, who visits the poet's dingy flat, asking for help to break up the couple. Waldemar and Aurora's catty exchanges reflect the tension between a spoiled heiress and a hardworking woman writer, particularly one who refuses to respect class hierarchy. Waldemar loves Romney because they are of the same class, not because she shares his social mission. Aurora refuses the heiress's request to interfere in Romney's nuptial plans but, out of concern for him, goes to meet Marian. The story of the seamstress's abusive childhood, escape from a sexual predator and path to self-sufficiency earns Aurora's sympathy and respect. Aurora also learns that her cousin's marriage proposal arises out of a desire to effect social change rather than to make a deep romantic attachment official. After Romney himself interrupts Aurora's visit, the two walk together in conversation and offer a swift portrait of issues current to the autumn of 1846.[5] It is their last conversation before the wedding.

Aurora receives a 'notice' (or invitation) for the marriage ceremony, and upon her arrival at the church, she sees that the guests come from both extremes of London society: the very rich and the very poor. Her grotesque and infernal description of the guests coming from the most neglected areas of the city often prompts students to accuse the author of being insensitive to or ignorant of poverty. Cora Kaplan attributes the source of EBB's description of the oozing masses to Charles Kingsley's novel, *Alton Locke, Tailor and Poet* (1885).[6] Kingsley was a Christian Socialist and Anglican clergyman, who worked to effect social reform through journalism and education. But both *Alton Locke* and *Aurora Leigh* draw on the infernal rhetoric and language of contamination from the Parliamentary Papers of the 1850s and Thomas Carlyle's *Latter-Day*

Pamphlets (1850), which is excerpted in this *Guide*.[7] Carlyle laments that 'supply-and-demand' has eroded the relationship between employers and workers (including those who may have once been masters and slaves), resulting in a caste of people subject not only to atrocious living conditions and inhumane work environments but also to moral laxity and criminal behaviour (29). EBB's observation of 'an ugly crest / Of faces [. . .] / From the crammed mass' (lines 569–71) captures Carlyle's picture of collective degradation.

Two of the excerpts chosen from these books also reflect *Aurora Leigh*'s incorporation of epistles or letters, a form of fictional narrative that originated with the Roman poet Ovid and was immensely popular in eighteenth-century verse and the novel. Although not solely composed of letters, *Aurora Leigh* contains numerous extended quotations of correspondence sent and received, which in the poem's first-person narrative offers a way to represent the minds of other characters. From Book III, the excerpts showcase Aurora's attitude toward her various correspondents and provide glimpses into Victorian literary culture. Aurora's letter from Vincent Carrington is a playful, erudite epistle from an old friend. As he seeks Aurora's opinion of his mythological drawings, Carrington's sketches and attraction to his model Kate Ward tap into ideas about the erotic origins of artistic inspiration. (EBB had a less sexually charged epistolary friendship with the Royal Academician Robert Benjamin Haydon but also socialised with the painters Dante Gabriel Rossetti and Frederic Leighton, for whom eroticism was an important component of their art.) Carrington seems to be a composite of various artist types whom EBB knew in Florence.

Never burn

Your letters, poor Aurora! for they stare
With red seals* from the table, saying each,
'Here's something that you know not.' Out alas,
'Tis scarcely that the world's more good and wise   45
Or even straighter and more consequent
Since yesterday at this time – yet, again,
If but one angel spoke from Ararat,*
I should be very sorry not to hear:
So open all the letters! let me read.   50
Blanche Ord, the writer in the 'Lady's Fan,'*

Line 43. Red sealing wax kept a letter closed before the introduction of self-adhesive envelopes.
Line 48. See Genesis 8–9. Ararat is the mountainous region where Noah's Ark landed after the flood.
Line 51. An invented title for a periodical or keepsake annual aimed at female readers.

Requests my judgment on . . that, afterwards.
Kate Ward desires the model of my cloak,
And signs, 'Elisha to you.'* Pringle Sharpe
Presents his work on 'Social Conduct,' craves   55
A little money for his pressing debts . .
From me, who scarce have money for my needs;
Art's fiery chariot* which we journey in
Being apt to singe our singing-robes to holes,
Although you ask me for my cloak, Kate Ward!   60
Here's Rudgely knows it, – editor and scribe;
He's 'forced to marry where his heart is not,
Because the purse lacks where he lost his heart.'
Ah, – lost it because no one picked it up!
That's really loss! – (and passable impudence.)   65
My critic Hammond flatters prettily,
And wants another volume like the last.
My critic Belfair wants another book
Entirely different, which will sell, (and live?)
A striking book, yet not a startling book,   70
The public blames originalities.
(You must not pump spring-water unawares
Upon a gracious public, full of nerves:)
Good things, not subtle, new yet orthodox,
As easy reading as the dog-eared page   75
That's fingered by said public fifty years,
Since first taught spelling by its grandmother,
And yet a revelation in some sort:
That's hard, my critic, Belfair! So – what next?
My critic Stokes objects to abstract thoughts;   80
'Call a man, John, a woman, Joan,' says he,
'And do not prate so of *humanities*:'
Whereat I call my critic, simply Stokes.
My critic Jobson recommends more mirth,
Because a cheerful genius suits the times,   85
And all true poets laugh unquenchably
Like Shakspeare and the gods.* That's very hard,
The gods may laugh, and Shakspeare; Dante smiled
With such a needy heart on two pale lips,
We cry, 'Weep rather, Dante.'* Poems are   90

Line 54. See 2 Kings 2:1–15. The prophet Elijah's cloak fell to his disciple Elisha, upon his assumption into heaven.
Line 58. See 2 Kings 2:11. Elijah and Elisha are separated by a fiery chariot.
Line 87. In Homer's *Iliad* and *Odyssey*, the Olympian gods possess inextinguishable laughter.
Line 90. Dante's typically solemn demeanour offers a stark contrast to Homer and Shakespeare.

Men, if true poems: and who dares exclaim
At any man's door, 'Here, 'tis probable
The thunder fell last week, and killed a wife,
And scared a sickly husband – what of that?
Get up, be merry, shout, and clap your hands,   95
Because a cheerful genius suits the times –'?
None says so to the man, and why indeed
Should any to the poem? A ninth seal;
The apocalypse is drawing to a close.*
Ha, – this from Vincent Carrington, – 'Dear friend,   100
I want good counsel. Will you lend me wings
To raise me to the subject, in a sketch
I'll bring to-morrow – may I? at eleven?
A poet's only born to turn to use;
So save you! for the world . . and Carrington.'   105
'(Writ after.) Have you heard of Romney Leigh,
Beyond what's said of him in newspapers,
His phalansteries* there, his speeches here,
His pamphlets, pleas, and statements, everywhere?
He dropped me long ago; but no one drops   110
A golden apple* – though, indeed, one day,
You hinted that, but jested. Well, at least,
You know Lord Howe, who sees him . . whom he sees,
And *you* see, and I hate to see, – for Howe
Stands high upon the brink of theories,   115
Observes the swimmers, and cries 'Very fine,'
But keeps dry linen equally, – unlike
That gallant breaster, Romney. Strange it is,
Such sudden madness, seizing a young man,
To make earth over again, – while I'm content   120
To make the pictures. Let me bring the sketch.
A tiptoe Danae,* overbold and hot:
Both arms a-flame to meet her wishing Jove
Halfway, and burn him faster down; the face
And breasts upturned and straining, the loose locks   125
All glowing with the anticipated gold.

Line. 99. See Revelation 5:1.
Line 108. See note 66 in Chapter 1.
    Line 111. In the legend of Atalanta, a suitor drops a golden apple to distract her during a
running contest and wins both her hand and the race. It is possible that Aurora has joked with
Carrington about his way with women.
    Line 122. An oracle tells Danae's father, Acrisius of Argos, that she will give birth to a son
who will kill him. He locks her in a prison to avoid that fate, but Zeus impregnates her in the
form of a golden shower. She conceives Perseus, who tries to avoid fulfilling the prophecy, but
fails.

Or here's another on the self-same theme.
She lies here – flat upon her prison-floor,
The long hair swathed about her to the heel,
Like wet sea-weed. You dimly see her through   130
The glittering haze of that prodigious rain,
Half blotted out of nature by a love
As heavy as fate. I'll bring you either sketch.
I think, myself, the second indicates
More passion.'
              Surely. Self is put away,   135
And calm with abdication. She is Jove,
And no more Danae – greater thus. Perhaps
The painter symbolises unawares
Two states of the recipient artist-soul,
One, forward, personal, wanting reverence,   140
Because aspiring only. We'll be calm,
And know that, when indeed our Joves come down.
We all turn stiller than we have ever been.*

         *   *   *

A lady called upon me on such a day.
She had the low voice of your English dames,   345
Unused, it seems, to need rise half a note
To catch attention, – and their quiet mood,
As if they lived too high above the earth
For that to put them out in anything:
So gentle, because verily so proud;   350
So wary and afeared of hurting you,
By no means that you are not really vile,
But that they would not touch you with their foot
To push you to your place; so self-possessed
Yet gracious and conciliating, it takes   355
An effort in their presence to speak truth:
You know the sort of woman, – brilliant stuff,
And out of nature. 'Lady Waldemar.'
She said her name quite simply, as if it meant
Not much indeed, but something, – took my hands,   360
And smiled, as if her smile could help my case,
And dropped her eyes on me, and let them melt.

Lines 122–41. Carrington's sketches portray two different ideas about Danae's sexual encounter with Zeus (or Jove in Latin literature): the first is active and willing, the second passive and oppressive. Aurora takes the drawings to be symbolic of artistic inspiration and prefers the passive Danae because she seems to absorb Jove's power.

'Is this,' she said, 'the Muse?'
                                    'No sibyl even,'*
I answered, 'since she fails to guess the cause
Which taxed you with this visit, madam.'
                                    'Good,'   365
She said, 'I like to be sincere at once;
Perhaps, if I had found a literal Muse,
The visit might have taxed me. As it is,
You wear your blue so chiefly in your eyes,
My fair Aurora, in a frank good way,   370
It comforts me entirely for your fame,
As well as for the trouble of my ascent
To this Olympus.'*
                            There, a silver laugh
Ran rippling through her quickened little breaths
The steep stair somewhat justified.
                                    'But still   375
Your ladyship has left me curious why
You dared the risk of finding the said Muse?'

'Ah, – keep me, notwithstanding, to the point
Like any pedant. Is the blue in eyes
As awful as in stockings, after all,   380
I wonder, that you'd have my business out
Before I breathe – exact the epic plunge
In spite of gasps? Well, naturally you think
I've come here, as the lion-hunters go
To deserts, to secure you, with a trap   385
For exhibition in my drawing-rooms
On zoologic soirées? Not in the least.
Roar softly at me; I am frivolous,
I dare say; I have played at lions, too
Like other women of my class, – but now   390
I meet my lion simply as Androcles
Met his . . when at his mercy.'*

Line 363. Aurora rejects her visitor's light flattery with a witty repost. A sibyl typically has oracular power.

Lines 368–73 and 380. The blue in Aurora's eyes suggest her bluestocking pursuit of learning. By the 1840s, 'bluestocking' was a pejorative term for an educated woman, even though its origin was in celebrated eighteenth-century London salons. Waldemar also snidely refers to Aurora's modest garret flat as the seat of the gods.

Lines 388–92. The term 'lion' for a celebrity was current in the nineteenth century. The tale of 'Androcles and the Lion' appears in *Aesop's Fables*. In short, Androcles is an escaped Roman slave who encounters a wounded lion in the forest. After removing a thorn from the lion's paw, which was causing him great distress, Androcles is recaptured by the Emperor's henchmen. His punishment is to be fed to a lion, but it so happens that the very animal released to kill Androcles is the

So, she bent
Her head, as queens may mock, – then lifting up
Her eyelids with a real grave queenly look,
Which ruled, and would not spare, not even herself,   395
'I think you have a cousin: – Romney Leigh.'

'You bring a word from *him*?' – my eyes leapt up
To the very height of hers, – 'a word from *him*?'

'I bring a word about him, actually.
But first,' (she pressed me with her urgent eyes)   400
'You do not love him, – you?'
                              'You're frank at least
In putting questions, madam,' I replied.
'I love my cousin cousinly – no more.'

'I guessed as much. I'm ready to be frank
In answering also, if you'll question me,   405
Or even with something less. You stand outside,
You artist women, of the common sex;
You share not with us, and exceed us so
Perhaps by what you're mulcted* in, your hearts
Being starved to make your heads: so run the old   410
Traditions of you. I can therefore speak,
Without the natural shame which creatures feel
When speaking on their level, to their like.
There's many a papist* she, would rather die
Than own to her maid she put a ribbon on   415
To catch the indifferent eye of such a man,
Who yet would count adulteries on her beads
At holy Mary's shrine, and never blush;
Because the saints are so far off, we lose
All modesty before them. Thus, to-day.   420
'Tis *I*, love Romney Leigh.'
                              'Forbear,' I cried.
'If here's no muse, still less is any saint;
Nor even a friend, that Lady Waldemar
Should make confessions' . .
                              'That's unkindly said.
If no friend, what forbids to make a friend   425
To join to our confession ere we have done?
I love your cousin. If it seems unwise

one he had previously assisted. The lion recognises his rescuer and fawns upon (rather than eats)
him. Impressed with the episode and its cause, the Emperor frees Androcles on the spot.
  Line 409. Punished; subjected to a penalty. See Book IX, line 564.
  Line 414. Roman Catholic.

To say so, it's still foolisher (we're frank)
To feel so. My first husband left me young,
And pretty enough, so please you, and rich enough,   430
To keep my booth in May-fair* with the rest
To happy issues. There are marquises
Would serve seven years to call me wife,* I know:
And, after seven, I might consider it,
For there's some comfort in a marquisate   435
When all's said, – yes, but after the seven years;
I, now, love Romney. You put up your lip,
So like a Leigh! so like him! – Pardon me,
I'm well aware I do not derogate*
In loving Romney Leigh. The name is good,   440
The means are excellent; but the man, the man –
Heaven help us both, – I am near as mad as he
In loving such an one.'
                    She slowly wrung
Her heavy ringlets till they touched her smile,
As reasonably sorry for herself,   445
And thus continued.
                    'Of a truth, Miss Leigh,
I have not, without a struggle, come to this.
I took a master in the German tongue,
I gamed* a little, went to Paris twice;
But, after all, this love! . . . you eat of love,   450
And do as vile a thing as if you ate
Of garlic – which, whatever else you eat,
Tastes uniformly acrid, till your peach
Reminds you of your onion! Am I coarse?
Well, love's coarse, nature's coarse – ah there's the rub!   455
We fair fine ladies, who park out our lives
From common sheep-paths, cannot help the crows
From flying over, – we're as natural still
As Blowsalinda.* Drape us perfectly
In Lyons' velvet,* – we are not, for that,   460

Line 431. 'A fashionable and expensive district of London. The allusion to the "booth" in May is yet another of Lady Waldemar's extravagant plays with words, pivoting here on the idea of a fair' (Reynolds, p. 85, n. 1).
Line 433. See Genesis 29:18–20.
Line 439. Condescend.
Line 449. Gambled.
Line 459. A shepherdess in John Gay's *Shepherd's Week* (1714), a series of pastorals in which the rustic nature of the characters is exaggerated.
Line 460. Lyons, located in central France, was a major centre of silk manufacture in the nineteenth century.

Lay-figures, like you! we have hearts within,
Warm, live, improvident, indecent hearts,
As ready for distracted ends and acts
As any distressed sempstress* of them all
That Romney groans and toils for. We catch love   465
And other fevers, in the vulgar way.
Love will not be outwitted by our wit,
Nor outrun by our equipages: – mine
Persisted, spite of efforts. All my cards
Turned up but Romney Leigh; my German stopped   470
At germane Wertherism*; my Paris rounds
Returned me from the Champs Elysées just
A ghost, and sighing like Dido's.* I came home
Uncured, – convicted rather to myself
Of being in love . . . in love! That's coarse you'll say   475
I'm talking garlic.'
                    Coldly I replied.
'Apologise for atheism, not love!
For, me, I do believe in love, and God.
I know my cousin: Lady Waldemar
I know not: yet I say as much as this: 480
Whoever loves him, let her not excuse
But cleanse herself; that, loving such a man,
She may not do it with such unworthy love
He cannot stoop and take it.'
                            'That is said
Austerely, like a youthful prophetess,   485
Who knits her brows across her pretty eyes
To keep them back from following the grey flight
Of doves between the temple-columns.* Dear,
Be kinder with me. Let us two be friends.
I'm a mere woman – the more weak perhaps   490

Line 464. The plight of the seamstress was well known: they were poorly paid due to an over-supply of workers and had trouble finding good employment as a result. Many turned to prostitution to supplement their income. See the extracts by Anna Jameson and W. R. Greg in Chapter 3.

Line 471. A cultural phenomenon resulting from the fame throughout Europe of Goethe's early novel, *Die Leiden des jungen Werther* [*The Sorrows of Young Werther* (1774)], a semi-autobiographical work about a sensitive artist, melancholy, rebellious and hopelessly in love with a girl, Charlotte (Lotte), who was engaged to someone else. Carlyle recognised the popularity of Werther-like youth in his essay 'Goethe' (1828).

Line 473. See Virgil's *Aeneid*, Book 6, lines 450–76. During his journey through the under-world, Aeneas meets the shade of Dido, the Carthaginian queen whom he had reluctantly aban-doned and who (to his surprise) had committed suicide. Reynolds points out the pun on Champs Elysées, which is a principal street in Paris and means Elysian Fields, the site of the virtuous dead in the underworld (p. 86, n. 9).

Line 488. In ancient Greece the priestess of a temple might use the release and observation of doves as a form of divination.

Through being so proud; you're better; as for him,
He's best. Indeed he builds his goodness up
So high, it topples down to the other side,
And makes a sort of badness; there's the worst
I have to say against your cousin's best!   495
And so be mild, Aurora, with my worst,
For his sake, if not mine.'
                              'I own myself
Incredulous of confidence like this
Availing him or you.'
                        'And I, myself,
Of being worthy of him with any love: 500
In your sense I am not so – let it pass.
And yet I save him if I marry him;
Let that pass too.'
                    'Pass, pass, we play police
Upon my cousin's life, to indicate
What may or may not pass?' I cried. 'He knows   505
What's worthy of him; the choice remains with *him*;
And what he chooses, act or wife, I think
I shall not call unworthy, I, for one.'
''Tis somewhat rashly said,' she answered slow;
'Now let's talk reason, though we talk of love.   510
Your cousin Romney Leigh's a monster! there,
The word's out fairly; let me prove the fact.
We'll take, say, that most perfect of antiques,
They call the Genius of the Vatican,*
Which seems too beauteous to endure itself   515
In this mixed world, and fasten it for once
Upon the torso of the Dancing Fawn,*
(Who might limp surely, if he did not dance,)
Instead of Buonarroti's mask*: what then?
We show the sort of monster Romney is,   520
With god-like virtue and heroic aims
Subjoined to limping possibilities
Of mismade human nature. Grant the man

Line 514. 'Also known as the contemplative Amor, the Eros of Centocelle, or Thanatos. The statue, which was thought to be a copy of a work by Praxiteles, stood during the 1850s in the Gallery of Statues in the Vatican Museum' (Reynolds, p. 87, n. 2).
   Line 517. The statue of the Dancing Faun stands (as it did in the nineteenth century) in the Tribune of the Uffizi Gallery in Florence. It plays both the *crotala* (a cymbal-like instrument) and the *scabellum* (or *croupezion*) under his right foot. The faun appears to be limping as he steps on the latter.
   Line 519. 'Buonarroti' scans in the pentameter line better than the more famous first name 'Michelangelo', who was thought to have restored the head and arms of the statue.

Twice godlike, twice heroic, – still he limps,
And here's the point we come to.'
                    'Pardon me,   525
But, Lady Waldemar, the point's the thing
We never come to.'
                'Caustic, insolent
At need! I like you' – (there, she took my hands)
'And now my lioness, help Androcles,
For all your roaring. Help me! for myself   530
I would not say so – but for him. He limps
So certainly, he'll fall into the pit
A week hence, – so I lose him – so he is lost!
And when he's fairly married, he a Leigh,
To a girl of doubtful life, undoubtful birth,   535
Starved out in London, till her coarse-grained hands
Are whiter than her morals, - even you
May call his choice most unworthy.'

            *   *   *

From Book IV

We had a strange and melancholy walk:
The night came drizzling downward in dark rain;
And, as we walked, the colour of the time,   395
The act, the presence, my hand upon his arm,
His voice in my ear, and mine to my own sense,
Appeared unnatural. We talked modern books,
And daily papers; Spanish marriage-schemes,*
And English climate – was 't so cold last year?   400
And will the wind change by to-morrow morn?
Can Guizot* stand? is London full? is trade
Competitive?* has Dickens turned his hinge
A-pinch upon the fingers of the great?*

Line 399. In August 1846 the Queen of Spain, Isabella, and her sister, the Infanta Maria Luisa, announced their plans to marry the Duke of Cadiz and the Duc de Montpensier, the son of Louis-Philippe of France, respectively. The English government objected to the Infanta's alliance, as it would mean Spain might come under French control, should Isabella be childless. *The Times* covered the controversy throughout September 1846. The scandal offers an ironic contrast to Romney and Marian's controversial marriage plans.

Line 402. François Pierre Guillaume Guizot (1787–1874) was an authoritarian French minister of Foreign Affairs during the time of the Spanish marriages, which he saw as advantageous for France. His resistance to reform eventually led to the revolutionary uprisings and his dismissal from office in 1848.

Line 403. Since the 1830s Free Traders and the Anti-Corn Law League had been campaigning for the repeal of the Corn Laws, which severely restricted the importation of foreign corn to England.

Line 404. Charles Dickens elicited charges of sedition for his criticism of upper-class attitudes toward the poor. See his Christmas book of 1844 called *The Chimes*.

And are potatoes to grow mythical   405
Like moly?* will the apple die out too?
Which way is the wind to-night? south-east? due east?*
We talked on fast, while every common word
Seemed tangled with the thunder at one end,
And ready to pull down upon our heads   410
A terror out of sight. And yet to pause
Were surelier mortal: we tore greedily up
All silence, all the innocent breathing-points,
As if, like pale conspirators in haste,
We tore up papers where our signatures   415
Imperilled us to an ugly shame or death.

I cannot tell you why it was. 'Tis plain
We had not loved nor hated: wherefore dread
To spill gunpowder on ground safe from fire?
Perhaps we had lived too closely, to diverge   420
So absolutely: leave two clocks, they say,
Wound up to different hours, upon one shelf,
And slowly, through the interior wheels of each,
The blind mechanic motion sets itself
A-throb, to feel out for the mutual time.*   425
It was not so with us, indeed. While he
Struck midnight, I kept striking six at dawn,
While he marked judgment, I, redemption-day;*
And such exception to a general law,
Imperious upon inert matter even,   430
Might make us, each to either insecure,
A beckoning mystery, or a troubling fear.

I mind me, when we parted at the door,
How strange his good-night sounded, – like good-night
Beside a deathbed, where the morrow's sun   435
Is sure to come too late for more good days:
And all that night I thought . . 'Good-night,' said he.

                    *   *   *

Lines 405–6. The Irish potato crop failed a second time in 1846, due to a parasitic fungus, and
resulted in a devastating famine. 'Moly' is an herb described by Homer, which allows Odysseus to
free himself from the enchantments of Circe. See *Odyssey*, Book 10, lines 302–6.
   Line 407. In the Bible the east wind heralds evil. See Exodus 10:13, Psalms 48:7, Ezekiel 19:12
and Hosea 12:1.
   Lines 421–5. EBB refers to Gottfried Wilhelm Leibniz's theory of the universal governing influence of pre-established harmony and draws specifically from his remarks on natural influence, in
which he uses two clocks as an example. See Reynolds, pp. 119–20, n. 3.
   Line 428. Ostensibly, the same day, but Romney's emphasis on retribution and Aurora's on
redemption casts the difference in their outlooks.

They clogged the streets, they oozed into the church
In a dark slow stream, like blood.* To see that sight,
The noble ladies stood up in their pews,   555
Some pale for fear, a few as red for hate,
Some simply curious, some just insolent,
And some in wondering scorn, – 'What next? what next?'
These crushed their delicate rose-lips from the smile
That misbecame them in a holy place,   560
With broidered hems of perfumed handkerchiefs;
Those passed the salts with confidence of eyes
And simultaneous shiver of moiré silk:
While all the aisles, alive and black with heads,
Crawled slowly toward the altar from the street,   565
As bruised snakes crawl and hiss out of a hole
With shuddering involution, swaying slow
From right to left, and then from left to right,
In pants and pauses. What an ugly crest
Of faces, rose upon you everywhere,   570
From that crammed mass! you did not usually
See faces like them in the open day:
They hide in cellars, not to make you mad
As Romney Leigh is. – Faces? O my God,
We call those, faces? men's and women's . . ay,   575
And children's; – babies, hanging like a rag
Forgotten on their mother's neck, – poor mouths,
Wiped clean of mother's milk by mother's blow
Before they are taught her cursing. Faces? . . phew,
We'll call them vices festering to despairs,   580
Or sorrows petrifying to vices: not
A finger-touch of God left whole on them;
All ruined, lost – the countenance worn out
As the garments, the will dissolute as the acts,
The passions loose and draggling in the dirt   585
To trip the foot up at the first free step!
Those, faces? 'twas as if you had stirred up hell
To heave its lowest dreg-fiends uppermost
In fiery swirls of slime, – such strangled fronts,
Such obdurate jaws were thrown up constantly,   590
To twit you with your race, corrupt your blood,
And grind to devilish colours all your dreams
Henceforth, – though, haply, you should drop asleep

Lines 553–4. The oozing blood suggests the opening of a wound. See the extract from Carlyle in this *Guide*. On Victorian metaphors that imply the appalling conditions of the urban poor, see Avery and Stott, pp. 190–7.

By clink of silver waters, in a muse
On Raffael's mild Madonna of the Bird.   595
I've waked and slept through many nights and days
Since then, – but still that day will catch my breath
Like a nightmare. There are fatal days, indeed,
In which the fibrous years have taken root
So deeply, that they quiver to their tops   600
Whene'er you stir the dust of such a day.

In contrast to Carrington's epistle, the apologetic, yet dignified letter from Marian Erle in Book IV explains why she left Romney waiting at the altar. Marian's mixture of regret, desire and determination recalls one of Ovid's mythological heroines from *Heroides*, a collection of verse epistles in which women (for example, Ariadne, Dido, Helen, Medea and so on) voice their despair over being separated from their beloved men. But far from simply lovelorn, Marian's letter expresses gratitude for Romney's care but also offers a reality check on his idealism. Although Lady Waldemar has confirmed her feeling that the union is socially taboo, Marian also insists that her love for him is solely platonic.

Here's Marian's letter, which a ragged child   885
Brought running, just as Romney at the porch
Looked out expectant of the bride. He sent
The letter to me by his friend Lord Howe
Some two hours after, folded in a sheet
On which his well-known hand had left a word.   890
Here's Marian's letter.
                        'Noble friend, dear saint
Be patient with me. Never think me vile,
Who might to-morrow morning be your wife
But that I loved you more than such a name.
Farewell, my Romney. Let me write it once, –   895
My Romney.
            ''Tis so pretty a coupled word,
I have no heart to pluck it with a blot.*
We say 'my God' sometimes, upon our knees,
Who is not therefore vexed: so bear with it . .
And me. I know I'm foolish, weak, and vain;   900
Yet most of all I'm angry with myself
For losing your last footstep on the stair,
The last time of your coming, – yesterday!

Line 897. Marian draws attention to the physical act of writing in these lines, which is typical of Ovid's letter-writers. The 'blot' of ink appears here notionally, but in line 967 Marian's tears create a real blot on the inked page. See Kauffman, pp. 36–7.

The very first time I lost step of yours,
(Its sweetness comes the next to what you speak)   905
But yesterday sobs took me by the throat,
And cut me off from music.
                 'Mister Leigh,
You'll set me down as wrong in many things.
You've praised me, sir, for truth, – and now you'll learn
I had not courage to be rightly true.   910
I once began to tell you how she* came,
The woman . . and you stared upon the floor
In one of your fixed thoughts . . which put me out
For that day. After, some one spoke of me,
So wisely, and of you, so tenderly,   915
Persuading me to silence for your sake . . .
Well, well! it seems this moment I was wrong
In keeping back from telling you the truth:
There might be truth betwixt us two, at least,
If nothing else. And yet 'twas dangerous.   920
Suppose a real angel came from heaven
To live with men and women! he'd go mad,
If no considerate hand should tie a blind
Across his piercing eyes.* 'Tis thus with you:
You see us too much in your heavenly light;   925
I always thought so, angel, – and indeed
There's danger that you beat yourself to death
Against the edges of this alien world,
In some divine and fluttering pity.
                   'Yes
It would be dreadful for a friend of yours,   930
To see all England thrust you out of doors
And mock you from the windows. You might say,
Or think (that's worse), 'There's some one in the house
I miss and love still.' Dreadful!*
                'Very kind,
I pray you mark, was Lady Waldemar.   935
She came to see me nine times, rather ten –
So beautiful, she hurts me like the day
Let suddenly on sick eyes.
               'Most kind of all,
Your cousin! – ah, most like you! Ere you came
She kissed me mouth to mouth: I felt her soul   940

Line 911. Lady Waldemar.
Lines 922–4. The lines foreshadow Romney's fate, which is revealed in Book IX.
Line 934. Aurora's interjection.

Dip through her serious lips in holy fire.
God help me, but it made me arrogant;
I almost told her that you would not lose
By taking me to wife: though, ever since,
I've pondered much a certain thing she asked . .   945
'He loves you, Marian?' . . in a sort of mild
Derisive sadness . . as a mother asks
Her babe, 'You'll touch that star,* you think?'
                         'Farewell!
I know I never touched it.
                         'This is worst:*
Babes grow, and lose the hope of things above;   950
A silver threepence sets them leaping high –
But no more stars! mark that.
                         'I've writ all night,
And told you nothing. God, if I could die,
And let this letter break off innocent
Just here! But no – for your sake . .
                         'Here's the last: 955
I never could be happy as your wife,
I never could be harmless as your friend,
I never will look more into your face,*
Till God says, 'Look!' I charge you, seek me not,
Nor vex yourself with lamentable thoughts   960
That peradventure I have come to grief;
Be sure I'm well, I'm merry, I'm at ease,
But such a long way, long way, long way off,
I think you'll find me sooner in my grave;
And that's my choice, observe. For what remains,   965
An over-generous friend* will care for me,
And keep me happy . . happier . .
                         'There's a blot!
This ink runs thick . . we light girls lightly weep . .
And keep me happier . . was the thing to say,
Than as your wife I could be! – O, my star,   970
My saint, my soul! for surely you're my soul,

Line 948. The image of Romney as a star begins here and continues throughout the poem. The symbolism becomes important in the last two books.
Lines 948–9. The breaking up of these lines suggests a dramatic change in Marian's heart, as she denies herself the right to dream of marrying a man higher in status than her and admits that even babies learn to lower their desires from heaven to earth. The analogy anticipates Marian's fate later in the poem.
Lines 956–8, 962. The parallel sentence structure, called anaphora, emphasises Marian's determination.
Line 966. Lady Waldemar.

Through whom God touched me! I am not so lost
I cannot thank you for the good you did,
The tears you stopped, which fell down bitterly,
Like these – the times you made me weep for joy   975
At hoping I should learn to write your notes
And save the tiring of your eyes, at night;
And most for that sweet thrice you kissed my lips
And said 'Dear Marian.'
     "Twould be hard to read,
This letter, for a reader half as learn'd,   980
But you'll be sure to master it, in spite
Of ups and downs. My hand shakes, I am blind;*
I'm poor at writing, at the best, – and yet
I tried to make my gs the way you showed.
Farewell. Christ love you. – Say 'Poor Marian' now.'   985

Epic and Society: Book V, lines 139–222, 627–771, 1266–78

In what is considered the central book of the poem, the narrator Aurora pauses to explain her ideals of poetry and describe her chilling experience at a party hosted by her wealthy patron, Lord Howe. At Book V's conclusion, Aurora, dissatisfied with being a literary lion, decides to leave England for Italy. The divide in the book between poetry and society, speculation and observation, seeing and hearing (or more precisely overhearing), optimism and disillusionment enacts the kind of 'double vision' (line 184 below) that Aurora believes all poets should have.

The first excerpt comes from Aurora's *ars poetica*, which comprises roughly the first half of Book V. Laying out what style and subject matter are suitable for serious writers, Aurora's mini-verse treatise focuses on epic, a genre that, in the mid-nineteenth century, was thought to be dead and the exclusive provenance of male writers. The critic Holly Laird points out that, 'although [*Aurora Leigh*'s] poetics appears to emerge primarily from a (male) Aristotelian tradition, its *ars* emerges from the modern (woman's) novel.'[8] But not even Victorian women's fiction foregrounds the body – particularly a maternal one – in the visually arresting way Aurora does in her discussion of epic. For while epics are always about society – typically at war or in its aftermath – Aurora believes women's lives and unique experiences, especially mothering, to be important subjects in a modern epic poem.

Line 982. With tears.

The density of annotation in the first excerpt reflects both Aurora's classical learning and engagement with Victorian literary trends. Her main point is this: a modern epic need not elevate its protagonists to the status of demi-gods nor wear the trappings of heroes from an earlier era. After all, Aurora argues, not only does Homer feature the human (and therefore imperfect) nature of his mortals, but the idealised subjects of later epic *chansons* (*La Chanson de Roland*; *Le Morte d'Arthur*) also have nothing to do with the age of Victoria. Rather, Aurora claims, poets should exert a 'double vision', stepping back from the events and actors of one's age in order to see them better. The extended analogy (lines 166–83) recounting Alexander's idea to carve a supine male figure into a mountain exemplifies the conqueror's hubris, as well as the pastoral plenitude of the ancient world. Moreover, it prepares the way for the metaphor of maternal energy and passion that Aurora believes represents her 'Age' and vitalises her art. In rejecting the vogue for medieval revivalism promoted by Tennyson and the Pre-Raphaelite poets and artists, EBB embraces instead the 'heroic heat' of 'true life' (line 205, 222).

> The critics say that epics have died out*
> With Agamemnon* and the goat-nursed gods;*   140
> I'll not believe it. I could never dream
> As Payne Knight* did, (the mythic mountaineer
> Who travelled higher than he was born to live,
> And showed sometimes the goitre* in his throat
> Discoursing of an image seen through fog,)   145
> That Homer's heroes measured twelve feet high.
> They were but men: – his Helen's* hair turned grey
> Like any plain Miss Smith's, who wears a front:
> And Hector's infant blubbered at a plume*
> As yours last Friday at a turkey-cock.   150

Line 139. A critical commonplace of the 1830s and 1840s.

Line 140. As recounted in Homer's *Iliad*, Agamemnon, King of Mycenae, was one of the generals who led the great siege of Troy.

Line 140. Zeus, head of the Greek gods, was nursed by the goat Amalthea. See Hyginus, *Poetica Astronomica*, II.13.

Line 142. Richard Payne Knight (1750–1824), classical scholar and connoisseur, whom EBB criticised for (among other things) cutting lines from his edition of the *Iliad* and the *Odyssey*.

Line 144. An enlargement of the thyroid gland, called bronchocoele, found in the necks of high mountain-dwellers.

Line 147. In Homer's *Iliad*, Helen was a Greek woman married to Agamemnon's brother, Menelaus. Her abduction by Paris, the son of Priam of Troy, is regarded as the cause of the Trojan War. Her beauty remains a feminine ideal.

Line 149. Hector was a valiant Trojan warrior, whose son Astyanax cries when he sees his father dressed for battle. See the *Iliad*, Book VI, lines 556–62.

All men are possible heroes: every age,
Heroic in proportions, double-faced,
Looks backward and before, expects a morn
And claims an epos.
      Ay, but every age   155
Appears to souls who live in it, (ask Carlyle)
Most unheroic.* Ours, for instance, ours!
The thinkers scout it, and the poets abound
Who scorn to touch it with a finger-tip:
A pewter age, – mixed metal, silver-washed;   160
An age of scum, spooned off the richer past;
An age of patches for old gabardines;
An age of mere transition,* meaning nought,
Except that what succeeds must shame it quite,
If God please. That's wrong thinking, to my mind, 165
And wrong thoughts make poor poems.*
         Every age,
Through being beheld too close, is ill-discerned
By those who have not lived past it. We'll suppose
Mount Athos carved, as Alexander schemed,
To some colossal statue of a man:*   170
The peasants, gathering brushwood in his ear,
Had guessed as little of any human form
Up there, as would a flock of browsing goats.
They'd have, in fact, to travel ten miles off
Or ere the giant image broke on them,   175
Full human profile, nose and chin distinct,
Mouth, muttering rhythms of silence up the sky,
And fed at evening with the blood of suns;
Grand torso, – hand, that flung perpetually
The largesse of a silver river down   180
To all the country pastures. 'Tis even thus
With times we live in, – evermore too great
To be apprehended near.

Line 157. See the introduction to Thomas Carlyle's 'The Hero as Divinity' from *On Heroes* (1841), vol. 28, p. 327.

Line 163. See John Stuart Mill, 'The Spirit of the Age', *The Examiner*, no. 1197 (9 January 1831), p. 21.

Line 166. Aurora seems to dislike Mill's pessimism about the current age, which he says is inclined to dispense with old doctrines and institutions because (as Aurora's imagery suggests) they are diluted, base and out of date.

Lines 168–70. Alexander the Great (356–323 BC), King of Macedon, conquered the known world and ushered in a flowering of Greek, Middle Eastern and Indian cultures. In Plutarch's *Lives*, 72, the sculptor Stasicrates suggests that Mount Athos be carved into the shape of the king, his left hand holding a city of 10,000 and his right pouring a river into the sea.

But poets should

Exert a double vision;* should have eyes
To see near things as comprehensibly   185
As if afar they took their point of sight,
And distant things, as intimately deep,
As if they touched them. Let us strive for this.
I do distrust the poet who discerns
No character or glory in his times,*   190
And trundles back his soul five hundred years,
Past moat and drawbridge, into a castle-court,
Oh not to sing of lizards or of toads
Alive i' the ditch there, – 'twere excusable;
But of some black chief, half knight, half sheep-lifter   195
Some beauteous dame, half chattel and half queen,
As dead as must be, for the greater part,
The poems made on their chivalric bones.
And that's no wonder:* death inherits death.
Nay, if there's room for poets in the world   200
A little overgrown, (I think there is)
Their sole work is to represent the age,
Their age, not Charlemagne's,* – this live, throbbing age,
That brawls, cheats, maddens, calculates, aspires,
And spends more passion, more heroic heat,   205
Betwixt the mirrors of its drawing-rooms,
Than Roland with his knights, at Roncesvalles.*
To flinch from modern varnish, coat or flounce,
Cry out for togas and the picturesque,
Is fatal, – foolish too. King Arthur's self   210
Was commonplace to Lady Guenever;*

Line 184. Reynolds (p. 148, n. 3) and Donaldson (p. 293, n. 22) trace this idea to Robert Browning's essay on Shelley, in which he describes 'the poet's double faculty of seeing objects more clearly, widely, and deeply than is possible to the average mind, at the same time that he is so acquainted and in sympathy with its narrower comprehension as to be careful to supply it with no other materials than it can combine into an intelligible whole' (*Letters of Percy Bysshe Shelley*, 1).

Lines 188–90. EBB elaborates on an argument initiated in Tennyson's poem 'The Epic', lines 27–37.

Lines 191–9. EBB mocks the vogue for medievalism that Tennyson inaugurated in the 1830s and the Pre-Raphaelite artists extended into the mid-nineteenth century.

Line 203. Charlemagne (c. 742–814) was King of the Franks and considered the prototype of a Christian king throughout medieval Europe.

Line 207. The historical Roland, comte de la Marche de Bretagne, died in 778 in the valley of Roncevaux, when the Basques attacked the battalions of Charlemagne's army under his command. The epic poem *La Chanson de Roland* (c. 1100–1225) elevates this incident to the status of a holy war and represents Roland as the type of the chivalric Christian hero.

Lines 210–11. King Arthur and Queen Guinevere are legendary rulers of medieval Britain. Arthur's cadre of chivalric knights gathered at Arthur's Round Table in Camelot. Tennyson wrote many Arthurian poems, which were published between 1832 and 1885.

And Camelot to minstrels seemed as flat
As Fleet Street to poets.*
                                    Never flinch,
But still, unscrupulously epic, catch
Upon a burning lava of a song,   215
The full-veined, heaving, double-breasted Age:*
That, when the next shall come, the men of that
May touch the impress with reverent hand, and say
'Behold, – behold the paps we all have sucked!
That bosom seems to beat still, or at least   220
It sets ours beating. This is living art,
Which thus presents and thus records true life.'

Central to Aurora's (and EBB's) defence of epic is her belief that poetry is a powerful vehicle for expressing contemporary ideas about art and society and depicting the spirit of the age. Echoes of Thomas Carlyle and John Stuart Mill in the first excerpt demonstrate an intense engagement with social and political thought. Carlyle was a transcendentalist who did not lose sight of the labouring man. Mill advocated educational and political reform and argued later in the century for universal suffrage and egalitarian marriage. Although Aurora seems to think Mill scornful of the nineteenth century as 'an age of mere transition', she rehearses the positive side of his assertion, which is that 'large subjects are discussed more, and longer, by more minds'.[9] Book V enters into ongoing discussions about the relevance of poetry to modern society and the sexual politics of socialism. As an author, Aurora takes on the authority of a sage in the first instance, but as a woman she leaves debate about the latter to a group of men, some scandalised by and some envious of Romney's affairs.

In the following excerpt, EBB lightly satirises three types of intellectual whom she either encountered in her London and Florentine circles or found in popular novels of the day: a long-haired undergraduate sensitive to female beauty, a self-righteous Anglo-Catholic aesthete and a vampiric literary reviewer. Their gossip focuses on the suitability of Lady Waldemar and Marian Erle as wives for Romney Leigh and what appears to be their meretricious beauty. The men's interest in female

---

Line 213. Traditionally, the home of London's newspaper offices.
Line 213–16. One of EBB's contemporaries attacked this mixed metaphor, associating lava with a woman's breast (not to mention the explicit breastfeeding reference), as shocking and indelicate (Roscoe, p. 245). But to link epic song and breastmilk is EBB's daring statement on the life-giving and sustaining power of poetry. That the 'Age' has a female monarch, Queen Victoria, serves to underscore EBB's point.

sexuality reflects a widely held but misguided concern that socialism would result in the abolition of marriage and sexual freedom for women. Socialist reformers such as Robert Owen and Charles Fourier certainly advocated greater individual freedom for women but not necessarily sexual licence.

I heard

The young man with the German student's look –
A sharp face, like a knife in a cleft stick,
Which shot up straight against the parting line   630
So equally dividing the long hair, –
Say softly to his neighbour, (thirty-five
And mediæval) 'Look that way, Sir Blaise.
She's Lady Waldemar – to the left, – in red –
Whom Romney Leigh, our ablest man just now,   635
Is soon to marry.'
Then replied
Sir Blaise Delorme, with quiet, priest-like voice,
Too used to syllable damnations round
To make a natural emphasis worth while:
'Is Leigh your ablest man? the same, I think,   640
Once jilted by a recreant pretty maid
Adopted from the people?* Now, in change,
He seems to have plucked a flower from the other side
Of the social hedge.'
'A flower, a flower,' exclaimed
My German student, – his own eyes full-blown   645
Bent on her. He was twenty, certainly.

Sir Blaise resumed with gentle arrogance,
As if he had dropped his alms into a hat,
And had the right to counsel, – 'My young friend,
I doubt your ablest man's ability   650
To get the least good or help meet for him,
For pagan phalanstery or Christian home,*
From such a flowery creature.'
'Beautiful!'
My student murmured, rapt, – 'Mark how she stirs!
Just waves her head, as if a flower indeed,   655
Touched far off by the vain breath of our talk.'

At which that bilious Grimwald, (he who writes
For the Renovator) who had seemed absorbed

Line 642. That is, Marian Erle. See Books III and IV above.
Line 652. See Chapter 1, note 66.

Upon the table-book of autographs,*
(I dare say mentally he crunched the bones   660
Of all those writers, wishing them alive
To feel his tooth in earnest) turned short round
With low carnivorous laugh, – 'A flower, of course!
She neither sews nor spins, - and takes no thought
Of her garments* . . falling off.'
                The student flinched;   665
Sir Blaise, the same; then both, drawing back their chairs
As if they spied black-beetles on the floor,
Pursued their talk, without a word being thrown
To the critic.
          Good Sir Blaise's brow is high
And noticeably narrow; a strong wind,   670
You fancy, might unroof him suddenly,
And blow that great top attic off his head
So piled with feudal relics. You admire
His nose in profile, though you miss his chin;
But, though you miss his chin, you seldom miss   675
His golden cross worn innermostly, (carved
For penance, by a saintly Styrian monk*
Whose flesh was too much with him,) slipping through
Some unaware unbuttoned casualty
Of the under-waistcoat. With an absent air   680
Sir Blaise sate fingering it and speaking low,
While I, upon the sofa, heard it all.

'My dear young friend, if we could bear our eyes
Like blessedest St. Lucy, on a plate,*
They would not trick us into choosing wives,   685
As doublets, by the colour. Otherwise
Our fathers chose, – and therefore, when they had hung
Their household keys about a lady's waist,
The sense of duty gave her dignity:

Line 659. A guest-book in which famous friends and acquaintances would leave quips and illustrations.

Lines 664–5. See Matthew 6:28–9. 'And why are you anxious about clothing? Consider the lilies of the field, how they grow; they neither toil nor spin; yet I tell you, even Solomon in all his glory was arrayed like one of these.'

Line 677. Styria, formerly a duchy of the Austro-Hungarian empire, became a federal state of Austria after World War I. Mainly Catholic, its population over the centuries resisted invasion from Turks and Protestants.

Lines 683–4. According to legend, Lucia of Syracuse suffered martyrdom in AD 303. She is traditionally depicted carrying her eyes on a plate because, having vowed to remain chaste, she removed them for a suitor, who claimed they tormented him. See Jameson, *Sacred and Legendary Art*, vol. 2, pp. 236–7.

She kept her bosom holy to her babes;   690
And, if a moralist reproved her dress,
'Twas, 'Too much starch!' – and not, 'Too little lawn!'*

'Now, pshaw!' returned the other in a heat,
A little fretted by being called 'young friend,'
Or so I took it, – 'for St. Lucy's sake,   695
If she's the saint to curse by, let us leave
Our fathers, – plagued enough about our sons!'
(He stroked his beardless chin) 'yes, plagued, sir, plagued:
The future generations lie on us
As heavy as the nightmare of a seer;   700
Our meat and drink grow painful prophecy:
I ask you, – have we leisure, if we liked,
To hollow out our weary hands to keep
Your intermittent rushlight* of the past
From draughts in lobbies? Prejudice of sex,   705
And marriage-laws . . the socket* drops them through
While we two speak, – however may protest
Some over-delicate nostrils, like your own,
'Gainst odours thence arising.'*
                              'You are young,'
Sir Blaise objected.
                              'If I am,' he said   710
With fire, – 'though somewhat less so than I seem.
The young run on before, and see the thing
That's coming. Reverence for the young, I cry.
In that new church for which the world's near ripe,
You'll have the younger in the elder's chair,   715
Presiding with his ivory front* of hope
O'er foreheads clawed by cruel carrion birds
Of life's experience.'
                              'Pray your blessing, sir,'
Sir Blaise replied good-humouredly, – 'I plucked
A silver hair this morning from my beard,   720
Which left me your inferior. Would I were
Eighteen, and worthy to admonish you!
If young men of your order run before

Lines 686–92. Sir Blaise expresses a preference for arranged marriage over modern courtship, as he thinks that men's eyes are seduced by beauty rather than modesty.
    Line 704. A light used by the poor, consisting of a rush dipped in wax or oil and ignited.
    Line 706. Of the light; the container for the light.
    Lines 705–9. That is, however much you may protest the sexual liberties associated with socialism, the movement is upon us.
    Line 716. Forehead.

To see such sights as sexual prejudice
And marriage-law dissolved, – in plainer words,   725
A general concubinage expressed
In a universal pruriency,* – the thing
Is scarce worth running fast for, and you'd gain
By loitering with your elders.'
                              'Ah,' he said,
'Who, getting to the top of Pisgah-hill,*   730
Can talk with one at the bottom of the view,
To make it comprehensible? Why Leigh
Himself, although our ablest man, I said,
Is scarce advanced to see as far as this,
Which some are: he takes up imperfectly   735
The social question – by one handle – leaves
The rest to trail. A Christian socialist,*
Is Romney Leigh, you understand.'
                              'Not I.
I disbelieve in Christians-pagans, much
As you in women-fishes. If we mix   740
Two colours, we lose both, and make a third
Distinct from either. Mark you! to mistake
A colour is the sign of a sick brain,
And mine, I thank the saints, is clear and cool:
A neutral tint is here impossible.   745
The church, – and by the church, I mean, of course,
The catholic, apostolic, mother-church,* –
Draws lines as plain and straight as her own wall;
Inside of which, are Christians, obviously,
And outside . . dogs.'
                              'We thank you. Well I know   750
The ancient mother-church would fain still bite
For all her toothless gums, – as Leigh himself
Would fain be a Christian still, for all his wit;
Pass that; you two may settle it, for me.

Lines 725–7. Sir Blaise expresses the fear, noted above, that socialism will lead to the dissolution of marriage and increased sexual license.

Line 730. Moses saw the Promised Land from the summit of Pisgah. See Deuteronomy 2:27 and 34:1–4.

Line 737. Writers and social activists, including F. D. Maurice, Charles Kingsley and Thomas Hughes, headed the Christian socialist movement in England, issuing the first Tract on Christian Socialism in 1849. Kingsley's novels, *Alton Locke* (1850) and *Yeast* (1851), illustrated the principles of Christian socialism, which, for the most part, EBB opposed.

Line 747. Reynolds attributes this description to the dissenting church created by Edward Irving in 1833 (p. 166, n. 2). However, I think Blaise's emphasis on the 'mother-church' refers to the Roman Catholic one and reflects widespread Catholic revivalism and Tractarianism in England of the 1830s.

You're slow in England. In a month I learnt   755
At Göttingen,* enough philosophy
To stock your English schools for fifty years;
Pass that, too. Here, alone, I stop you short,
Supposing a true man like Leigh could stand
Unequal in the stature of his life   760
To the height of his opinions. Choose a wife
Because of a smooth skin? – not he, not he!
He'd rail at Venus' self for creaking shoes,
Unless she walked his way of righteousness:
And if he takes a Venus Meretrix*   765
(No imputation on the lady there)
Be sure that, by some sleight of Christian art,
He has metamorphosed and converted her
To a Blessed Virgin.'
           'Soft!' Sir Blaise drew breath
As if it hurt him, – 'Soft! no blasphemy,   770
I pray you!'

Having heard of Romney's affairs secondhand and been cruelly taunted by Lady Waldemar, Aurora seeks an escape from Lord Howe's party. She is disgusted by the idea that Romney would be engaged to someone like Waldemar, whose vanity seems to know no bounds. But she takes heart in the fact that the manuscript of her 'long poem' is finished (Book V, line 1213) and that if she sells her father's books she can afford a train journey to Florence. In the final excerpt (and verse paragraph) from Book V, Aurora apostrophises Italy as though it were a Muse. The thirteen lines compose an abbreviated sonnet in which Aurora addresses Italy as a nursing mother in the first five-and-a-half lines, and then as a sublime entity indifferent to human want. The divide rehearses the connection between maternal solicitude and divine power initiated in Book I.

          And now I come, my Italy,
My own hills! are you 'ware of me, my hills,
How I burn toward you? do you feel to-night
The urgency and yearning of my soul,
As sleeping mothers feel the sucking babe   1270
And smile?* – Nay, not so much as when, in heat,

Line 756. Home of the university founded in 1734 and famous for scholars sceptical towards events in the Bible.
Line 765. From the Latin word meaning 'prostitute'.
Line 1271. Italian sonnets typically comprise fourteen iambic pentameter lines divided between eight (octave), which sets up a subject, and six (sestet), which addresses it in some fashion. Usually,

Vain lightnings catch at your inviolate tops,
And tremble while ye are stedfast. Still, ye go
Your own determined, calm, indifferent way
Toward sunrise, shade by shade, and light by light,   1275
Of all the grand progression nought left out;
As if God verily made you for yourselves,
And would not interrupt your life with ours.

Motherhood and Sexual Transgression. Book VI, lines 560–81, 1182–274; Book VII, lines 92–196

Aurora's journey to Italy begins with a stop in Paris, where she makes a discovery that alters the course of her plan. While walking through a crowded city street, the face of Marian Erle, whom Aurora has not seen since the ill-fated wedding day, swims into her line of vision. At first she thinks she has hallucinated the visage, but Aurora decides to stay longer in Paris in order to confirm her suspicion. One morning in the Quai aux Fleurs, she hears Marian's voice. To keep the frightened seamstress from running away, Aurora charges her to stay for Romney's sake and pleads with her to talk. Marian agrees, but only if they can return to her place where 'there's one at home [. . .] has need of me' (Book VI, line 488).

The first of the three excerpts below is a description of what Aurora sees in Marian's room. It is important that the description of Marian's baby comes before her account of how he came to be. First, it establishes the baby's innocence and vulnerability as well as Marian's unconditional love for the child. Second, Aurora's description of the baby, which makes allusions to classical mythology, also suggests that Marian has suffered greatly bringing him into the world. The question that presses upon this passage, as well as the subsequent one, is: can motherhood redeem what the Victorians called a fallen woman?[10] In mid-nineteenth-century England, the outright condemnation of unwed motherhood – especially in the case of rape victims – was commonplace but starting to be challenged by social reformers and literary writers, especially EBB.[11] Marian's belief that she is a lost soul, or member of the walking dead, reflects society's negative view of unmarried mothers. Aurora, however, defends Marian's virtue because she was a victim of sexual violence, and, unlike Marian's own mother, she expresses a saint-like devotion to her child. In other words, Marian's character defies Victorian stereotypes

---

there is a turn of thought or *volta* at line 9. Line 1271 serves as the *volta* in EBB's adaptation of the sonnet here, as the lyric divides between infantile desire and mature contemplation. The lyric moment encapsulates the double vision and growing emotional maturity of the poet-narrator.

of working-class mothers: she is not a prostitute nor neglectful of her child. Moreover, she is a committed mother who chooses not to send her infant to a baby farm in order to work.[13]

> Alone? She threw her bonnet off,   560
> Then sighing as 'twere sighing the last time,
> Approached the bed, and drew a shawl away:
> You could not peel a fruit you fear to bruise
> More calmly and more carefully than so, –
> Nor would you find within, a rosier flushed   565
> Pomegranate –*
>   There he lay, upon his back,
> The yearling creature, warm and moist with life
> To the bottom of his dimples, – to the ends
> Of the lovely tumbled curls about his face;
> For since he had been covered over-much   570
> To keep him from the light glare, both his cheeks
> Were hot and scarlet as the first live rose
> The shepherd's heart blood ebbed away into,
> The faster for his love.* And love was here
> As instant! in the pretty baby-mouth,   575
> Shut close as if for dreaming that it sucked;
> The little naked feet drawn up the way
> Of nestled birdlings; everything so soft
> And tender, – to the little holdfast hands,
> Which, closing on a finger into sleep,   580
> Had kept the mould of't.

The next excerpt comes from Marian's account of Lady Waldemar's betrayal and her abduction by white slave traders, as well as her horrific experience of rape and its aftermath. The opening description of a treacherous procuress reminds readers that being female does not mean maternal or humane instincts come naturally. Rather, circumstances of desperate poverty and constant abuse incited women to do terrible things to one another. Marian's feeling of helplessness is conveyed through the corpse and grave imagery, which captures the moral corruption in her midst and recalls Proserpina's underworld habitation.

Line 566. Pomegranates are associated with the rape of Proserpina, who ate the seeds of that fruit, which were forbidden by her captor Pluto. As a result, Proserpina spends half a year in the underworld and the other half on earth with her mother, Ceres. See Ovid, *Metamorphoses*, Book V.

Line 574. The shepherd Adonis, beloved of Aphrodite, was wounded in the thigh by a boar, and though the goddess flew to his aid, she was unable to save him. As he lay dying, the drops of his blood turned into roses, and Aphrodite's tears into anemones. EBB translated Bion's 'Lament for Adonis' from the *Idylls*.

While the excerpt constitutes the final verses of Book VI, Marian's story does not end here but continues into Book VII. (There is no end quotation mark at the end of the passage.) Aurora seems purposely to carry the narrative over into the next book, as the final image of Book VI is Marian's thought of her own sepulchre. The allusion to Matthew 28 raises an important parallel to Marian's seemingly irreversible, death-like state: Christ's burial and resurrection. Although Marian is pessimistic about redemption, the allusion suggests that the precedent is worth bearing in mind, especially as Aurora increasingly assumes the role of prophet-poet in the narrative.

'A woman . . hear me, let me make it plain, . .
A woman . . not a monster . . both her breasts
Made right to suckle babes . . she took me off,
A woman also, young and ignorant,   1185
And heavy with my grief, my two poor eyes
Near washed away with weeping, till the trees,
The blessed unaccustomed trees and fields,
Ran either side the train like stranger dogs
Unworthy of any notice, – took me off,   1190
So dull, so blind, and only half alive,
Not seeing by what road, nor by what ship,
Nor toward what place, nor to what end of all.
Men carry a corpse thus, – past the doorway, past
The garden-gate, the children's playground, up   1195
The green lane, – then they leave it in the pit,
To sleep and find corruption, cheek to cheek
With him who stinks since Friday.
                              'But suppose;
To go down with one's soul into the grave,
To go down half dead, half alive, I say,   1200
And wake up with corruption, . . cheek to cheek
With him who stinks since Friday! There it is,
And that's the horror of't, Miss Leigh.
                              'You feel?
You understand? – no, do not look at me,
But understand. The blank, blind, weary way,   1205
Which led, where'er it led, away at least;
The shifted ship*, to Sydney or to France,
Still bound, wherever else, to another land;
The swooning sickness on the dismal sea,

Line 1207. Marian has been placed on a ship sailing for either England's Australian colony or France. In either place, the implication is that she is destined for the sex trade.

The foreign shore, the shameful house, the night,   1210
The feeble blood, the heavy-headed grief, . . .
No need to bring their damnable drugged cup,
And yet they brought it! Hell's so prodigal
Of devil's gifts, hunts liberally in packs,
Will kill no poor small creature of the wilds   1215
But fifty red wide throats must smoke at it,
As HIS at me . . when waking up at last . .
I told you that I waked up in the grave.

'Enough so! – it is plain enough so. True,
We wretches cannot tell out all our wrong,   1220
Without offence to decent happy folk.
I know that we must scrupulously hint
With half-words, delicate reserves, the thing
Which no one scrupled we should feel in full.
Let pass the rest, then; only leave my oath   1225
Upon this sleeping child, – man's violence,
Not man's seduction, made me what I am,*
As lost as . . I told *him* I should be lost.
When mothers fail us, can we help ourselves?*
That's fatal! – And you call it being lost,   1230
That down came next day's noon and caught me there,
Half gibbering and half raving on the floor,
And wondering what had happened up in heaven,
That suns should dare to shine when God Himself
Was certainly abolished.
                              'I was mad,   1235
How many weeks, I know not, – many weeks.
I think they let me go, when I was mad,
They feared my eyes and loosed me, as boys might
A mad dog which they had tortured. Up and down
I went, by road and village, over tracts   1240
Of open foreign country, large and strange,
Crossed everywhere by long thin poplar-lines*
Like fingers of some ghastly skeleton hand
Through sunlight and through moonlight evermore
Pushed out from hell itself to pluck me back,   1245
And resolute to get me, slow and sure;
While every roadside Christ upon his cross*

Line 1227. Marian is quite clear that she was not seduced but raped.
    Line 1229. Marian may be thinking of her own mother, who, when Marian was a teenager, handed her over to a brutish man. She barely escaped being violated that time.
    Line 1242. Rows of poplars are a characteristic feature of rural France.
    Line 1247. Crucifixes were typical of crossroads in France, a predominantly Catholic country.

Hung reddening through his gory wounds at me,
And shook his nails in anger, and came down
To follow a mile after, wading up   1250
The low vines and green wheat, crying 'Take the girl!
She's none of mine from henceforth.' Then, I knew,
(But this is somewhat dimmer than the rest)
The charitable peasants gave me bread
And leave to sleep in straw: and twice they tied,   1255
At parting, Mary's image* round my neck –
How heavy it seemed! as heavy as a stone;
A woman has been strangled with less weight:
I threw it in a ditch to keep it clean
And ease my breath a little, when none looked;   1260
I did not need such safeguards: – brutal men
Stopped short, Miss Leigh, in insult, when they had seen
My face, – I must have had an awful look.
And so I lived: the weeks passed on, – I lived.
'Twas living my old tramp-life o'er again,   1265
But, this time, in a dream, and hunted round
By some prodigious Dream-fear at my back,
Which ended, yet: my brain cleared presently,
And there I sate, one evening, by the road,
I, Marian Erle, myself, alone, undone,   1270
Facing a sunset low upon the flats,
As if it were the finish of all time,
The great red stone upon my sepulchre,
Which angels were too weak to roll away.*

The last excerpt from Book VII constitutes Aurora's response to
Marian's story and her solution to the stigma of being an unwed,
working mother. The passage begins with Aurora's outrage over the
harsh response of a miller's wife, who, having accepted Marian as a
lodger and found her a job as a servant, sends her away once she discovers that Marian is pregnant. The woman's hypocrisy is particularly
vexing, as Marian reveals that she is an adulteress.

Aurora's invitation to Marian and her baby to come and live with
her in Italy is a noble solution and mutually beneficial to both women.
Aurora has a companion for (what promises to be) a lonely journey, and
Marian gains respectability travelling with a middle-class 'sister' (Book

Line 1256. A medallion depicting the Virgin Mary.
Line 1274. See Matthew 28:2. 'The angel of the Lord descended from heaven, and came and
rolled back the stone from the door, and sat upon it.' A reference to the burial of Christ, whose
tomb was closed by a great stone, which the angel came and rolled away in anticipation of the
Resurrection.

VII, line 117). What may seem an unorthodox family arrangement to some Victorian readers – especially because of class difference – was not uncommon among EBB's expatriate community in Florence and Rome. Women, sometimes quietly lesbian, cohabited as a family unit with no questions asked. In her own expatriate circle, EBB had friends who were members of same-sex partnerships, including the American sculptor Harriet Hosmer (1830–1908) and the American actress Charlotte Cushman (1816–76). More radical than these relationships, however, is Aurora's statement: 'henceforth, thou and I / Being still together, will not miss a friend, / Nor he a father, since two mothers shall / Make that up to him' (lines 122–5). That a fatherless household is not only desirable but also viable demonstrates how far ahead of its time the sexual politics of *Aurora Leigh* are.

> 'O crooked world,' I cried, 'ridiculous
> If not so lamentable! It's the way
> With these light women of a thrifty vice,
> My Marian, – always hard upon the rent   95
> In any sister's virtue!* while they keep
> Their chastity so darned with perfidy,
> That, though a rag itself, it looks as well
> Across a street, in balcony or coach,
> As any stronger stuff* might. For my part,   100
> I'd rather take the wind-side of the stews*
> Than touch such women with my finger-end
> They top the poor street-walker by their lie,
> And look the better for being so much worse
> The devil's most devilish when respectable.   105
> But you, dear, and your story.'
>   'All the rest
> Is here,' she said, and sighed upon the child.
> 'I found a mistress-sempstress who was kind
> And let me sew in peace among her girls;
> And what was better than to draw the threads   110
> All day and half the night for him and him?

Line 96. See *King Lear*, IV, vi, 166–7.

Line 100. Cloth, material, fabric.

Line 101. Brothels. EBB's reference to houses of prostitution troubled many readers, but she insisted on acknowledging the grim reality for many poor women. 'If a woman ignores these wrongs, then may women as a sex continue to suffer them; there is no help for any of us—let us be dumb and die. I have spoken therefore, and in speaking have used plain words . . . which, if blurred or softened, would imperil perhaps the force and righteousness of the moral influence' (Letter to Mrs Martin, February [1857], *Letters of EBB*, vol. II, p. 254).

And so I lived for him, and so he lives,
And so I know, by this time, God lives too.'

She smiled beyond the sun, and ended so,
And all my soul rose up to take her part   115
Against the world's successes, virtues, fames.
'Come with me, sweetest sister,' I returned,
'And sit within my house, and do me good
From henceforth, thou and thine! ye are my own
From henceforth. I am lonely in the world,   120
And thou art lonely, and the child is half
An orphan. Come, – and, henceforth, thou and I
Being still together, will not miss a friend,
Nor he a father, since two mothers shall
Make that up to him. I am journeying south,   125
And, in my Tuscan home I'll find a niche,
And set thee there, my saint,* the child and thee,
And burn the lights of love before thy face,
And ever at thy sweet look cross myself
From mixing with the world's prosperities;   130
That so, in gravity and holy calm,
We too may live on toward the truer life.'

She looked me in the face and answered not,
Nor signed she was unworthy, nor gave thanks,
But took the sleeping child and held it out   135
To meet my kiss, as if requiting me
And trusting me at once. And thus, at once,
I carried him and her to where I lived;
She's there now,* in the little room, asleep,
I hear the soft child-breathing through the door;   140
And all three of us, at to-morrow's break,
Pass onward, homeward, to our Italy.
Oh, Romney Leigh, I have your debts to pay,
And I'll be just and pay them.
                              But yourself!
To pay your debts is scarcely difficult;   145
To buy your life is nearly impossible,
Being sold away to Lamia.* My head aches;
I cannot see my road along this dark;
Nor can I creep and grope, as fits the dark,

Line 127. The mother and child in a niche evoke an image of the Madonna and Child. 'Marian'
is a derivation of Mary.
Line 139. Aurora's narrative catches up to the present.
Line 147. See the note to Book I, lines 161–3.

For these foot-catching robes of womanhood: 150
A man might walk a little .. but I! – He loves
The Lamia-woman,* – and I, write to him
What stops his marriage, and destroys his peace, –
Or what, perhaps, shall simply trouble him,
Until she only need to touch his sleeve   155
With just a finger's tremulous white flame,
Saying, 'Ah, – Aurora Leigh! a pretty tale,
'A very pretty poet! I can guess
'The motive' – then, to catch his eyes in hers,
And vow she does not wonder, – and they two   160
To break in laughter, as the sea along
A melancholy coast, and float up higher,
In such a laugh, their fatal weeds of love!
Ay, fatal, ay. And who shall answer me,
Fate has not hurried tides; and if to-night   165
My letter would not be a night too late,
An arrow shot into a man that's dead,
To prove a vain intention? Would I show
The new wife vile, to make the husband mad?*
No, Lamia! shut the shutters, bar the doors   170
From every glimmer on thy serpent-skin!
I will not let thy hideous secret out
To agonise the man I love – I mean
The friend I love .. as friends love.

                              It is strange,
To-day while Marian told her story like   175
To absorb most listeners, how I listened chief
To a voice not hers, not yet that enemy's,
Nor God's in wrath, .. but to one that mixed with mine
Long years ago among the garden-trees,
And said to *me*, to *me* too, 'Be my wife,   180
Aurora.' It is strange with what a swell
Of yearning passion, as a snow of ghosts
Might beat against the impervious door of heaven,
I thought, 'Now, if I had been a woman, such
As God made women, to save men by love, –   185
By just my love I might have saved this man,
And made a nobler poem for the world
Than all I have failed in.' But I failed besides
In this; and now he's lost! through me alone!

Line 152. That is, Lady Waldemar.
Line 169. See Keats's *Lamia* (1820), lines 239–311.

And, by my only fault, his empty house   190
Sucks in, at this same hour, a wind from hell
To keep his hearth cold, make his casements creak
For ever to the tune of plague and sin –
O Romney, O my Romney, O my friend,
My cousin and friend! my helper, when I would,   195
My love, that might be! mine!

Poetry and Prophecy. Book VIII, lines 316–37, 592–636; Book IX, lines 486–659, 737–60, 907–64

In these final books of the poem, Aurora writes about events soon after they transpire; narrator and subject are nearly synchronous. Having established a harmonious household in a village outside Florence, Aurora supports Marian and her son through authorship. One evening, Romney unexpectedly arrives at their home and unsettles Aurora, who thinks he has married Lady Waldemar and has come to confront her about an angry letter she sent on the subject of Marian's mistreatment. Rather, Romney seeks reconciliation, raising the subject of their 'June-day' conversation in Book II and explaining his own recent adversity (Book VIII, line 320). He also shares how Aurora's recently published long poem has 'moved' him and initiated a change in his view about the relationship between poetry and society.

The two excerpts from Book VIII revive the imagery and setting of the June-day debate and transfer the star imagery, found in Marian's letter (Book IV), from Romney to Aurora. Perhaps, most importantly, Romney calls Aurora 'My Miriam' (line 334), acknowledging that the world needs a poet-prophetess, such as the one Moses had in Exodus 15:20–1. Yet what Aurora sings about is not the triumph of an oppressed people, as Miriam did.[14] Rather, her poetry serves as a medium between body and spirit, imparting 'truths not yours, indeed, / But set within my reach by means of you' (lines 610–11). In a letter to her sister, Arabella, EBB names the source of Aurora's theology: Emanuel Swedenborg (b. 1688), a Christian mystic and philosopher, whose work drew great interest in the mid-nineteenth century.[15]

Swedenborg claimed that Scripture should be interpreted strictly as an expression of God in man and that the soul (or spirit) dictates the actions of the body (or matter).[16] For mankind to focus solely on the material world at the expense of the spirit is to fail in 'any project of social or political reformation'.[17] Just such an estrangement between spirit and matter can be seen in Romney's arguments from Book II; there, he argues vehemently for the primacy of material necessity over spiritual regeneration. But as we can see in the second excerpt below, Romney, in the wake of personal hardship and Aurora's poem, has experienced a change of heart and delivers a Swedenborgian sermon on the refreshing power of spirit in a world choking on 'clay' (lines 630, 632, 633). The echo of Carlyle in lines 635–6 raises Romney's speech to the level of 'sage discourse': a term that describes the writings of England's great social reformers who spoke to the major moral issues of the age.

But if Romney comes to a Carlylean view by the end of the poem, Aurora maintains a prophetic stance from the beginning (Ecclesiastes) to the end (Revelation). Although she and Romney have invoked Eve and Adam, as well as Miriam and Moses, throughout the poem, Aurora resists an exact correspondence, calling her beloved 'my Romney' (Book IX, line 950), even when he has pronounced her 'my Miriam' (Book VIII, line 334), and 'my morning star' (Book IX, line 908). The latter epithet suggests not only her final identification with the Biblical singer David, but also the incarnational power of her poetry (Davies, pp. 58–9). In Revelation 22:16, Christ proclaims: 'I Jesus have sent mine angel to testify unto you these things in the churches. I am the root and the offspring of David, and the bright morning star' (King James Version). In an instance of typological interpretation, the word of the Messiah is born of the Old Testament prophet, whom Aurora invokes for a newly found purpose. United with Romney in 'work', her poetry becomes a means to renew and redeem the 'old world' (Book IX, lines 925, 942).[18]

> 'You have the stars,' he murmured, – 'it is well:
> Be like them! shine, Aurora, on my dark,
> Though high and cold and only like a star,
> And for this short night only, – you, who keep
> The same Aurora of the bright June-day   320
> That withered up the flowers before my face,
> And turned me from the garden* evermore
> Because I was not worthy. Oh, deserved,
> Deserved! That I, who verily had not learnt
> God's lesson half, attaining as a dunce   325
> To obliterate good words with fractious thumbs
> And cheat myself of the context, – I should push
> Aside, with male ferocious impudence,
> The world's Aurora who had conned* her part
> On the other side the leaf! ignore her so,   330

Line 322. Romney's banishment recalls Adam and Eve's from Eden in Genesis.
Line 329. Learned; memorised by heart.

Because she was a woman and a queen,
And had no beard to bristle through her song, –
My teacher, who has taught me with a book,
My Miriam, whose sweet mouth, when nearly drowned
I still heard singing on the shore!* Deserved,   335
That here I should look up unto the stars
And miss the glory' . .

    * * *

    You have written poems, sweet,
Which moved me in secret as the sap is moved
In still March branches, signless as a stone:
But this last book o'ercame me like soft rain   595
Which falls at midnight, when the tightened bark
Breaks out into unhesitating buds,
And sudden protestations of the spring.
In all your other books I saw but *you*:
A man may see the moon so, in a pond,   600
And not the nearer therefore to the moon,
Nor use the sight . . except to drown himself
And so I forced my heart back from the sigh
For what had I, I thought, to do with her, –
Aurora . . Romney? But, in this last book,   605
You showed me something separate from yourself,
Beyond you; and I bore to take it in,
And let it draw me. You have shown me truths,
O June-day friend, that help me now at night,
When June is over! truths not yours, indeed,   610
But set within my reach by means of you:
Presented by your voice and verse the way
To take them clearest. Verily I was wrong;
And verily many thinkers of this age,
Ay, many Christian teachers, half in heaven,   615
Are wrong in just my sense, who understood
Our natural world too insularly, as if
No spiritual counterpart completed it
Consummating its meaning, rounding all
To justice and perfection, line by line,   620
Form by form, nothing single, nor alone, –
The great below clenched by the great above;
Shade here authenticating substance there,

Line 335. After the drowning of the Egyptians in the Red Sea, the Israelites rejoiced: 'And Miriam, the prophetess, the sister of Aaron, took a timbrel in her hand; and all the women went out after her with timbrels and with dances' (Exodus 15:20). See *Aurora Leigh*, Book II, line 171.

The body proving spirit, as the effect
The cause:* we, meantime, being too grossly apt   625
To hold the natural, as dogs a bone,
(Though reason and nature beat us in the face),
So obstinately, that we'll break our teeth
Or ever we let go. For everywhere
We're too materialistic, – eating clay,   630
(Like men of the west)* instead of Adam's corn
And Noah's wine;* clay by handfuls, clay by lumps,
Until we're filled up to the throat with clay,
And grow the grimy colour of the ground
On which we are feeding. Ay, materialist   635
The age's name is.*

In Book IX Romney and Aurora confess their love for one another and express new feelings about their respective roles. While the blank verse continues at its normal clip, especially in Romney's revelation of his blindness and Aurora's reaction to it, smaller lyric units, particularly ones that are sonnet-like, appear in the verse paragraphs. Monique R. Morgan has argued that the last two books contain more lyric moments than the rest of the poem in order to capture the immediacy of the narrator's feeling.[19] The commentary below designates lyric extracts within the verse narrative, which contribute to a sense of Book IX as a devotional lyric sequence. The popular lyric known as a sonnet typically comprises a fourteen-line unit and has a deep history in English and Italian literature of expressing the poet's love for God or another person. Lines 649–59, 907–14 and 924–36 are sonnet-like in their language of spiritual awakening, affectionate exhortation and revelatory vision. These selected short lyric units, which, while only approximately the length of a true sonnet, enact a turn of thought (or *volta*) between something like an octave and a sestet, the traditional Italian division.[20] The excerpts express Aurora and Romney's feelings of joy and awe as they embark upon a mission dedicated to Art and Love, a quest they hope will renew society.

There are also verbal echoes of the sonnets of John Milton, which

---

Line 625. Romney rehearses Swedenborg's idea of mutually constitutive spiritual and material worlds, which Aurora has been advocating.

Line 631. The Philistines, enemies of the children of Israel, lived in the west. See Isaiah 11:14. The serpent who tempted Eve was also condemned to eat dust. See Genesis 3:14.

Line 632. Genesis 3:17–18, 9:20. Adam's corn and Noah's wine are God-given and therefore good things.

Line 636. See Thomas Carlyle, 'Signs of the Times' (1829): 'This is not a Religious age. Only the material, the immediately practical, not the divine and spiritual, is important to us' (*Works of Thomas Carlyle*, vol. III, p. 111).

are flagged in the footnotes below. Milton's long poem in blank verse, *Paradise Lost*, was an important precedent for *Aurora Leigh*, and his sonnets, both devotional and occasional, were equally so. In the poems that EBB echoes, Milton tempers his youthful poetic ambition with a form of Protestant patience in God's will ('How Soon Hath Time'), and in another one written during the years of his blindness ('To Mr. Cyriack Skinner Upon His Blindness') commiserates with a friend who has also lost his sight. As a man who seems to have lost everything, Romney Leigh, like Milton, feels he has a divinely directed purpose and by means of his love for Aurora 'realizes' that there is hope for him in a sighted world.

Lines 737–59 describe a moment of intimacy between Aurora and Romney, conveying the power of their attraction to one another and the feeling that their first kiss has brought them to a higher spiritual state. In the quoted passage there are echoes of EBB's *Sonnets from the Portuguese*, a sonnet sequence written while her future husband Robert Browning courted her, as well as the Book of Revelation. The conflation of EBB's intensely personal record of her amatory passion with apocalyptic vision suggests the importance of erotic love to spiritual understanding.

<pre>
                    Now, at last,
I own heaven's angels round her* life suffice
To fight the rats of our society,
Without this Romney: I can see it at last;
And here is ended my pretension which   490
The most pretended. Over-proud of course,
Even so! – but not so stupid . . blind . . that I,
Whom thus the great Taskmaster* of the world
Has set to meditate mistaken work,
My dreary face against a dim blank wall   495
Throughout man's natural lifetime, – could pretend
Or wish . . O love, I have loved you! O my soul,
I have lost you! – but I swear by all yourself,
And all you might have been to me these years,
If that June-morning had not failed my hope, –   500
I'm not so bestial, to regret that day
This night, – this night, which still to you is fair;
</pre>

Line 487. Romney refers to Marian Erle, who has just rejected his second marriage proposal, which he has offered in friendship (to protect her and the baby) rather than love.

Line 493. Romney's word choice recalls Milton's sonnet 'How Soon Hath Time', which expresses the poet's resignation to God's 'will'. The Miltonic echo anticipates Romney's plight, as the author went blind at age 44.

Nay, not so blind, Aurora. I attest
Those stars above us, which I cannot see . . .'

'You cannot' . .
     'That if Heaven itself should stoop,   505
Remix the lots, and give me another chance,
I'd say, 'No other!' – I'd record my blank.
Aurora never should be wife of mine.'

'Not see the stars?'
     ''Tis worse still, not to see
To find your hand, although we're parting, dear. 510
A moment let me hold it, ere we part:
And understand my last words – these at last!
I would not have you thinking, when I'm gone,
That Romney dared to hanker for your love,
In thought or vision, if attainable,   515
(Which certainly for me it never was)
And wish to use it for a dog to-day,
To help the blind man stumbling. God forbid!
And now I know he held you in his palm,
And kept you open-eyed to all my faults,   520
To save you at last from such a dreary end.
Believe me, dear, that if I had known like Him,
What loss was coming on me, I had done
As well in this as He has. – Farewell, you,
Who are still my light, – farewell! How late it is: 525
I know that, now: you've been too patient, sweet.
I will but blow my whistle toward the lane,
And some one comes, – the same who brought me here.
Get in – Good night.'
     'A moment. Heavenly Christ!
A moment. Speak once, Romney. 'Tis not true. 530
I hold your hands, I look into your face –
You see me?'
     'No more than the blessed stars.
Be blessed too, Aurora. Ah, my sweet,
You tremble. Tender-hearted! Do you mind
Of yore, dear, how you used to cheat old John, 535
And let the mice out slyly from his traps,
Until he marvelled at the soul in mice
Which took the cheese and left the snare? The same
Dear soft heart always! 'Twas for this I grieved
Howe's letter never reached you. Ah, you had heard 540
Of illness, – not the issue, – not the extent:

My life long sick with tossings up and down,
The sudden revulsion in the blazing house,
The strain and struggle both of body and soul,
Which left fire running in my veins, for blood: 545
Scarce lacked that thunderbolt of the falling beam,
Which nicked me on the forehead as I passed
The gallery door with a burden. Say heaven's bolt,
Not William Erle's; not Marian's father's; tramp
And poacher, whom I found for what he was,   550
And, eager for her sake to rescue him,
Forth swept from the open highway of the world,
Road-dust and all, – till, like a woodland boar
Most naturally unwilling to be tamed,
He notched me with his tooth. But not a word   555
To Marian! and I do not think, besides,
He turned the tilting of the beam my way, –
And if he laughed, as many swear, poor wretch,
Nor he nor I supposed the hurt so deep.
We'll hope his next laugh may be merrier,   560
In a better cause.'
                    'Blind, Romney?'*
                                      'Ah, my friend,
You'll learn to say it in a cheerful voice.
I, too, at first desponded. To be blind,
Turned out of nature, mulcted* as a man,
Refused the daily largesse of the sun   565
To humble creatures! When the fever's heat
Dropped from me, as the flame did from my house,
And left me ruined like it, stripped of all
The hues and shapes of aspectable* life,
A mere bare blind stone in the blaze of day,   570
A man, upon the outside of the earth,
As dark as ten feet under, in the grave, –
Why that seemed hard.'
                       'No hope?'
                                  'A tear! you weep,
Divine Aurora? tears upon my hand!
I've seen you weeping for a mouse, a bird, –   575

Line 561. Reynolds (p. 301, n. 8) and others have noted that Romney's blinding and Aurora's love for him strongly resemble the conclusion of Charlotte Brontë's *Jane Eyre* (1847). EBB denied remembering these events at the time of *Aurora Leigh*'s composition. However, EBB did have a personal interest in a blind hero, based on her friendship with the Greek scholar Hugh Stuart Boyd. See Carpenter; Jones; and Rodas.
Line 564. Punished; subjected to a penalty. See Book III, line 409.
Line 569. Capable of being seen, visible (*OED*).

But, weep for me, Aurora? Yes, there's hope.
Not hope of sight, – I could be learned, dear,
And tell you in what Greek and Latin name
The visual nerve is withered to the root,
Though the outer eyes appear indifferent,   580
Unspotted in their crystals.* But there's hope.
The spirit, from behind this dethroned sense,
Sees, waits in patience till the walls break up
From which the bas-relief and fresco have dropt.*
There's hope. The man here, once so arrogant   585
And restless, so ambitious, for his part,
Of dealing with statistically packed
Disorders, (from a pattern on his nail,)
And packing such things quite another way, –
Is now contented. From his personal loss   590
He has come to hope for others when they lose,
And wear a gladder faith in what we gain . .
Through bitter experience, compensation sweet,
Like that tear, sweetest. I am quiet now,
As tender surely for the suffering world,   595
But quiet, – sitting at the wall to learn,
Content, henceforth, to do the thing I can:
For, though as powerless, said I, as a stone,
A stone can still give shelter to a worm,
And it is worth while being a stone for that: 600
There's hope, Aurora.'
                  'Is there hope for me?
For me? – and is there room beneath the stone
For such a worm? – And if I came and said . .
What all this weeping scarce will let me say,
And yet what women cannot say at all,   605
But weeping bitterly . . (the pride keeps up,
Until the heart breaks under it) . . I love, –
I love you, Romney' . . .

Line 581. EBB describes Romney's blindness in a letter to Anna Jameson, dated 26 December 1856, and attributes the cause to a fever, not injury from the fire: 'the eyes, the visual nerve, perished, showing no external strain—perished as Milton's did' (*Letters of EBB*, vol. 2, p. 246). The lines also echo Milton's 'To Mr. Cyriack Skinner on His Blindness', lines 1–3: 'Cyriack, this three years' day these eyes, though clear / To outward view of blemish or of spot, / Bereft of light thir seeing have forgot.' On the Victorian association of Milton's blindness with inward vision, see Flint, pp. 78–80.

Line 584. Bas (or 'low') relief sculpture features figures that have been partially carved out of a flat surface, such as on a frieze or wall. A fresco is 'a kind of painting executed in water-colour on a wall, ceiling, etc. of which the mortar or plaster is not quite dry, so that the colours sink in and become more durable' (*OED*). The art references recall Aurora's Italian scene and suggest the façades that house the soul or spirit.

'Silence!' he exclaimed.
'A woman's pity sometimes makes her mad.
A man's distraction must not cheat his soul   610
To take advantage of it. Yet, 'tis hard –
Farewell, Aurora.'
         'But I love you, sir;
And when a woman says she loves a man,
The man must hear her, though he love her not.
Which . . hush! . . he has leave to answer in his turn;   615
She will not surely blame him. As for me,
You call it pity, – think I'm generous?
'Twere somewhat easier, for a woman proud,
As I am, and I'm very vilely proud,
To let it pass as such, and press on you   620
Love born of pity, – seeing that excellent loves
Are born so, often, nor the quicklier die,
And this would set me higher by the head
Than now I stand. No matter: let the truth
Stand high; Aurora must be humble: no,   625
My love's not pity merely. Obviously
I'm not a generous woman, never was,
Or else, of old, I had not looked so near
To weights and measures, grudging you the power
To give, as first I scorned your power to judge   630
For me, Aurora. I would have no gifts
Forsooth, but God's, – and I would use *them*, too,
According to my pleasure and my choice,
As He and I were equals, you, below,
Excluded from that level of interchange   635
Admitting benefaction. You were wrong
In much? you said so. I was wrong in most.
Oh, most! You only thought to rescue men
By half-means, half-way, seeing half their wants,
While thinking nothing of your personal gain.   640
But I who saw the human nature broad,
At both sides, comprehending, too, the soul's,
And all the high necessities of Art,
Betrayed the thing I saw, and wronged my own life
For which I pleaded. Passioned to exalt   645
The artist's instinct in me at the cost
Of putting down the woman's, I forgot
No perfect artist is developed here
From any imperfect woman. Flower from root,
And spiritual from natural, grade by grade   650

In all our life. A handful of the earth
To make God's image!* the despised poor earth,
The healthy odorous earth, – I missed, with it,
The divine Breath that blows the nostrils out
To ineffable inflatus – ay, the breath   655
Which love is. Art is much, but love is more.
O Art, my Art, thou'rt much, but Love is more!*
Art symbolises heaven, but Love is God
And makes heaven.

         *   *   *

                        What he said,
I fain would write. But if an angel spoke
In thunder,* should we, haply, know much more
Than that it thundered? If a cloud came down   740
And wrapt us wholly,* could we draw its shape,
As if on the outside, and not overcome?
And so he spake. His breath against my face
Confused his words, yet made them more intense.
As when the sudden finger of the wind   745
Will wipe a row of single city-lamps
To a pure white line of flame, more luminous
Because of obliteration; more intense
The intimate presence carrying in itself
Complete communication, as with souls   750
Who, having put the body off, perceive
Through simply being. Thus, 'twas granted me
To know he loved me to the depth and height
Of such large natures,* ever competent
With grand horizons by the sea or land,   755
To love's grand sunrise. Small spheres hold small fires
But he loved largely, as a man can love
Who, baffled in his love, dares live his life,

Line 652. See Genesis 1:26–7 and 2:7.

Lines 656–7. These lines epitomise the controversy about whether Aurora expresses subservience to patriarchy, placing 'love' above 'Art' at the poem's conclusion (see David, pp. 143–58). However, one should consider that the reiteration of the sentiment in lines 658–9 suggests a correction: Art is less than Love (with a capital 'L') because it only 'symbolizes heaven' not 'makes' it. See also Stone, *Elizabeth*, pp. 184–8.

Line 739. Revelation 10:3.

Line 741. Revelation 10:1. 'And I saw another mighty angel came down from heaven, clothed with a cloud.'

Line 753–4. See *Sonnets from the Portuguese* (1850), poem 43, lines 1–4: 'How do I love thee? Let me count the ways. / I love thee to the depth and breadth and height / My soul can reach, when feeling out of sight / For the ends of Being and ideal Grace' (*Works*, vol. II, p. 478). The reference to spatial dimensions also echoes Ephesians 3:17–18 and Romans 8:39.

Accept the ends which God loves, for his own,
And lift a constant aspect.   760

              *   *   *

Come thou, my compensation, my dear sight,
My morning-star, my morning!* rise and shine,
And touch my hills with radiance not their own
Shine out for two, Aurora, and fulfil   910
My falling-short that must be! work for two,
As I, though thus restrained, for two, shall love!*
Gaze on, with inscient* vision toward the sun,
And, from his visceral heat, pluck out the roots
Of light beyond him. Art's a service, – mark: 915
A silver key is given to thy clasp,
And thou shalt stand unwearied, night and day,
And fix it in the hard, slow-turning wards,*
And open, so, that intermediate door
Betwixt the different planes of sensuous form   920
And form insensuous, that inferior men
May learn to feel on still through thee to those,
And bless thy ministration. The world waits
For help. Beloved, let us love so well,
Our work shall still be better for our love,   925
And still our love be sweeter for our work,
And both, commended, for the sake of each,
By all true workers and true lovers, born.
Now press the clarion on thy woman's lip
(Love's holy kiss shall still keep consecrate)   930
And breathe the fine keen breath along the brass,
And blow all class-walls level as Jericho's
Past Jordan,* – crying from the top of souls
To souls, that they assemble on earth's flats
To get them to some purer eminence   935
Than any hitherto beheld for clouds!
What height we know not, – but the way we know,

Line 908. A play on Aurora's name, which means the dawn.
Line 912. Due in part to his blindness, Romney embraces a reversal of traditional gender roles, declaring that Aurora will work and he will love.
Line 913. Having inward knowledge or insight (*OED*). EBB's use of this definition is the only instance cited in the *OED*.
Lines 916–18. The metaphor makes Aurora instrumental in unlocking the door to a higher plane of consciousness. Wards are 'the ridges projecting from the inside plate of a lock, serving to prevent the passage of any key the bit of which is not provided with incisions of corresponding form and size' (*OED* 2, 24a).
Line 933. See Joshua 6:1–20.

And how by mounting aye, we must attain,
And so climb on. It is the hour for souls,
That bodies, leavened by the will and love,   940
Be lightened to redemption. The world's old;
But the old world waits the hour to be renewed,
Toward which, new hearts in individual growth
Must quicken, and increase to multitude
In new dynasties of the race of men*, –   945
Developed whence, shall grow spontaneously
New churches, new economies, new laws
Admitting freedom, new societies
Excluding falsehood: HE shall make all new.'

My Romney! – Lifting up my hand in his,   950
As wheeled by Seeing spirits toward the east,
He turned instinctively, – where, faint and far,
Along the tingling desert of the sky,
Beyond the circle of the conscious hills,
Were laid in jasper-stone as clear as glass   955
The first foundations of that new, near Day
Which should be builded out of heaven to God.
He stood a moment with erected brows,
In silence, as a creature might, who gazed, –
Stood calm, and fed his blind, majestic eyes   960
Upon the thought of perfect noon: and when
I saw his soul saw, – 'Jasper first,' I said,
'And second, sapphire; third, chalcedony;
The rest in order, – last, an amethyst.'*

Notes

1. See David, pp. 114–27, and Avery and Stott, pp. 197–9, on images of wounding
   in the poem.
2. Reynolds, pp. 22–3, nn. 7–9.
3. Cooper, pp. 153–4.
4. Ibid. pp. 154–5.
5. Reynolds dates these events and explains that they are contemporary with the
   Brownings' secret marriage and departure for Italy. See p. 118, n. 3.
6. Kaplan, pp. 29–32.

Line 945. An instance of evolutionary thought pervasive in writing of the 1850s. Charles
Lyell introduced the evolutionary theory of J. B. Lamarck in his *Principles of Geology* (1830–3).
Charles Darwin built on the work of Lamarck and others in *On the Origin of Species by Means of
Natural Selection, or the Preservation of Favoured Races in the Struggle for Life* (1859).
  Lines 962–4. The foundation of the New Jerusalem consists of precious stones. See Revelation
21:19–20. Aurora enumerates the first three and last stones, but there are twelve altogether.

7. See David, pp. 124–5; Walsh, pp. 171–7; and Avery and Stott, pp. 192–4. Parliamentary Papers were published government-sponsored studies that recorded the extreme poverty and horrific working conditions of English industrial labourers. Friedrich Engel in Manchester and Henry Mayhew in London also documented the lives of urban street dwellers and workers in the 1840s and 1850s.

8. Laird, p. 363.

9. Mill, p. 21.

10. The term 'fallen woman' was a morally fraught epithet current in the mid-nineteenth century, which implied the sinful nature of a woman who may have engaged in illicit (pre- or extra-marital sex) or illegal (prostitution) sexual behaviour. In a society that valued women's chastity and fidelity, sexual abuse and rape victims were also regarded as 'fallen', since offenders were not prosecuted as criminals until the Offences against the Person Act was passed in 1861.

11. A series of legislative acts in the 1860s and 1870s sought to regulate women's sexuality and monitor the welfare of unwanted offspring. See Smart, pp. 7–32; and Walkowitz, 32–47. Fictions that complicate simple moral binaries toward sexual women include Nathaniel Hawthorne's *The Scarlet Letter* (1850) and Elizabeth Gaskell's *Ruth* (1853). EBB's positive portrayal of a sexual woman in 'Lord Walter's Wife' (1862) prompted William M. Thackeray not to publish it. In its representation of a woman's body as a desirable / desiring commodity, Christina Rossetti's *Goblin Market* (1861) reflects on the reform of a fallen woman through sisterhood.

12. See Logan, pp. 298–9.

13. Working women sometimes had no choice but to send their infants to impoverished caregivers, who accepted too many children and treated them badly. The name 'baby farm' describes the animal-like treatment of the children, which often resulted in their deaths.

14. See also Book II, line 171. Aurora's invocation of the prophetess Miriam is complicated, as Cynthia Scheinberg has shown. In Jewish history, Miriam provides a rare instance of female poetic authority, but she is also punished for her singing (she is struck with leprosy and exiled for seven days from her Israelite camp. See Numbers 10–15). In her use of Miriam as a type for a female Christian poet, EBB elides the singer's punishment and converts her into a modern ideal represented by Aurora. Interpreting Hebrew scripture to anticipate Christian characters or events is called typology and a practice common in Victorian literature.

15. [. . .] and there's one sort of compliment which would please you particularly . . people are fond of calling [*Aurora Leigh*] a 'gospel' – That's happy—is'nt [*sic*] it? [. . .] Is it entirely prophane [*sic*], or simply ridiculous? I leave you to choose. Still, that there *is* an amount of spiritual truth in the book to which the public is unaccustomed, I know very well, only I was helped to it—did not originate—it [. . .] the naming of the name of Swedenborg, that great Seer into the two worlds, would have utterly destroyed any hope of general acceptance & consequent utility. Instead of M^rs. Browning's 'gospel', it w^d. have been M^rs. Browning's rhodomontade! What! that imposter Swedenborg! that madman, Swedenborg. But that imposter & madman, such as he is, holds sublime truths in his right hand, & most humbly I have used them as I could. My desire is that the weakness in *me*, may not hinder the influence. (Letter to Arabella, [10–18 December 1856] in Lewis, vol. II, pp. 275)

16. See Swedenborg's *Arcana Coelestia quae in Scriptura Sacra seu Verbo Domini sunt detecta* [Heavenly Secrets contained in Holy Scripture or the Word of

God unfolded], 8 vols (1749–56) and *De Nova Hierosolyma et Ejus Doctrina Coelesti* [The New Jerusalem and its Heavenly Doctrine] (1758).
17. Camp, p. 65.
18. As Barbara Taylor has shown, the figure of a female messiah comes from social-ist millennarian thought, particularly the Owenite and Fourierian movements that Aurora so dislikes (161–80). Marjorie Stone draws out the pragmatic and political implications of this figure in *Aurora Leigh* (*Elizabeth*, pp. 181–4).
19. Morgan, pp. 132–5.
20. EBB may have been drawn to the Italian form because of Dante Alighieri's *Vita Nuova* (*The New Life*), an autobiographical sequence devoted to the praise of a woman named Beatrice, who directs the poet's heart towards God.

Chapter 3

Contexts for Reading *Aurora Leigh*

The selection of primary documents in this chapter voice the aesthetic, feminist and social ideas with which *Aurora Leigh* was vitally engaged. They explain (among other things) the recurrent allusions to Wordsworth's poetry in *Aurora Leigh*, the narrator's passionate descriptions of rural England and Italy, the realities of Marian Erle's hardships and the viability of Romney Leigh's cooperative ideal. Categorised into three groups – 'Poetry, Nature and Landscape', 'Women's Duties and Women's Work' and 'The Condition of England' – these excerpts are drawn from longer pieces that have been chosen for their direct relevance to *Aurora Leigh*. An instructor should be able to give students extracts from the poem in Chapter 2 of this *Guide*, in addition to selected primary material included below.

Poetry, Nature and Landscape

When in the 1840s EBB was developing the character of her title protagonist, there were two writers whose influence she found inescapable: William Wordsworth (1770–1850) and John Ruskin (1819–1900). When EBB was born in 1816, Wordsworth was a middle-aged poet and a national treasure. By the time she was in her thirties and emerging into literary celebrity, Wordsworth lived in laurelled retirement, producing great numbers of sonnets and working tirelessly on his major long poem, *The Prelude*, which was published in the year of his death in 1850. In 1843, EBB was asked to co-author biographical essays with Richard Hengist Horne for his *A New Spirit of the Age* (1844), a compendium of England's best contemporary writers.[1] The moment to reassess Queen Victoria's favourite poet seemed to have come, and as an anonymous contributor to Horne's collection, EBB seized the opportunity to do so.

The excerpt from EBB's essay included here analyses the cultural climate that enabled Wordsworth's stellar ascent and meditates on the brightness of that star. In her commentary she affirms Wordsworth's status as a prophet-poet, a role we see Aurora Leigh aspire to and assume by the end of her narrative. Yet EBB also expresses reservations about her hero's prodigious verse output and poetic voice, particularly the expression of 'egotistical sublime' that ostensibly turns nature and all things into Wordsworth alone.[2] Yet, despite the criticism, it is clear that EBB admires and at times emulates Wordsworth's plain style of verse and careful attention to the meanest aspects of nature. Aurora's conversational, observant voice (in the opening books and throughout the poem) is clearly inspired by the man EBB calls 'a poet of detail'.

John Ruskin was EBB's exact contemporary in age and disposition: a child of the Romantic age and a Victorian-era grownup. Encouraged to read widely and taught to draw by his father, Ruskin took a keen interest in nature from an early age and recounts that interest in 'On the Moral of Landscape' (1856), which is part of his great work of aesthetic and social criticism, *Modern Painters* (1843–60). In the excerpt included in this *Guide*, Ruskin describes the sentiments that nature, or 'landscape' (as he calls it), excites within him and attempts to understand their origin. While he is profoundly moved by the reflection on childhood and nature in Wordsworth's *Ode: Intimations on Immortality from Recollections of Early Childhood* (1807), Ruskin has trouble believing the poet's claim that a child perceives nature unmediated by culture, arguing that literary texts read in childhood have a profound influence on one's perception. Despite his insistence that books greatly influence the experience of landscape, however, Ruskin also believes that it possesses a kind of innate 'Sanctity', which can be perceived first in childhood and then recollected in later life.

What does it mean that Ruskin refers to 'nature' as 'landscape', a term that derives from the art of painting? Pauline Fletcher emphasises that the term does not refer simply to the countryside: 'it was countryside viewed as scenery, an artefact that the sophisticated urban visitor was able to constitute as a painting by Claude Lorrain or Salvator Rosa'.[3] In nineteenth-century England, landscapes – whether painted or natural – typically belonged to landowners and industrialists, who sought to display their sophisticated taste. Although Ruskin did not belong to either class, his education gave him a connoisseur's eye for nature and the visual arts. The 'moral' that he perceives in landscape reflects the values and sensibilities of that education. But it should be noted that, elsewhere in his writings, Ruskin's merchant-class background also kept him mindful of the labourer or worker often marginalised in picturesque views.

EBB was greatly influenced by Ruskin's ideas about landscape, and they vitalise the narrator's recollection of her own upbringing and intellectual development in Book I of *Aurora Leigh*. Ruskin sent Robert Browning a copy of *Modern Painters*, volume 3, in January 1856, and it is striking how much EBB and Ruskin are both engaged with Wordsworth's *Immortality* ode and the role of books in perceiving nature. Yet, while Ruskin detects only tacit evidence of the divine in landscape, Aurora Leigh's descriptions comprise a kind of green Christianity in which evidence of the Holy Spirit can be perceived in nature and then preserved in poetry. In some sense, *Aurora Leigh* extrapolates the devotional in Ruskin's prose and espouses an emphatic gospel of nature.

Elizabeth Barrett Browning and Richard Hengist Horne, 'William Wordsworth', *A New Spirit of the Age*, vol. I, London: Smith, Elder & Co., 1844, pp. 308–14

When Mr. Wordsworth first stood before the world as a poet, he might as well, for the soriness of his reception, have stood before the world as a prophet. In some such position, perhaps, it may be said he actually did stand; and he had prophet's fare in a shower of stones. For several generations, had the cadences of our poets (so called) moved to them along the ends of their fingers. Their language had assumed a conventional elegance, spreading smoothly into pleonasms or clipped nicely into elisions.* The point of an antithesis had kept perpetual sentry upon the 'final pause;' and while a spurious imagination made a Name stand as a personification, Observation only looked out of window ('with extensive view' indeed . . . 'From China to Peru!') and refused very positively to take a step out of doors.* A long and dreary decline of poetry it was, from the high-rolling sea of Dryden, or before Dryden, when Waller first began to 'improve' (bona verba!) our versification down to the time of Wordsworth. Milton's far-off voice, in the meantime, was a trumpet,

---

* elisions: a 'pleonasm' is a redundancy of expression that can be a deliberate rhetorical strategy or a stylistic flaw. An 'elision' is an omission or suppression, such as a syllable in pronunciation or spelling.

* doors: in rhetoric, an 'antithesis' expresses 'an opposition or contrast of ideas, expressed by using as the corresponding members of two contiguous sentences or clauses, words which are the opposites of, or strongly contrasted with, each other; as "*he* must *increase*, but *I* must *decrease*," "in *newness* of spirit, not in the *oldness* of the *letter*"' (*OED*). The 'final pause' ostensibly refers to the end-stop of a line of verse, especially in a heroic couplet. 'Personification' refers to the humanisation of an abstract noun, such as 'Observation' above. For EBB these rhetorical and formal verse strategies are hackneyed.

which the singing-birds could not take a note from: his genius was a lone island in a remote sea, and singularly uninfluential on his contemporaries and immediate successors. The decline sloped on. And that edition of the poets which was edited by Dr. Johnson for popular uses, and in which he and his publishers did advisedly obliterate from the chronicles of the people, every poet before Cowley, and force the Chaucers, Spencers, and Draytons to give to 'Pomfret's Choice' and the 'Art of Cookery,' is a curious proof of poetical and critical degradation.* 'Every child is graceful,' observes Sir Joshua Reynolds, with a certain amount of truth, 'until he has learnt to dance.'* We had learned to dance with a vengeance—we could not move except we danced—the French school pirouetted in us most anti-nationally. The age of Shakspere [*sic*] and our great ancestral writers had grown to be rococo—*they* were men of genius and deficient in 'taste,' but *we* were wits and classics we exceeded in civilization, and wore wigs. It was not, however, to end so.*

Looking back to the experiences of nations, a national literature is seldom observed to recover its voice after an absolute declension: the scattered gleaners may be singing in the stubble, but the great song of the harvest sounds but once. Into the philosophy of this fact, it would take too much space to enquire. That genius comes as a periodical effluence, and in dependence on unmanifest causes, is the confession of grave thinkers, rather than fanciful speculators; and perhaps if the Roman empire, for instance, could have endured in strength, and held its mighty breath until the next tide, some Latin writer would have emerged from the onward flood of inspiration which was bearing Dante to the world's wide shores. Unlike Dante, indeed, would have been that writer for no author, however influential on his contemporaries, can be perfectly independent himself of their influences but he would have been a Latin writer, and his hexameters worth waiting for.* And England

---

* degradation: EBB refers to Dr Samuel Johnson's *Lives of the Most Eminent English Poets* (1779–81), a collection of biographical essays on poets from the time of the English Civil War to the reign of George III. Thus, Geoffrey Chaucer, Edmund Spenser and Michael Drayton would not have been included. John Pomfret's *The Choice: a Poem written by a Person of Quality* (1699) was a popular, but unexceptional, meditation on the good life. William King published *The Art of Cookery, in Imitation of Horace's Art of Poetry* in 1709. EBB dislikes these imitative and mannered compositions typical of eighteenth-century neoclassical verse.

* 'Every . . . dance': Joshua Reynolds (1723–92) was a portrait artist and the first president of London's Royal Academy of Art.

* so: EBB's comments derive from the decorative arts and contrast the rococo, 'a light, elegant, and sensuous style' with the neoclassical movement, which has been characterised as 'stern and moralizing' (*Grove Art Online*). As applied to English literature, EBB thinks critics have favoured the polished classicism of Georgian poetry rather than the passionate originality of the Elizabethans.

* for: Dante Alighieri (1265–1321), political exile and author of the *Divine Comedy*, was Italy's first great vernacular poet. EBB suggests that, regardless of historical fortune, a great writer

did not wait in vain for a *new* effluence of genius it came at last like the morning—a pale light in the sky, an awakening bird, and a sunburst— we had Cowper—we had Burns—that lark of the new grey dawn; and presently the early-risers of the land could see to spell slowly out the name of William Wordsworth. They saw it and read it clearly with those of Coleridge and Leigh Hunt,—and subsequently of Shelley and Keats, notwithstanding the dazzling beams of lurid power which were in full radiation from the engrossing name of Byron.*

Mr. Wordsworth began his day with a dignity and determination of purpose, which might well have startled the public and all its small poets and critics, his natural enemies. He laid down fixed principles in his prefaces, and carried them out with rigid boldness, in his poems; and when the world laughed, he bore it well, for his logic apprized him of what should follow: nor was he without the sympathy of Coleridge and a few other first-rate intellects.* With a severe hand he tore away from his art, the encumbering artifices of his predecessors; and he walked upon the pride of criticism with greater pride. No toleration would he extend to the worst laws of a false critical code; nor any conciliation to the critics who had enforced them. He was a poet, and capable of poetry, he thought, only as he was a man and faithful to his humanity. He would not separate poetry and nature, even in their forms. Instead of being 'classical' and a 'wit,' he would be a poet and a man, and 'like a man,' (not-withstanding certain weak moments) he spoke out bravely, in language free of current phraseology and denuded of conventional adornments, the thought which was in him. And the thought and the word witnessed to that verity of nature, which is eternal with variety. He laid his hand upon the Pegasean* mane, and testified that it was no floss silk. He testified that the ground was not all lawn or bowling-green; and that the forest trees were not clipped upon a pattern. He scorned to be contented with a tradition of beauty, or with an abstraction of the beautiful. He refused to work, as others had done, like those sculptors, who make

---

of Dante's calibre would have emerged from the Latin-speaking world; likewise, England had not waited in vain, since Wordsworth emerged after a decline in English poetry. A feature of Latin poetry, a 'hexameter' is a line of verse containing six metrical feet.

   * Byron: EBB enumerates the primary male Romantic poets, including the proto-Romantic William Cowper and the Scottish poet Robert Burns. Samuel Taylor Coleridge was Wordsworth's collaborator on *Lyrical Ballads* (1798) and lifelong interlocutor about poetry. Leigh Hunt was a poet, critic and journalist.

   * intellects: for *Lyrical Ballads* Wordsworth wrote a 1798 advertisement and an 1800 preface, which was revised and extended in 1802. He also wrote prefaces to *The Excursion* (1814) and *Poems* (1815).

   * Pegasean mane: Pegasus was the winged horse that created the fountain on Mt Helicon, the home of the Muses.

all their noises in the fashion of that of the Medicaean Venus*; until no one has his own nose; nature being 'cut to order.' William Wordsworth would accept no type for nature, he would take no leap at the generalization of the natural; and the brown moss upon the pale should be as sacred to him and acceptable to his song, as the pine-clothed mountain. He is a poet of detail, and signs of what is closest to his eye; as small starting points for far views, deep sentiment, and comprehensive speculation. 'The meanest flower that blows' is not too deep for him; exactly because 'thoughts too deep for tears' lie for him in the mystery of its meanness.* He has proved this honor on the universe; that in its meanest natural thing is no vulgarism, unconveyed by the artificiality of human manners. That such a principle should lead to some puerilities at the outset, was not surprising.

A minute observer of exterior nature, his humanity seems nevertheless to stand between it and him; and he confounds those two lives—not that he loses himself in the contemplation of things, but that he absorbs them in himself, and renders them Wordsworthian. They are not what he wishes, until he has brought them home to his own heart. Chaucer and Burns made the most of a daisy, but left it still a daisy; Mr. Wordsworth leaves it transformed into *his* thoughts. This is the sublime of egotism, disinterested as extreme. It is on the entity of the man Wordsworth, that the vapour creeps along the hill—and 'the mountains are a feeling.'* To use the language of the German schools, he makes a subjectivity of his objectivity. Beyond the habits and purposes of his individuality, he cannot carry his sympathies; and of all powerful writers, he is the least dramatic. Another reason, however, for his dramatic inaptitude, is his deficiency in passion. He is passionate in his will and reason, but not in his senses and affections; and perhaps scarcely in his fancy and imagination. He has written, however, one of the noblest odes in the English language, in his 'Recollections of Childhood[,]' and his chief poem 'The Excursion,' which is only a portion of a larger work (to be published hereafter) called 'The Recluse,' has passages of very glorious exaltation. Still, he is seldom impulsive; and his exaltation is rather the nobly-acquired habit of his mind than the prerogative of his temperament. A great Christian moralist and teacher, he is sacerdotal both in gravity and

---

   * Venus: the Venus de' Medici (Hellenistic, 1 BC) was a touchstone for neoclassical artists in the nineteenth century and resided in the Tribune of the Uffizi in Florence, Italy.
   * 'The meanest . . . meanness': the quotations are from the last two lines of the *Intimations* ode: 'To me the meanest flower that blows can give / Thoughts that do often lie too deep for tears' (lines 203–4).
   * 'the . . . feeling': George Gordon, Lord Byron, *Childe Harold's Pilgrimage*, canto 3, line 681.

purity; he is majestic and self-possessed. Like many other great men he *can* be dull and prolix. If he has not written too many sonnets, it may be doubted if he has not burned too few: none are bad, it is true; but the value of the finest would be enhanced by separation from so much fatiguing good sense. They would be far more *read*. Perhaps, his gravity and moral aim are Mr. Wordsworth's most prevailing characteristics. His very cheerfulness is a smile over the altar,—a smile of benediction which no one dares return,—and expression of good will rather than sympathy.

These remarks have doubtless occurred to many students and admirers of Wordsworth; but it is more remarkable that he is what he is, not unconsciously or instinctively, as many other men of genius have developed their idiosyncracies; but consciously, to all appearance, and determinately, and by a particular act of the will. Moreover, he is not only a self-conscious thinker and feeler; but he is conscious, apparently, of this self-consciousness.

John Ruskin, 'On the Moral of Landscape' (1856), from *Modern Painters*, vol. 3, part 4, *The Works of John Ruskin*, vol. 5, ed. E. T. Cook and Alexander Wedderburn, London: George Allen, 1904, pp. 363–70

We saw above that Wordsworth described the feeling* as independent of thought, and, in the particular place then quoted, he *therefore* speaks of it depreciatingly. But in other places he does not speak of it depreciatingly, but seems to think the absence of thought involves a certain nobleness [. . .]

> 'In such high hour
> Of visitation from the living God
> *Thought* was not.'*

And he refers to the intense delight which he himself felt, and which he supposes other men feel, in nature, during their thoughtless youth, as an intimation of their immortality, and a joy which indicates their having come fresh from the hand of God.*

Now if Wordsworth be right in supposing this feeling to be in some

---

* feeling: that is, a love of nature.

* 'In such . . . not': William Wordsworth, *The Excursion*, Part I, lines 211–13. Ruskin's emphasis.

* hand of God: see the *Intimations* ode: 'But trailing clouds of glory do we come / From God, who is our home: / Heaven lies about us in our infancy' (lines 64–66).

degree common to all men, and most vivid in youth, we may question if it can be *entirely* explained as I have now tried to explain it. For if it entirely depended on multitudes of ideas, clustering about a beautiful object, it might seem that the youth could not feel it so strongly as the man, because the man knows more, and must have more ideas to make the garland of. Still less can we suppose the pleasure to be of that melancholy and languid kind, which Scott defines as 'Resignation' and 'Content'*; boys being not distinguished for either of those characters, but for eager effort and delightsome discontent. If Wordsworth is at all right in this matter, therefore, there must surely be some other element in the feeling not yet detected.

Now, in a question of this subtle kind, relating to a period of life when self-examination is rare, and expression imperfect, it becomes exceedingly difficult to trace, with any certainty, the movements of the minds of others, nor always easy to remember those of our own. I cannot, from observation, form any decided opinion as to the extent in which this strange delight in nature influences the hearts of young persons in general; and, in stating what has passed in my own mind, I do not mean to draw any positive conclusion as to the nature of the feeling in other children; but the inquiry is clearly one in which personal experience is the only safe ground to go upon, though a narrow one; and I will make no excuse for talking about myself with reference to this subject, because, though there is much egotism in the world, it is often the last thing a man thinks of doing,—and, though there is much work to be done in the world, it is often the best thing a man can do,—to tell the exact truth about the movements of his own mind, and there is this farther reason, that whatever other faculties I may or may not possess, this gift of taking pleasure in landscape I assuredly possess in a greater degree than most men; it having been the ruling passion of my life, and the reason for the choice of its field of labour.

The first thing which I remember, as an event in life, was being taken by my nurse to the brow of Friar's Crag on Derwent Water; the intense joy, mingled with awe, that I had in looking through the hollows in the mossy roots, over the crag, into the dark lake, has associated itself more or less with all twining roots of trees ever since. Two other things I remember as, in a sort, beginnings of life;—crossing Shapfells* (being let

---

* 'Content': the full quotation is 'But, in a bosom thus prepared, / Its still small voice is often heard, / Whispering a mingled sentiment / 'Twixt resignation and content', from Walter Scott's *Marmion* (1808), introduction to canto 2, lines 142–5.

* Friar's Crag, Derwent Water and Shapfells: famous features of Cumbria in the area of northern England known as the Lake District.

out of the chaise to run up the hills), and going through Glenfarg, near Kinross*, in a winter's morning, when the rocks were hung with icicles; these being culminating points in an early life of more travelling than is usually indulged to a child. In such journeyings, whenever they brought me near hills, and in all mountain ground and scenery, I had a pleasure, as early as I can remember, and continuing till I was eighteen or twenty, infinitely greater than any which has been since possible to me in anything; comparable for intensity only to the joy of a lover in being near a noble and kind mistress, but not more explicable or definable than that feeling of love itself. Only thus much I can remember, respecting it, which is important to our present subject.

First: it was never independent of associated thought. Almost as soon as I could see or hear, I had got reading enough to give me associations with all kinds of scenery; and mountains, in particular, were always partly confused with those of my favourite book, Scott's *Monastery*; so that Glenfarg and all other glens were more or less enchanted to me, filled with forms of hesitating creed about Christie of the Clint Hill, and monk Eustace; and with a general presence of White Lady everywhere.* I also generally knew, or was told by my father and mother, such simple facts of history as were necessary to give more definite and justifiable association to other scenes which chiefly interested me, such as the ruins of Lochleven and Kenilworth; and thus, my pleasure in mountains or ruins was never, even in earliest childhood, free from a certain awe and melancholy, and general sense of the meaning of death, though, in its principal influence, entirely exhilarating and gladdening.

Secondly, it was partly dependent on contrast with a very simple and unamused mode of general life; I was born in London, and accustomed, for two or three years, to no other prospect than that of the brick walls over the way; had no brothers nor sisters, nor companions; and though I could always make myself happy in a quiet way, the beauty of the mountains had an additional charm of change and adventure which a country-bred child would not have felt.

Thirdly: there was no definite religious feeling mingled with it. I partly believed in ghosts and fairies; but supposed that angels belonged entirely to the Mosaic dispensation, and cannot remember any single thought or feeling connected with them. I believed that God was in heaven, and could hear me and see me; but this gave me neither pleasure nor pain,

---

* Glenfarg: a small village in the central Scottish county of Perth and Kinross.

* everywhere: Walter Scott's *The Monastery* (1820) is set around 1550 at the dawn of the Scottish Reformation. The plot illustrates the clash in Scotland between landowning families and marauders and involves the mysterious intercession of a spectral lady.

and I seldom thought of it at all. I never thought of nature as God's work, but as a separate fact or existence.

Fourthly: it was entirely unaccompanied by powers of reflection or invention. Every fancy that I had about nature was put into my head by some book; and then, the more I reflected, the less nature was precious to me: I could then make myself happy, by thinking, in the dark, or in the dullest scenery; and the beautiful scenery became less essential to my pleasure.

Fifthly: it was, according to its strength, inconsistent with every evil feeling, with spite, anger, covetousness, discontent, and every other hateful passion; but would associate itself deeply with every just and noble sorrow, joy or affection. It had not, however, always the power to repress what was inconsistent with it; and, though only after stout contention, might at last be crushed by what it had partly repressed. And as it only acted by setting one impulse against another, though it had much power in moulding of the character, it had hardly any in strengthening it; it formed temperament but never instilled principle; it kept me generally good-humoured and kindly, but could not teach me perseverance or self-denial: what firmness or principle I had was quite independent of it; and it came itself nearly as often in the form of a temptation as of a safeguard, leading me to ramble over hills when I should have been learning lessons, and lose days in reveries which I might have spent doing kindnesses.

Lastly: although there was no definite religious sentiment mingled with it, there was a continual perception of Sanctity in the whole of nature, from the slightest thing to the vastest;—an instinctive awe, mixed with delight; an indefinable thrill, such as we sometimes imagine to indicate the presence of a disembodied spirit. I could only feel this perfectly when I was alone; and it would often make me shiver from head to foot with the joy and fear of it, when after being some time away from hills, I first got to the shore of a mountain river, where the brown water circled among the pebbles, or when I first saw the swell of distant land against the sunset, or the first low broken wall, covered with mountain moss. I cannot in the least *describe* the feeling; but I do not think this is my fault, nor that of the English language, for I am afraid, no feeling *is* describable. If we had to explain even the sense of bodily hunger to a person who had never felt it, we should be hard to put it into words; and the joy in nature seemed to me to come of a sort of heart-hunger, satisfied with the presence of a Great and Holy Spirit. These feelings remained in their full intensity till I was eighteen or twenty, and then, as the reflective and practical power increased, and the 'cares of this world'* gained upon me, faded gradually away, in the manner described by Wordsworth in his *Intimations of Immortality*.

I cannot, of course, tell how far I am justified in supposing that these sensations may be reasoned upon as common to children in general. In the same degree they are not of course common, otherwise children would be, most of them, very different from what they are in their choice of pleasures. But, as far as such feelings exist, I apprehend they are more or less similar in their nature and influence; only producing different characters according to the elements with which they are mingled. Thus, a very religious child may give up many pleasures to which its instincts lead it, for the sake of irksome duties; and an inventive child would mingle its love of nature with watchfulness of human sayings and doings; but I believe the feelings I have endeavoured to describe are the pure landscape-instinct; and the likelihoods of good or evil resulting from them may be reasoned upon as generally indicating the usefulness or danger of the modern love and study of landscape.

And, first, observe that the charm of romantic association can be felt only by the modern European child. It rises eminently out of the contrast of the beautiful past with the frightful and monotonous present; and it depends for its force on the existence of ruins and traditions, on the remains of architecture, the traces of battlefields, and the precursorship of eventful history. The instinct to which it appeals can hardly be felt in America, and every day that either beautifies our present architecture and dress, or overthrows a stone of medieval monument, contributes to weaken it in Europe. Of its influence on the mind of Turner and Prout,* and the permanent results which, through them, it is likely to effect, I shall have to speak presently.

Again: the influence of surprise in producing the delight, is to be noted, as a suspicious or evanescent element in it. Observe, my pleasure was chiefly when I *first* got into beautiful scenery out of London. The enormous influence of novelty the way in which it quickens observation, sharpens sensation, and exalts sentiment is not half enough taken note of by us, and is to me a very sorrowful matter. I think that what Wordsworth speaks of as a glory in the child, because it has come fresh

---

* 'cares of this world': Mark 4:19.
* Turner and Prout: J. M. W. Turner (1775–1851), a landscape and history painter, is the central subject of *Modern Painters*. Ruskin championed Turner's subjective, impressionistic style in response to nature, ruins and modernity. Samuel Prout (1783–1852), a watercolour painter and lithographer. Ruskin admired Prout's lithograph drawings of the Rhine country and southern English counties.

from God's hands,* is in reality nothing more than the freshness of all things to its newly opened sight. I find that by keeping long away from hills, I can in great part still restore the old childish feeling about them; and the more I live and work among them, the more it vanishes.

This evil is evidently common to all minds; Wordsworth himself mourning over it in the same poem:

'Custom hangs upon us, with a weight
Heavy as frost, and deep almost as life.'*

And if we grow impatient under it, and seek to recover the mental energy by more quickly repeated and brighter novelty, it is all over with our enjoyment. There is no cure for this evil, any more than for the weariness of the imagination already described, but in patience and rest: if we try to obtain perpetual change, change itself will become monotonous; and then we are reduced to that old despair, 'If water chokes, what will you drink after it?' And the two points of practical wisdom in this matter are, first, to be content with as little novelty as possible at a time; and secondly, to preserve, as much as possible in the world, the sources of novelty.

[. . .] Observe: the whole force of education, until very lately, has been directed in every possible way to the destruction of the love of nature. The only knowledge which has been considered essential among us is that of words, and, next after it, of the abstract sciences; while every liking shown by children for simple natural history has been either violently checked, (if it took an inconvenient form for the housemaids,) or else scrupulously limited to hours of play: so that it has really been impossible for any child earnestly to study the works of God but against its conscience; and the love of nature has become inherently the characteristic of truants and idlers. While also the art of drawing, which is of more real importance to the human race than that of writing (because people can hardly draw anything without being of some use both to themselves and others, and can hardly write anything without wasting their own time and that of others), this art of drawing, I say, which on plain and stern system should be taught to every child, just as writing is, has been so neglected and abused, that there is not one man in a thousand, even of its professed teachers, who knows its first principles; and thus it needs much ill-fortune or obstinancy—much neglect on the part of its teachers, or rebellion on his own before a boy can get leave to use

---

* God's hands: another echo of the *Intimations* ode: 'But trailing clouds of glory do we come / From God, who is our home: / Heaven lies about us in our infancy' (lines 64–6).

* 'Custom . . . life': ibid. 'And custom lie upon thee with a weight / Heavy as frost and deep almost as life' (lines 128–9). Note Ruskin's alteration.

his eyes or his fingers; so that those who *can* use them are for the most part neglected or rebellious lads runaways and bad scholars passionate, erratic, self-willed, and restive against all forms of education; while your well-behaved and amiable scholars are disciplined into blindness and palsy of half their faculties. Wherein here is at once a notable ground for what difference we have observed between the lovers or nature and its despisers; between the somewhat immoral and unrespectable watchfulness of the one, and the moral and respectable blindness of the other.

One more argument remains, and that, I believe, an unanswerable one. As, by the accident of education, the love of nature has been, among us, associated with *wilfulness*, so, by the accident of time, it has been associated with *faithlessness*. I traced, above, the peculiar mode in which this faithlessness was indicated; but I never intended to imply, therefore, that it was an invariable concomitant of the love. Because it happens that, by various concurrent operations of evil, we have been led according to those words of the Greek poet already quoted, to 'dethrone the gods, and crown the whirlwind,'* it is no reason that we should forget there was once a time when 'the Lord answered Job *out* of the whirlwind.'* And if we now take final and full view of the matter, we shall find that the love of nature, wherever it has existed, has been a faithful and sacred element of human feeling; that is to say, supposing all circumstances otherwise the same with respect to two individuals, the one who loves nature most will be *always* found to have more *faith in God* than the other. It is intensely difficult, owing to the confusion and counter influences which always mingle in the data of the problem, to make this abstraction fairly, but so far as we can do it, so far, I boldly assert, the result is constantly the same: the nature-worship will be found to bring with it such a sense of the presence and power of a Great Spirit as no mere reasoning can either induce or controvert; and where that nature-worship is innocently pursued, *i.e.* with due respect to other claims on time, feeling, and exertion, and associated with the higher principles of religion, it becomes the channel of certain sacred truths, which by no other means can be conveyed.

Women's Duties and Women's Work

'I know I have not ground you down enough / To flatten and bake you to a wholesome crust / For household uses and proprieties' (*Aurora*

---

* 'dethrone . . . whirlwind': Aristophanes, *Clouds*, line 828.
* 'the Lord . . . whirlwind': Job 38:1.

Leigh, Book I, lines 1040–2). In thinking of her aunt's desire to make her a proper woman, Aurora imagines her mind to be a pile of grain soon to be processed for domestic consumption. The poet's outrage over her English and decidedly female education is palpable in the opening book of the poem in part because it necessitates the poet 'nibbl[ing]' knowledge from her father's books like a 'small nimble mouse' (Book I, lines 837–8). Aurora's individualistic pursuit of learning fuels her desire to be a poet, which, in the view of her aunt and Romney Leigh, is contrary to her destiny as an Englishwoman, who typically rules the household and serves her husband and family.

Writing on the role of middle-class women at the dawn of the Victorian Age, Mrs Ellis, as she was known, was a major exponent of separate spheres ideology, which limited women's influence to the home, while allowing men to traverse between private and public. Yet the excerpt below from *The Women of England, their Social Duties and Domestic Habits* (1839), which comes from the very beginning of the text, does not view domesticity as disengaged from the wider national scene. Rather, the English home, or hearth, Ellis claims, is the very foundation of the nation's moral character, and on this basis she feels a patriot's duty to ensure Englishwomen's moral superiority through proper conduct. With greater numbers of women seeking higher education by the late 1830s, Ellis detects female dissatisfaction with the status quo and a feeling of frivolity and idleness in others. But rather than promote wider opportunity for women's education and employment, Ellis recommends suppressing the desire for individual advancement and turning one's concern solely to family members or those in need. As the excerpt makes clear, a woman's influence – rather than public words or action – is the most powerful way to shape the character of the nation. Although Ellis stresses that women should perform all duties with kindness and benevolence, contemporary critics thought her advice resulted in a passive-aggressive female type, one who manipulated men and betrayed fellow women. EBB suggests that the haughty demeanour and angry gaze of Aurora's English aunt is the result of a limited education and bitter selflessness. Aurora is ostensibly the antitype to Ellis's angel in the house, as she speaks her mind openly, lives alone (and then with a woman of a different class) and makes a living by her pen.

In contrast to the temerity Ellis advocates, the review article by Anna Jameson (1794–1860), a novelist, travel writer and journalist, outspokenly seeks to improve conditions for industrial workers, especially women and children. Richard Dugard Grainger's report on children's employment was the first of two investigative parliamentary studies, which contributed to the passing of two Factory Acts (1844, 1847), limiting the hours children were required to work and prohibiting the labour of children under eight. The excerpt on millinery workers reveals some of the facts behind the story of Marian Erle, who finds work as a seamstress both before (Books III–IV) and after (Book VII) her life takes a turn for the worse. Jameson's anger toward the upper classes – for remaining indifferent to the plight of those making ladies' ornate and delicate dresses on short notice – is palpable. In the portrayal of Lady Waldemar in *Aurora Leigh*, EBB suggests the savage exploitation of the less privileged, while appearing virtuous in a flawless wardrobe.

Marian Erle not only experiences the hardship of being a seamstress but also becomes drawn into the dangerous world of prostitution. W. R. Greg's lengthy *Westminster Review* essay on that subject forthrightly addresses a pressing social problem that was a source of shame, suffering and despair to thousands of women in Paris and London. Greg's consideration of the causes and circumstances of the urban sex trade in two major European cities attempts to reach social conservatives who blamed women for indulging in erotic excess and wantonly spreading sexually transmitted diseases. In Greg's analysis, prostitution arises because of the vulnerability of working women, who struggled to make ends meet and had few employment opportunities. Whether duped or desperate, prostitutes were regarded as fallen women and irredeemable sinners.[4] Against such uninformed moralising, Greg and EBB, through Marian's story of abduction in Book VI, argue that such women deserve Christian charity and the opportunity to improve their lives.

Sarah Stickney Ellis, *The Women of England*, Philadelphia: E. L. Carey & A. Hart, 1839, pp. 13–17, 21–2, 27–31, 35–7, 40–3

Every country has its peculiar characteristics, not only of climate and scenery, of public institutions, government, and laws; but every country has also its *moral characteristics*, upon which is founded its true title to a station, either high or low, in the scale of nations.

The national characteristics of England are the perpetual boast of her patriotic sons; and there is one especially which it behoves all British subjects not only to exult in, but to cherish and maintain. Leaving the justice of her laws, and the extent of her commerce, and the amount of her resources, to the orator, the statesman, and the political economist, there yet remains one of the noblest features in her national character, which may not improperly be regarded as within the compass of a woman's understanding, and the province of a woman's pen. It is the domestic character of England the home comforts, and fireside virtues for which she is so justly celebrated. These I hope to be able to speak of without presumption, as intimately associated with, and dependent upon, the moral feelings and habits of the women of this favoured country.

It is therefore in reference to these alone that I shall endeavour to treat the subject of England's nationality; and in order to do this with more precision, it is necessary to draw the line of observation within a narrower circle, and to describe what are the characteristics of the women of England. I ought, perhaps, in strict propriety, to say what *were* their characteristics; because I would justify the obtrusiveness of a work like this by first premising that the women of England are deteriorating in their moral character, and that false notions of refinement are rendering them less influential, less useful, and less happy than they were.

In speaking of what English women were, I would not be understood to refer to what they were a century ago. Facilities in the way of mental improvement have greatly increased during this period. In connexion with moral discipline, these facilities are invaluable; but I consider the two excellencies as having been combined in the greatest perfection in the general average of women who have now attained to middle, or rather advanced age. When the cultivation of the mental faculties had so far advanced as to take precedence of the moral, by leaving no time for domestic usefulness, and the practice of personal exertion in the way of promoting general happiness, the character of the women of England assumed a different aspect, which is now beginning to tell upon society in the sickly sensibilities, the feeble frames, and the useless habits of the rising generation.

In stating this humiliating fact, I must be blind indeed to the most cheering aspect of modern society, not to perceive that there are signal instances of women who carry about with them into every sphere of domestic duty, even the most humble and obscure, the accomplishments and refinements of modern education; and who deem it rather an honour than a degradation to be permitted to add to the sum of human happiness, by diffusing the embellishments of mind and manners over the homely and familiar aspect of every-day existence.

Such, however, do not constitute the majority of the female population of Great Britain. By far the greater portion of the young ladies (for they are no longer *women*) of the present day, are distinguished by a morbid listlessness of mind and body, except when under the influence of stimulus, a constant pining for excitement, and an eagerness to escape from every thing like practical and individual duty. Of course, I speak of those whose minds are not under the influence of religious principle. Would that the exception could extend to all who *profess* to be governed by this principle!

Gentle, inoffensive, delicate, and passively amiable as many young ladies are, it seems an ungracious task to attempt to rouse them from their summer dream; and were it not that wintry days will come, and the surface of life be ruffled, and the mariner, even she who steers the smallest bark, be put upon the inquiry for what port she is really bound were it not that the cry of utter helplessness is of no avail in rescuing from the waters of affliction, and the pleas of ignorance unheard upon the far-extending and deep ocean of experience, and the question of accountability perpetually sounding, like the voice of a warning spirit, above the storms and the billows of this lower world I would be one of the very last to call the dreamer back to a consciousness of present things. But this state of listless indifference, my sisters, must not be. You have deep responsibilities, you have urgent claims; a nation's moral wealth is in your keeping. Let us inquire then in what way it may be best preserved. Let us consider what you are, and have been, and by what peculiarities of feeling and habit you have been able to throw so much additional weight into the scale of your country's worth.

*   *   *

There is a principle in woman's love, that renders it impossible for her to be satisfied without actually *doing* something for the object of her regard. I speak only of woman in her refined and elevated character. Vanity can satiate itself with admiration, and selfishness can feed upon services received; but woman's love is an overflowing and inexhaustible fountain, that must be perpetually imparting from the source of its own blessedness. It needs but slight experience to know, that the mere act of loving our fellow-creatures does little towards the promotions of their happiness. The human heart is not so credulous as to continue to believe in affection without practical proof. Thus the interchange of mutual kind offices begets a confidence which cannot be made to grow out of any other foundation; and while gratitude is added to the connecting link, the character on each side is strengthened by the personal energy required for the performance of every duty.

There may exist great sympathy, kindness, and benevolence of feeling, without the power of bringing any of these emotions into exercise for the benefit of others. They exist as emotions only. And thus the means which appear to us as the most gracious and benignant of any that could have been adopted by our heavenly Father for rousing us into necessary exertion, are permitted to die away, fruitless and unproductive, in the breast, where they ought to have operated as a blessing and a means of happiness to others.

          *   *   *

It is perhaps the nearest approach we can makes towards any thing like a definition of what is most striking in the characteristic of the women of England, to say, that the nature of their domestic circumstances is such as to invest their character with the threefold recommendation of *promptitude in action, energy of thought, and benevolence of feeling.* With all the responsibilities of family comfort and social enjoyment resting upon them, and unaided by those troops of menials who throng the halls of the affluent and the great, they are kept alive to the necessity of making their own personal exertions conducive to the great end of promoting the happiness of those around them. They cannot sink into supineness, or suffer any of their daily duties to be neglected, but some beloved member of the household is made to feel the consequences, by enduring inconveniences which it is alike their pride and their pleasure to remove. The frequently recurring avocations of domestic life admit no delay. When the performance of any kindly office has to be asked for, solicited, and re-solicited, it loses more than half its charm. It is therefore strictly in keeping with the fine tone of an elevated character to be beforehand with expectation, and thus to show, by the most delicate yet most effectual of all human means, that the object of attention, even when unheard and unseen, has been the subject of kind and affectionate solicitude.

By experience in these apparently minute affairs, a woman of kindly feeling and properly disciplined mind, soon learns to regulate her actions also according to the principles of true wisdom, and hence arises that energy of thought for which the women of England are so peculiarly distinguished. Every passing event, however insignificant to the eye of the world, has its crisis, every occurrence its emergency, every cause its effect; and upon these she has to calculate with precision, or the machinery of household comfort is arrested in its movements, and thrown into disorder.

Woman, however, would but ill supply the place appointed her by Providence, were she endowed with no other faculties than those of promptitude in action and energy of thought. Valuable as these may be, they would render her but a cold and cheerless companion, without the kindly affections and tender offices that sweeten human life. It is a high privilege, then, which the women of England enjoy, to be necessarily, and by force of circumstances, thrown upon their affections, for the rule of their conduct in daily life. 'What shall I do to gratify myself to be admired or to vary the tenor of my existence?' are not the questions which a woman of right feeling asks on first awaking to the avocations of the day. Much more congenial to the highest attributes of woman's character, are inquiries such as these: 'How shall I endeavour through this day to turn the time, the health, and the means permitted me to enjoy, to the best account? Is any one sick, I must visit their chamber without delay, and try to give their apartment an air of comfort, by arranging such things as the wearied nurse may not have thought of. Is any one about to set off on a journey, I must see that the early meal is spread, or prepare it with my own hands, in order that the servant, who was working late last night, may profit by unbroken rest. Did I fail in what was kind or considerate to any of the family yesterday; I will meet her this morning with a cordial welcome, and show, in the most delicate way I can, that I am anxious to atone for the past. Was any one exhausted by the last day's exertion, I will be an hour before them this morning, and let them see that their labour is so much in advance. Or, if nothing extraordinary occurs to claim my attention, I will meet the family with a consciousness that, being the least engaged of any member of it, I am consequently the most at liberty to devote myself to the general good of the whole, by cultivating cheerful conversation, adapting myself to the prevailing tone of feeling, and leading those who are least happy, to think and speak of what will make them more so.'

Who can believe that days, months, and years spent in a continual course of thought and action similar to this, will not produce a powerful effect upon the character, and not upon the individual who thinks and acts, alone, but upon all to whom her influence extends? In short, the customs of English society have so constituted women the guardians of the comforts of their homes, that, like the Vestals of old, they cannot allow the lamp they cherish to be extinguished, or to fail for want of oil, without an equal share of degradation attaching to their names.

*   *   *

Amongst their other characteristics, the women of England are frequently spoken of as plebeian in their manners, and cold in their affections; but their unpolished and occasionally embarrassed manner, as frequently conceals a delicacy that imparts the most refined and elevated sentiment to their familiar acts of duty and regard; and those who know them best are compelled to acknowledge that all the noblest passions, the deepest feelings, and the highest aspirations of humanity, may be found within the brooding quiet of an English woman's heart.

There are flowers that burst upon us, and startle the eye with the splendour of their beauty; we gaze until we are dazzled, and then turn away, remembering nothing but their gorgeous hues. There are others that refresh the traveller by the sweetness they diffuse but he has to search for the source of his delight. He finds it embedded amongst green leaves; it may be less lovely than he had anticipated, in its form and colour, but oh! how welcome is the memory of that flower, when the evening breeze is again made fragrant with its perfume.

It is thus that the unpretending virtues of the female character force themselves upon our regard, so that the woman *herself* is nothing in comparison with her attributes, and we remember less the celebrated belle, than her who made us happy.

*   *   *

But above all other characteristics of the women of England, the strong moral feeling pervading even their most trifling and familiar actions, ought to be mentioned as most conducive to the maintenance of that high place which they so justly claim in the society of their native land. The apparent coldness and reserve of English women ought only to be regarded as a means adopted for the preservation of their purity of mind, an evil, if you choose to call it so, but an evil of so mild a nature, in comparison with that which it wards off, that it may with truth be said to 'lean to virtue's side'.

I have said before, that the sphere of a domestic woman's observation is microscopic. She is therefore sensible of defects within that sphere, which, to a more extended vision, would be imperceptible. If she looked abroad for her happiness, she would be less disturbed by any falling off at home. If her interest and her energies were diffused through a wider range, she would be less alive to the minuter claims upon her attention. It is possible she may sometimes attach too much importance to the minutiae of her own domestic world, especially when her mind is imperfectly cultivated and informed: but, on the other hand, there arises, from the same cause, a scrupulous exactness, a studious observance of the means of happiness, a delicacy of perception, a purity of mind, and a dignified correctness of manner, for which the women of England are unrivalled by those of any other nation.

By a certain class of individuals, their general conduct may possibly be regarded as too prudish to be strictly in keeping with enlarged and liberal views of life. These are such as object to find the strict principles of female action carried out towards themselves. But let every man who disputes the right foundation of this system of conduct, imagine in the place of the woman whose retiring shyness provokes his contempt, his sister or his friend; and, while he substitutes another being, similarly constituted, for himself, he will immediately perceive that the boundary-line of safety, beyond which no true friend of a woman ever tempted her to pass, is drawn many degrees within which he has marked out for his own intercourse with the female sex. Nor is it in the small and separate deviations from this strict line of propriety, that any great degree of culpability exists. Each individual act may be simple in itself, and almost too insignificant for remark; it is habit that stamps the character, and custom that renders commons. Who then can guard too scrupulously against the first opening, the almost imperceptible change of manners, by which the whole aspect of domestic life would be altered? And who would not rather that the English women should be guarded by a wall of scruples, than allowed to degenerate into less worthy and less efficient supporters of their country's moral worth?

Were it only in their intercourse with mixed society that English women were distinguished by this strict regard to the proprieties of life, it might with some justice fall under the ban of prudery; but, happily for them, it extends to every sphere of action in which they move, discountenancing vice in every form, and investing social duty with that true moral dignity which it ought ever to possess.

I am not ignorant that this can only be consistently carried out under the influence of personal religion. I must, therefore, be understood to speak with limitations, and as comparing my own countrywomen with those of other nations as acknowledging melancholy exceptions and not only fervently desiring that every one professed a religion capable of leading them in a more excellent way, but that all who do profess that religion were studiously careful in these minor points. Still I do believe that the women of England are not surpassed by those of any other country for their clear perception of the right and the wrong of common and familiar things, for their reference to principle in the ordinary affairs of life, and for their united maintenance of that social order, sound integrity, and domestic peace, which constitute the foundation of all that is most valuable in the society of our native land.

Anna Jameson, 'The Milliners', *The Athenaeum*, vol. 801, 4 March 1843, pp. 203–5

Report and Appendices of the Children's Employment Commission. Presented to both Houses of Parliament, by Command of Her Majesty.

How little do people dream of the incidents and ills of that wide world of industry, with all its deeply interesting varieties of craft, skill, and condition, which surrounds and sustains our daily existence, unheeded and unseen by the throng of society! How fearful is the pain, toil, disease, and vice, convulsing the very class who supply some of the costliest pageantries of life! It is not so with all the trades which minister to pleasure; but some of the extremes of pain of production, and luxury of enjoyment, are fantastically and horribly coupled.

The report before us was last week presented to Parliament. It is an outpouring of facts full of warning; teeming with graphic narratives and discoveries of horror, which ought to have been long since known and remedied, and which, being to the world as novel as they are interesting, are a stigma on the mind and soul of our generation. There is something to us unintelligible, and almost contradictory, in the present growth and inactivity of intellect. Nobody questions this growth, and yet we see no fruits equal to the progressive sense of the need, as well as power, of improving society and the sources of its weal. Nevertheless, this is the use and design of all mental power. But it is our purpose to pourtray, and not to philosophize.

We mean to gather from these leviathan revelations the most striking and interesting of the descriptive passages relating to a variety of employments, of which the circumstances almost form a romance unlooked-for in the regions of labour, even by those who dwell in them. The very seats of fashion and easy opulence in this voluptuous London, present the worst instances of excessive toil in their service, of which the industry of empire has afforded any evidence throughout the whole scope of this very searching inquiry, in the case of

THE MILLINERS

After reading Mr. Grainger's Report, and the body of evidence he adduces, we can well appreciate the remark made to us by an individual, acquainted with the facts, on the morning of the last Court Fancy Ball,—'I shall have no pleasure there: I shall have before my eyes a score of the makers of those gay dresses in their coffins.'

We gather from the Report that there are about 15,000 milliners and dressmakers in the metropolis. They commence work usually at from 14 to 16,—that is to say, at an age when the future health and constitution is determined by the care it then receives. A very large portion of these girls are boarded and lodged by their employers, and they often come from the country healthy and strong. During the busy seasons— i.e., from April to August, and from October to Christmas—the regular hours of work 'at all the principal houses' are, *on the average, eighteen hours daily!* 'Long as these hours are,' adds Mr. Grainger, 'they are very often exceeded.' Sometimes fifty of these girls work together in a room almost always insufficiently ventilated. The sleeping apartments are generally overcrowded. In one instance, five slept in a single bed, and often ten in one room. They are fed chiefly, says an experienced witness, on cold mutton; but they subsist mostly on tea and bread and butter. Stimulants are often applied to keep them awake.

'Miss O'Neill, of Welbeck-street, (who has been a dress-maker and milliner several years, and employed in several of the London homes, is now in business for herself,) states, that the hours of work in the spring season are unlimited. The common hours are from 6 a.m. till 12 at night; sometimes from 4 a.m. till 12. Has herself often worked from 6 a.m. till 12 at night for 2 or 3 months together. It is not at all uncommon, especially in the dress-making business to work all night; just in the "drive of the season" the work occasionally continued all night, 3 times-a-week. Has worked herself twice in the week all night.'

Cases, such as follows, are not uncommon. Miss H. Baker says that—

'On the occasion of the general mourning, for his Majesty William IV, she worked without going to bed from 4 o'clock on Thursday morning till half-past 10 on Sunday morning; during this time witness did not sleep at all: of this she is certain. In order to keep awake she stood nearly the whole of Friday night, Saturday, and Saturday night, only sitting down for half an hour for rest. Two other young persons dozed occasionally in a chair. Witness, who was then 19, was made very ill by this great exertion; and when on Sunday she went to bed, she could not sleep.'

We will now extract a few facts from the evidence of some of the girls themselves. For obvious reasons the names are not given. Miss——, in the establishment, we are informed, of a first-rate milliner, states that—

'On special occasions, such as drawing-rooms, general mournings, and very frequently wedding orders, it is not uncommon to work all night: has herself worked 20 hours out of the 24 for 3 months together; at this time she was suffering from illness, and the medical attendant remonstrated against the treatment she received. He wished witness to remain in bed at least one day longer, which the employer objected to, required her to get up, and dismissed the surgeon.'

X.Y., in the same house, 'was told she ought to take her break-fast standing'; and 'M.D. has known several young persons so much exhausted that they were obliged to lie down either in the work-room or in their bed-room for an hour before they could undress.'

In consequence of giving this evidence, which Mr. Grainger was, owing to the interruptions of the mistress, obliged to obtain elsewhere,—

'M.D. was grossly abused before 3 or 4 persons: accused of improper motives in meeting with the Sub-Commissioner to give evidence, and at a moment's notice, turned out of doors without a character. She has a reason to believe that her employer has made false representations to her relations. These circumstances have caused witness deep mental suffering and anguish, and have also seriously interfered with her future prospects in life. She is at this time out of a situation. M.D. is ready to corroborate the truth of the whole of these statements on oath.'

It must not, however, be imagined that there are no instances of considerate humanity. 'In houses,' says one of the witnesses, 'where they profess to *study the health* of their young people, they begin at 8 a.m. and leave off at 11 p.m. Never earlier'! And houses which are 'regulated,' Miss Baker informed the Commissioner, 'mean those where they do not work all night.' How comforting to philanthropy to find health sometimes studied, by a limitation of labour in a close room to fifteen hours per diem *only!* The humanities among *modistes** occasionally assume even a higher range; and the benevolence of superintendents sometimes even exceeds the tender mercies of the regulations themselves. A witness says: 'If they get very sleepy they lie on the floor, on the cuttings if there are any. This indulgence depends on the kindness of the head of the room!'

Mr. Grainger, though he feels bound to state that his Report in some respects, owing to intimidation of witnesses, falls short of the truth, yet maintains 'that there is a strong desire on the part of many of the employers to promote the comfort of their workwomen, as far as the long hours permit.' But do they permit of comfort, or any approach it to? Are they not hours universally protracted to an extent necessarily painful at the time, and utterly destructive of future health and welfare?

The effects on general health are so disastrous, that one only had retained it out of the whole number, known to witness, who had been for years in the business. Indigestion, constitutional derangement, heart diseases, and, at last, consumption, seem to prevail in nearly every case. It is, in fact, a slow death.

One witness accounted for her approaching death by her excessive hours of work, and colds caught, at Bath, where her time for sleep was

---

* *modistes*: Jameson's irony reaches a pitch, as she exaggerates the compassion of the overseer milliners.

so short, that she used frequently to sleep on the rug, it not being 'worth while to go to bed.' Another, aged 25—

'Has been in the millinery business 8 years, in London. In the busy season, she began work at 7 a.m., and went on till 12 or 1 in the morning. She was so unwell she could not begin before 7; *but the principal wished it. Lately has not gone to bed before 2 or 3 in the morning:* for a good while has been in a bad state of health.'

This girl was ill at home, when the Commissioner visited her with her medical attendant. 'In fact,' says he, 'such was her state, that it seemed as if I were taking, not her evidence, but her dying declaration. It is very doubtful if she will recover.'

Medical evidence is not wanting to complete this picture, and authenticate its truth. Sir James Clark says, in his written evidence, of these poor girls:—

'—worked from 6 in the morning till 12 at night, with the exception of the short intervals allowed for their meals, in close rooms and passing the few hours allowed for rest in still more close and crowded apartments; a mode of life more completely calculated to destroy human health could scarcely be contrived, and this at a period of life when exercise in the open air, and a due proportion of rest, are essential to the development of the system.'

Dr. Devonald states that he—

'Is convinced that in no trade or manufactory whatever is the labour to be compared to that of the young dress-makers; no men work so long. It would be impossible for any animal to work so continuously with so little rest.'

*   *   *

Such is the condition of 15,000 of the inhabitants of London; a body, moreover, so quickly mouldering away, that during the span of an ordinary life full two generations have passed through the horrors of the craft, and perished in its services. Now, supposing these 15,000 beings, instead of being scattered over and lost sight of in the vortex of our Metropolitan millions, constituted the whole of a town, and a separate community, as large, for instance as Canterbury, or Dover, or Halifax, what outcries of indignation, what lamentations of sympathy, what a hurricane of virtuous reproach, would burst forth of the breadth and length of the land! And yet these towns of Canterbury, Dover, or Halifax, contain no larger population than that of the London milliners, and there would be not an atom more suffering than there is already.

The refinement and wealth of London is ever commemorating events, and efforts, and epochs; great men and great doings have their mementos in every square and nook; we erect palaces for our private pleasures, temples for our public pieties, galleries for art, and pillars and pedestals, great and small, for every sort and kind of hero; but oh, for a monument to remind us of our crushing crimes, our thousands and tens of thousands of fellow beings, the doomed slaves of our glittering grandeur, living a deathly life of torment for the gratification of wealth, which immolates them almost without a thought or care in the services of its paltry pomp, and silly pageantry. Of all the vanities of life, that of dress is at once the most inane and mindless, and its gratification the least defensible, if purchased at the cause of pain to any human being. We shall consider that this Report has done valuable service if, henceforth, where plumes wave and diamonds sparkle, and fashion disports herself in all the galaxy of her costliest trappings, a thought be now and then bestowed on the mass of suffering from which that splendour sprung. If the bloodless cheeks and attenuated frames of these poor milliner girls passed in array before the beauty their lives are sacrificed to adorn, it might, perhaps, induce them to abate a little of the brilliance of our ballrooms, for the preservation of the souls and bodies of fifteen thousand of our fellow beings.

William Rathbone Greg, *Westminster Review*, vol. 53 (July 1850), pp. 448–9, 451–3, 457–60, 474–6, 476–7, 478–9

1. *De la Prostitution dans la Ville de Paris* [1837]. Par [Alexis-Jean-Baptiste] Parent-Duchatelet.
2. *Miseries of Prostitution* [1844]. By James Beard Talbot.
3. *Prostitution in London* [1839]. By Dr. [Michael] Ryan.
4. *Letters in the Morning Chronicle—Metropolitan Poor.* [By Henry Mayhew]

There are some questions so painful and perplexing, that statesmen, moralists, and philanthropists shrink from them by common consent. The subject to which the following pages are devoted, is one of these. Of all the social problems which philosophy has to deal with, this is, we believe, the darkest, the knottiest, and the saddest. From whatever point of view it is regarded, it presents considerations so difficult and so grievous, that in this country no ruler or writer has yet been found with nerve to face the sadness, or resolution to encounter the difficulties. Statesmen see the mighty evil lying on the main pathway of the world, and, with a groan of pity and despair, 'pass by on the other side.' They act like the timid patient, who, fearing and feeling the existence of a terrible disease, dares not examine its symptoms or probe its depth, lest he should realise it too clearly, and possibly aggravate its intensity by the mere investigation. Or, like a more foolish animal still, they hide their head at the mention of the danger, as if they hoped, by ignoring it, to annihilate it.

*   *   *

Feeling, then, that it is a false and mischievous delicacy, and a culpable moral cowardice, which shrinks from the consideration of the great social vice of Prostitution, because the subject is a loathsome one; feeling, also, that no good can be hoped unless we are liberty to treat the subject, and all its collaterals, with perfect freedom, both of thought and speech; convinced that the evil must be probed with a courageous and unshrinking hand before a care can be suggested, or palliatives can safely be applied; we have deliberately resolved to call public attention to it, though we do so with pain, reluctance, and diffidence.

*   *   *

If the *extremity* of human wretchedness—if a condition which combines within itself every element of suffering, mental and physical, circumstantial and intrinsic—is a passport to our compassion, every heart should bleed for the position of an English prostitute, as it never bled at any form of woe before. We wish it were in our power to give a picture, simple, faithful, uncoloured, but 'too severely true', of the horrors which constitute the daily life of a woman of the town. The world—the unknowing world—is apt to fancy her revelling in the *enjoyment* of licentious pleasures; lost and dead to all sense of remorse and shame; wallowing in mire because she loves it. Alas! there is no truth in *this* conception, or only in the most exceptional cases. Passing over all the agonies of grief and terror she must have endured before she reached her present degradation; the vain struggles to retrieve the first false, fatal step; the feeling of her inevitable future pressing her down with all the hopeless weight of destiny; the dreams of a happy past that haunt her in the night-watches, and keep her ever trembling on the verge of madness;—passing over all this, what is her position when she has reached the last step, of her downward progress, and has become a common prostitute? Every calamity that can afflict human nature seems to have gathered round her,—cold, hunger, disease, often absolute starvation. Insufficiently fed, insufficiently clad, she is driven out alike by necessity and by the dread of solitude, to wander through the streets by night, for the chance of earning a meal by the most loathsome labour that imagination can picture, or a penal justice can inflict. For, be it remembered, desire has, by this time, long ceased; the mere momentary excitement of sexual indulgence is no longer attainable; repetition has changed pleasure into absolute repugnance; and these miserable women ply their wretched trade with a loathing and abhorrence which only perpetual semi-intoxication can deaden or endure. The curses, the blows, the nameless brutalities they have to submit to from their ruffianly associates of the brothel and saloon, are as nothing to the hideous punishment inherent in the daily practice of their sin. Their evidence, and the evidence of all who have come in contact with them, is unanimous at this point—that gin alone enables them to live or act; that without its constant stimulus and stupefaction, they would long since have died from the mere physical exhausting, or gone mad from mental horrors.* The reaction from the nightly excitement is too terrible to be borne, and gin is again resorted to as a morning draught. Even this wretched stimulus often fails; and there can be few of our readers who have not seen some of these unhappy creatures, after a winter's night spent in walking wearily to and fro for hours, amid snow, frost, or piercing winds, in dress too flimsy even for the hottest season, sink down upon a door-step, fainting and worn out; too feeble to be able, and too miserable to desire to rise. All this time, too, disease of many kinds is busy with its victim; and positive pain is added to severe privation and distracting thought. Do not let it be supposed that they are insensible to the horrors of their situation; we believe this is rarely the case altogether; where it is so, they owe it to the spirits in which they invariably indulge.

*　　*　　*

The causes which lead to the fall of women are various; but all of them are of a nature to move grief and compassion rather than indignation and contempt, in all minds cognizant of the strange composition of humanity the follies of the wise, the weakness of the strong, the lapses of the good; cognizant, also, of those surprising and deplorable inconsistencies 'by which faults may sometimes be found to have grown out of virtues, and very many of our heaviest offences to have been grafted by human imperfection upon the best and kindest of our affections.'

The first and perhaps the largest class of prostitutes are those who may fairly be said to have had no choice in the matter—who were born and bred in sin; whose parents were thieves and prostitutes before them;

---

* The evidence of all these poor girls is unanimous on this point. "No girl could lead the life we do without drink," is the common expression. (See the Letters in the *Morning Chronicle*, Letter XXIX. especially). [Author's note].

whose dwelling has always been in an atmosphere of squalid misery and sordid guilt; who have never had a glimpse or a hearing of a better life; whom fate has marked from their cradle for a course of degradation; for whom there is no *fall*, for they stood already on the lowest of existence; in whom there is no crime, for they had, and could have, neither an aspiration, a struggle, nor a choice. Such abound in London, in Dublin, in Glasgow; and, though to a less extent, in almost all large towns. Their families form the *classes dangereuses* of French statisticians; and it is from these that is recruited the population of the gaols, the lowest brothels, the hulks, and latterly, to some extent, the ragged schools. How this class is to be checked, controlled, diminished, and finally extirpated, presents one of the most difficult practical problems for English statesmen, and one, to the solution of which they must address themselves without delay; but it is one with which, at present, we have not to do. All that we wish to urge is, that the prostitutes who spring from this class, are clearly the victims of circumstances; and therefore must on all hands be allowed to be objects of the most unalloyed compassion.

Others, unquestionably, and alas! too many, fall from the snares of vanity. They are flattered by the attentions of those above them in station, and gratified by a language more refined and courteous than they hear from those of their own sphere. They enjoy the present pleasure, think they can secure themselves against being led on too far, and, like foolish moths, flutter round the flame which is to dazzle and consume them. For these we have no justification, and little apology to offer. Silly parents, and a defective or injudicious education, form their most frequent excuse. Still, even these are not worthy of the treatment they meet with, even from those of their own sex, who cannot be unconscious of the same foibles—still less from men. Let those who are without sin among us, cast the first stone at them.

Some, too, there are for whom no plea can be offered who voluntarily and deliberately sell themselves to shame, and barter, in a cold spirit of bargain, chastity and reputation for carriages, jewels, and a luxurious table. All that can here be urged is the simple fact—too notorious to be denied, too disgraceful for the announcement of it to be listed to with patience—that in this respect the unfortunate women who ultimately come upon the town, are far from being the chief or the most numerous delinquents. For one woman who thus, of deliberate choice, sells herself to a lover, ten sell themselves to a husband. Let not the world cry shame upon us for the juxtaposition. The barter is as naked and as cold in the one case as in the other; the thing bartered is the same; the difference between the two transactions lies in the price that is paid down.

Many—and these are commonly the most innocent and the most wronged of all—are deceived by unreal marriages; and in these cases their culpability consists in the folly which confided in their lover to the extent of concealing their intention from their friends—in all cases a weak and in most cases a blameable concealment; but surely not one worthy of the fearful punishment which overtakes it. Many—far more than would generally be believed—fall from pure unknowingness. Their affections are engaged, their confidence secured; thinking no evil themselves, they permit caresses which in themselves, and to them, indicate no wrong, and are led on ignorantly and thoughtlessly from one familiarity to another, not conscious where those familiarities must inevitably end, till ultimate resistance becomes almost impossible; and they learn, when it is too late—what women can never learn too early or impress too strongly on their minds—that a lover's encroachments, to be repelled successfully, must be repelled and negatived at the very outset.

We believe we shall be borne out by the observation of all who have inquired much into the antecedents of this unfortunate class of women—those, at least, who have not sprung from the *very* low, or the actually vicious sections of the community—in stating that a vast proportion of those who, after passing though the career of kept mistresses, ultimately come upon the town, fall in the first instance from a mere exaggeration and perversion of one of the best qualities of a woman's heart. They yield to desires in which they do not share, from a weak generosity which cannot refuse anything to the passionate entreaties of the man they love. There is in the warm fond heart of woman a strange and sublime unselfishness, which men too commonly discover only to profit by,—a positive love of self-sacrifice,—an active, so to speak, an *aggressive* desire to show their affection, by giving up to those who have won it something they hold very dear. It is an unreasoning and dangerous yearning of the spirit, precisely analogous to that which prompts the surrenders and self-tortures of the religious devotee. Both seek to prove their devotion to the idol they have enshrined, by casting down before his altar their richest and most cherished treasures. This is no romantic or over-coloured picture; those who deem it so have not known the better portion of the sex, or do not deserve to known them. We refer confidently to all whose memory unhappily may furnish an answer to the question, whether an appeal to this perverted generosity is not almost always the final resistless argument to which female virtue succumbs. When we consider these things, and remember also, as we must not proceed to show, how many thousands trace their ruin to actual want—*the want of those dependent on them*—we believe, upon our honour, that nine out of ten originally modest women who fall from virtue, fall from motives or feelings in which sensuality and self have no share; nay, under circumstances in which selfishness, had they not been of too generous a nature to listen to its dictates, would have saved them.

* * *

Let us now cast a short glance at the *extent* of this hideous gangrene of English society. We have given a sketch of the life of one prostitute; we have to multiply this by thousands for every large town, by tens of thousands for the metropolis. We shall not pretend to give any definite numbers; little is known with certainty; and the estimates, even among those likely to be best informed, vary enormously. Colquhoun, at the end of the last century, gave the numbers residing in London alone at 50,000. This is now admitted on all hands to have been a monstrous exaggeration. Mr. Mayne, one of the Commissioners of Police, states the number of regular prostitutes who might be traced, at from 8,000 to 10,000 in the metropolis, *exclusive of the city*; but he adds, 'There is no means of ascertaining the number of female servants, milliners, and women in the upper and middle ranks of society, who might properly be classed with prostitutes, or the women who frequent theatres exclusively, barracks, ships, prisons, &c., &c.' Mr. Talbot states, as the result of the most careful inquiries that have been made, that the number in Edinburgh is about 800; in Glasgow, 1,800; in Liverpool 2,900; in Leeds, 700; in Bristol, 1,300; in Manchester, about 700; and in Norwich, between 500 and 700. If to these we add the number furnished by other towns, and the numbers who everywhere escape the knowledge of the police, the impression among the best informed is, that the number who live by prostitution, whose sole profession it may be said to be, cannot be under 50,000 in Great Britain. This of course does not include those women of loose character who follow also some ostensible and honest occupation.

We are desirous of avoiding all needless details which would deter readers from following us to our conclusions. We shall therefore pass over many facts, which it might otherwise have been desirable to publish, and will refer to those who wish for further information, to the works of Dr. Ryan, and more especially to that of Mr. Talbot. We shall here content ourselves with three or four brief statements.

1. Most of the higher class of brothels are supplied by means of regularly-employed and highly-paid procuresses, whose occupation it is to entice to their house female servants and governesses applying in answer to advertisements, and young women—frequently young ladies—who

come to London for employment, and do not know where to fix their lodgings. Sometimes by cajolery, sometimes by force, sometimes by drugs, they are kept close prisoners till their ruin is effected; when they are handed over to the brothel-keepers, and their place supplied by fresh victims.

2. One of the most painful facts connected with the whole subject, is the tender age at which thousands of these poor creatures are seduced. On no point is the evidence more clear than this. Not only is a vast proportion of existing prostitutes under twenty, but the number who become prostitutes at the age of fifteen, twelve, and even ten years, is such as almost to exceed credibility. This is known from the testimony of the hospitals into which they are brought to be treated for syphilitic diseases. Mr. Laing (Talbot, p. 29) tells us of one child who died of a worn-out constitution at the age of thirteen! It is for the old and withered *débauché* that these youngest victims are ordinarily selected.

3. The extent to which the frequentation of brothels is carried among all classes and professions, and even among the married of both sexes, is little suspected by the public at large. On this topic some frightful disclosures have, from time to time, had to be hushed up; thought not soon enough to prevent an astounding glimpse of the hideous iniquity within.

*   *   *

4. It is notorious that nearly all prostitutes except the highest class are either thieves themselves, or are connected with and supporters of professional thieves. It is calculated, by those most conversant with police courts, that more than one half of those convicted of larceny are prostitutes or their associates.

5. One of the most important practical points connected with this painful subject, is the deplorable extent and virulence of disease which prostitution is the means of spreading throughout the community.* Sanitary matters occupy so large a share of public attention at the present moment, that so important a branch of them cannot be wholly overlooked. The amount of social evil arising from syphilitic maladies, statistics cannot measure, even if trustworthy statistics on the subject were within our reach, which they are not. All that we know with certainty is, that the Lock Hospitals (those devoted to syphilitic patients) throughout the country are always full, and generally insufficient. One witness affirms that not one man in ten goes through life without being

---

* community: on the sexual politics of treating venereal disease in the nineteenth century, see Walkowitz, pp. 48–66. The 1866 and 1869 Contagious Diseases Acts focused exclusively on women's sexual activity rather than that of both sexes.

diseased at one point or another of his career. We do not believe this statement: but we do know that the disease prevails to an extent that is perfectly appalling; and that where there are 50,000 prostitutes scattered over the country (a vast majority of whom are, or have been diseased), spreading infection on every side of them, quarantines against the plague, and costly precautions against cholera, seem very like straining at gnats and swallowing camels. It must not be imagined that the mischief of syphilis can be measured by the number of those who are ostensibly its victims, even could we ascertain this datum.

We must take into account the sufferings of those innocent individuals in private life who are infected through the sins of others; we must take into account the happiness of many families thus irretrievably destroyed; the thousands of children who are in consequence born into the world with a constitution incurably unsound; the certain, but incalculable deterioration of public health and of the vigour of the race, which must ensue in the course of a generation or two more. None but the medical men can have an adequate insight into the degree or the ramifications of this great social mischief; and medical men will tell us that it is not easy to overrate either. Surely this is a point which must soon command the most anxious attention of the state authorities.

*   *   *

Such being the evil we have to deal with, we now come to the practical and most painful questions—Can it be eradicated?—and, if not, what can and ought to be done to mitigate its mischief and diminish its amount? And is the *quasi*-sanction given to the practice, by such a recognition of it as is involved in the attempt to control it by certain administrative regulations, a greater or less evil than the consequences which at present flow from its unchecked prevalence?

Can Prostitution be eradicated?—At present, *per saltum* and *ab extra*, certainly not.* In a state of society like that which now prevails in England,—with livelihood so difficult, and marriage so impeded by scantiness of means, with so many thousands constantly on the verge, and sometimes beyond the verge, of starvation, and whose urgent poverty will therefore overrule their reluctant wills, with idleness so prevalent among the rich, and education so defective among the poor,— with the vice so sanctioned by the custom of centuries as to have become a thing of course,—with the hundred of female devils who prowl about day and night seeking for their prey, with the countless temptations

---

* *per saltum*: by a leap; *ab extra*: from without.

which beset the path of the innocent, and the countless obstacles which are cast in the backward steps of the repentant,—we fear that the extinction of the practice, or even its reduction from a rule to an exception, must be a slow, gradual, and incalculably difficult process. That it may, in time, and by bringing to bear upon it all the sound, moral, social, and economic influences in our power, be more and more discarded by the respectable, as a low and disreputable habit, and confined to the vulgar and the vicious, we are not without strong hopes; but at present we must be content, however reluctantly, to regard it as one of those admitted and established evils which the statist* has to accept and to deal with as he best may.

*   *   *

The Condition of England

In their commentary on England's economic and social problems, Thomas Carlyle (1795–1881) and Robert Owen (1771–1858) argued that improving the lives of labourers was critical for ensuring the nation's ongoing prosperity and integrity. Carlyle, a translator of German literature and a historian of the French Revolution, recognised the significance and necessity of social change but also abhorred violent conflict. Owen was a cotton-mill owner, whose 1816 socialist experiment, based in New Lanark, Scotland, initiated an activist workers' movement in the 1820s and 1830s. In some sense Owen's New Lanark anticipated Carlyle's call to revive a holistic, and decidedly paternalistic, relationship between master and worker, one that fosters social harmony while preserving hierarchy. But the 'Owenite' socialist movement did not produce great philanthropic managers, such as the kind Romney Leigh wants to become. Rather the worker–organizers and trade union leaders sought 'the emancipation of the labouring class from the tyranny of capitalism and monopoly'.[5] Neither Carlyle nor Owen wished to topple the social order. But it is fascinating to see that even as late as 1849 – a time when the Chartist[6] and 'labourist' Owenite movements were essentially defunct – Owen continued to promote his own brand of philanthropic management, as a viable solution to the economic chasm dividing England's prosperous and struggling classes.

Through her husband's friendship with Carlyle, EBB had become well acquainted with England's most famous social critic and histo-

* statist: statistician.

rian. In September 1851, the Brownings and Carlyle travelled together from London to Paris – just one year after *Latter-Day Pamphlets*, excerpted below, appeared as a collection. The two poets were familiar with Carlyle's grievances about English society, and it is clear from *Aurora Leigh* and EBB's co-authored essay on Carlyle in *A Spirit of the Age* (1844) that she shared some of his views. In the excerpt below from *Latter-Day Pamphlets*, Carlyle vents his frustrations in the form of a jeremiad, railing against what he perceived to be a steep decline in England's social commitments and values. The enemy was industrial capitalism, particularly the pursuit of the bottom line at the expense of the worker and his or her community. He laments the breakdown of the relationship between the English and the Irish, former masters and ex-slaves in the West Indies, and England's government and working-class women. Although Carlyle had the best interests of black West Indians and Irish Catholics at heart, his declarations about the laziness of these groups betray his racist disdain for workers' strikes and self-organisation. For Carlyle, performing one's job was paramount, even when employers and workers disagreed. His desire to revive a form of feudalism in the structure of the British Empire blinded him to the colonial subject's desire for both economic and political emancipation.

On the home front, Carlyle is much more sympathetic to the plight of the needlewoman and the prostitute, even if he views the latter as a lost soul. In the horrifying and apocalyptic language used to describe the dwellings of street-workers, Carlyle suggests the depths of depravation and sin to which these desperate women have sunk, and the rhetoric, excerpted below, is echoed in Aurora Leigh's description of the wedding guests who emerge from the impoverished parish of St Giles in Book IV. Carlyle blames English authorities for the appalling treatment of working women in English society. Their accursed condition is the result not of innate sinfulness but of a government that chooses to look the other way.

In contrast to Carlyle's deep pessimism, the ever-optimistic Owen reflects on his creation of a utopian community located in the cotton-mill village of New Lanark. From his father-in-law in 1816, Owen had bought the mill with several partners and become its manager. Anticipating the agriculture-based ideal of Charles Fourier's 'phalanx', Owen organised and improved all aspects of his mill workers' lives, from the quality of their homes, children's education and daily staples to the length of the average workday and the regularity of wages. The goal was to reform the character of the working man, such that vices were not a temptation and labour a genuine pleasure. The result seems to have been a community of contented, docile workers, who were loyal to their master for thirty years until he sold the operation.

Romney Leigh articulates his strong Carlylean / Owenite sense of a calling, especially a responsibility to those less privileged than him: 'Who / Being man, Aurora, can stand calmly by / And view these things, and never tease his soul / For some great cure?' (Book II, lines 279–82). We learn that he 'has parted Leigh Hall into almshouses' (Book V, line 575) and later that his 'vain phalanstery dissolved itself' (Book VIII, line 888). An almshouse is an institution that receives and supports the (typically elderly) poor, and it appears that Romney attempted to transform his charity into a phalanstery, an enterprise requiring the cooperation and work skills of the inhabitants. The violent dissolution of Romney's cooperative seems to affirm Aurora's Carlylean scepticism about the reform of people marred by poverty, vice and ignorance.

In his New Lanark experiment, however, Owen had successfully established a generous, familial dynamic between employer and worker, which appears to have prevented and even reversed any tendency towards vice. In Book II Romney expresses a similar desire to affect lives through individual care. He proclaims to Aurora: 'And hand in hand we'll go where yours shall touch / These victims, one by one! till, one by one, / The formless, nameless trunk of every man / Shall seem to wear a head with hair you know' (Book II, lines 386–9). By Book VIII, however, Romney sadly accepts the failure of his classless utopia and laments the revolt of his thankless dependents (lines 883–991). Through Romney's plot, EBB expresses her disapproval of paternalistic models of society that fail to address the spiritual as well as material needs of the impoverished: 'Ah your Fouriers failed, / Because not poets enough to understand / That life develops from within' (Book II, lines 483–5). Charles Fourier (1772–1837) was the French avatar of Owenite principles. EBB may name him instead of Owen in *Aurora Leigh* because his utopian ideal was agriculture-based and perhaps more feasible on Romney's country estate. Without attending to the soul in any social system, Aurora argues, one neglects the true source of virtue.

Thomas Carlyle, *Latter-Day Pamphlets*, London: Chapman & Hall, 1850, pp. 32–5

Supply-and-demand, Leave-it-alone, Voluntary principle, Time will mend it:—till British industrial existence seems fast becoming one huge poison-swamp of reeking pestilence physical and moral; a hideous *living* Golgotha of souls and bodies buried alive; such a Curtius' gulf,* communicating with the Nether Deeps, as the Sun never saw till now. These scenes, which the *Morning Chronicle* is bringing home to all minds of men,—thanks to it for a service such as Newspapers have seldom done,—ought to excite unspeakable reflections in every mind. Thirty-thousand outcast Needlewomen working themselves swiftly to death; three-million Paupers rotting in forced idleness, *helping* said Needlewomen to die: these are but items in the sad ledger of despair.

Thirty-thousand wretched women*, sunk in that putrefying well of abominations; they have oozed in upon London, from the universal Stygian quagmire of British industrial life; are accumulated in the *well* of the concern, to that extent. British charity is smitten to the heart, at the laying bare of such a scene; passionately undertakes, by enormous subscription of money, or by other enormous effort, to redress that individual horror; as I and all men hope it may. But, alas, what next? This general well and cesspool once baled clean out today, will begin before night to fill itself anew. The universal Stygian quagmire is still there; opulent in women ready to be ruined, and in men ready. Towards the same sad cesspool will these waste currents of human ruin ooze and gravitate as heretofore; except in draining the universal quagmire itself there is no remedy. 'And for that, what is the method?' cry many in an angry manner. To whom, for the present, I answer only, 'Not "emancipation," it would seem, my friends; not the cutting loose of human ties, something far the reverse of that!'

Many things have been written about shirtmaking; but here perhaps is the saddest thing of all, not written anywhere till now, that I know of. Shirts by the thirty-thousand are made at twopence-halfpenny each;—and in the meanwhile no needlewoman, distressed or other, can be procured in London by any housewife to give, for fair wages, fair help in sewing. Ask any thrifty house-mother, high or low, and she will answer. In high houses and in low, there is the same answer: No *real* needlewoman, 'distressed' or other, has been found attainable in any of the houses I frequent. Imaginary needlewomen, who demand considerable wages, and have a deepish appetite for beers and viands, I hear of everywhere; but their sewing proves too often a distracted puckering and botching; not sewing, only the fallacious hope of it, a fond imagination of the mind. Good sempstresses are to be hired in every village; and

---

* gulf: in Livy's account, after the gods opened a gap in the Roman forum, they demanded that Rome's most precious object be sacrificed to close it. The soldier Marcus Curtius understood their meaning and threw himself and his horse into the gap, which closed over them.

* abominations: prostitutes.

in London, with its famishing thirty-thousand, not at all, or hardly.—Is not No-government beautiful in human business? To such length has the Leave-alone principle carried it, by way of organising labour, in this affair of shirtmaking. Let us hope the Leave-alone principle has now got its apotheosis; and taken wing towards higher regions than ours, to deal henceforth with a class of affairs more appropriate for it!

Reader, did you ever hear of 'Constituted Anarchy?' Anarchy; the choking, sweltering, deadly and killing rule of No-rule; the consecration of cupidity, and braying folly, and dim stupidity and baseness, in most of the affairs of men? Slop-shirts attainable three-halfpence cheaper, by the ruin of living bodies and immortal souls? Solemn Bishops and high Dignitaries, *our* divine 'Pillars of Fire by night,' debating meanwhile, with their largest wigs and gravest look, upon something they call 'prevenient grace?'* Alas, our noble men of Genius, Heaven's *real* messengers to us, they also rendered nearly futile by the wasteful time;—preappointed they everywhere, and assiduously trained by all their pedagogues and monitors, to 'rise in Parliament,' to compose orations, write books, or in short speak *words,* for the approval of reviewers; instead of doing real kingly *work* to be approved of by the gods! Our 'Government,' a highly 'responsible' one; responsible to no God that I can hear of, but to the twenty-seven million *gods* of the shilling gallery. A Government tumbling and drifting on the whirlpools and mud-deluges, floating atop in a conspicuous manner, nowhither,—like the carcass of a drowned ass. Authentic *Chaos* come up into this sunny Cosmos again; and all men singing *Gloria in excelsis* to it. In spirituals and temporals, in field and workshop, from Manchester to Dorsetshire, from Lambeth Palace to the Lanes of Whitechapel, wherever men meet and toil and traffic together,—Anarchy, Anarchy; and only the street-constable (though with ever-increasing difficulty) still maintaining himself in the middle of it; that so, for one thing, this blessed exchange of slop-shirts for the souls of women may transact itself in a peaceable manner!—I, for my part, do profess myself in eternal opposition to this, and discern well that universal Ruin has us in the wind, unless we can get out of this.

Robert Owen, *New Lanark*, Great Britain?: s.n., 1849

In the present anarchical state of Europe, when no parties appear to know what to do, and when the human mind is dissatisfied with all old

---

* 'Pillars of fire by night': See Exodus 13:21. In Wesleyan theology, 'prevenient grace' is divine grace that precedes human decision. It exists regardless of what humans have done.

things, and a necessity has arisen for a change in the general system of society, it will be useful to recur to an experiment, made on a knowledge of these coming events, with a view to be prepared for them.* In my four essays on the theory of the formation of character, first published in 1812 and 1813;—in my discourse on opening the New Institution at New Lanark, for the practical formation of character;—in two memorials presented for me, by the late Lord Castlereagh, to the Congress of Sovereigns, assembled in Aix la Chapelle, in 1818;—and in innumerable other publication, lectures, and public meetings, I adopted every means in my power to forewarn all parties of these coming events, and to prepare both governments and people for the inevitable change that was rapidly approaching unheeded and little understood progress of mechanical invention, chemical discoveries, and of knowledge among the working class.

This natural growth of the mind of the world, with the immensity of the ever increasing new scientific power to aid manual power in the creation of wealth, were sure to meet at a point that would create an irresistible necessity for an entire change in the principles and practices of the world, and in the creation from birth, of a new character for the human race; a character based on a true fundamental principle, in direct opposition to the false one on which, until now, the character of all has been formed; and hence the past and present evils of humanity.

*　　*　　*

[. . .] the experiment at New Lanark was commenced and continued by me for thirty years, to prove the truth of the new fundamental principle which is to regenerate the world, by making man a new being in feeling and knowledge, and altogether changing the human-formed part of the character of all future generations and to re-construct society.

*　　*　　*

The particulars of this, the most important experiment ever yet made for humanity, shall be given in succeeding numbers; but, for the present, suffice it to say, that by acting consistently on this new fundamental principle for thirty years, commencing with a population of intemperate, idle, immoral, inefficient, dirty, full of religious differences and

---

* them: 1848 was a year of revolutions in France, Germany, Italy and Austria. The causes are attributable to a number of factors, among them dissatisfaction with political leadership, the rise of nationalism, calls for democratic rights, and a convergence of middle- and working-class militancy. In 1848 Chartists demonstrated in Kennington Common, London, and presented a petition with over two million signatures to parliament. The Irish Famine (1845–9) also created an international crisis that shamed England.

animosities, and at first greatly opposed to myself, being to them as a foreigner, and to the changes which they saw I was about to introduce; the following results were obtained:—

1. The character of the whole population was gradually greatly changed for the better, physically, mentally, morally, and practically.

2. Through a new invented infant school, and an institution for the formation of character, a new character was formed for the children of these workpeople, superior to any ever given to the working class, or, in some essential points, to the children of any class.

3. Gradually, many of the inferior, injurious, and vicious arrangements and external circumstances, which existed on my arrival, were removed, and superseded by others much better.

4. As these injurious circumstances were superseded by those which were superior, individual reward and punishments were diminished, until ultimately they nearly ceased. In the schools, with those trained from infancy within them, individual reward and punishments were unknown, and in a thoroughly well constituted society both would be for ever unknown.

5. Quarrelling and religious animosities were gradually made to cease, and the spirit of charity, even for those of different sects, was being generally made to pervade the whole population.

6. During the thirty years of this experiment, I did not apply once to a magistrate or lawyer; nor was there a legal punishment inflicted upon one of this new formed population.

7. The entire population was not only satisfied, but frequently declared publicly that they were content and most happy under the treatment they experienced, and with the principles by which they were governed. Their only wish was that all other workpeople might enjoy the same advantages.

8. The children received this new formation of character at an expense to the parents of three shillings per year for each child. These children were so happy during the whole period of their instruction within the institution, that they never desired or wished for one holiday.

9. This institution for the formation of character was divided into three schools, according to age and progress, and was supported by the company, at an expense of 1,200*l.* a-year, in addition to the payment by the parents of three shillings a-year for each child.

10. The time of working per day, without any reduction of wages, was

reduced for all ages to ten-and-a half hours, when competitors in the same kind of manufactures were causing their workpeople to be employed for 13, 14, and some 15 hours per day.

11. The whole population was supplied with the entire necessaries of life, and many of its comforts, of the most wholesome and best qualities, at prime cost, without profit to the company.

12. The houses, streets, and pleasure ground were kept for them in good order, and each family had a small garden given to them.

13. During four months of the American embargo, all the workpeople were paid, without reduction, their full wages; amounting to seven thousand pounds, for doing nothing during the whole period.

14. The institution for the formation of character, which consisted of two large buildings, with their fitting-up and furnishings, cost full ten thousand pounds.

15. And yet the pecuniary profits of this establishment, during these thirty years, after covering these extra expenses, and allowing five per cent per annum for the use of the capital employed, were upwards of three hundred thousand pounds, which were divided between the partners.

16. Both pecuniary profits, depending upon the more or less amount of gold in circulation, or upon the immediate demand over production, are no just or adequate criterion of the real or intrinsic wealth produced by the population of this establishment of two thousand five hundred persons. The fact is that the working part of this population produced during these thirty years as much intrinsic useful wealth as the working part of a population of six hundred thousand could have produced, of the same description, only twenty years before this manufacture was commenced at New Lanark.

17. That little as the world dreams of such result, this experiment has laid a foundation for an entire re-construction of society, upon rational principles, over the world.
London, Feb. 20th, 1849. ROBERT OWEN.

Notes

1. The composition of these essays was complex, for, although the compendium designates Horne as the sole author, EBB's more substantial contributions have been demonstrated. See Paroissien, pp. 274–81.

2. 'egotistical sublime': Keats's phrase is derived from William Hazlitt's essay on Wordsworth in *The Spirit of the Age, Or Contemporary Portraits* (1825). Keats uses the expression in his letter to Richard Woodhouse, 27 October 1818, in Forman, p. 227.

3. Fletcher, p. 493.

4. On the unease about agency and selfhood created by Victorian prostitutes, see Anderson, pp. 22–65.
5. *To Unionists*, p. 13.
6. Chartist: the Chartists were a collection of union and trade leaders who wrote and presented to parliament a People's Charter, which set forth the following six democratic goals:

   1. universal manhood suffrage
   2. annual elections for Parliament
   3. voting by secret ballot
   4. equal electoral districts
   5. abolition of property qualifications for members of parliament
   6. payment of members of Parliament.

   The Chartists presented their petition with millions of signatures in 1839, 1842 and 1848, only to be rejected all three times.

Chapter 4

Teaching *Aurora Leigh*

This chapter aims to provide instructors who are teaching the poem for the first time with ways of handling the poem's complexity. *Aurora Leigh* is a novel-poem set squarely in the hubbub of Victorian English life, but it resounds with literary echoes. While annotations definitely help with the poem's more allusive and densely figurative passages, it is helpful to be aware that the poem's autobiographical (and novel-like) narrative immediately engages students. A typical undergraduate is not much younger than Aurora when the poem begins, and her alternately mournful, ecstatic and sardonic recollections of childhood loss, haphazard education, thwarted love and poetic calling resonate with many college-age readers. Moreover, the poem's *Bildungsroman* plot introduces students to various Victorian types, whose lives intersect with and energise Aurora's: the philanthropic socialist Romney Leigh, the struggling seamstress Marian Erle, the scheming aristocrat Lady Waldemar and the aesthete-painter Vincent Carrington, among others. These characters transform Aurora's monologic history into a dialogic performance full of social observation and critique that focuses sharply on two pressing problems of the 1840s: the amelioration of widespread poverty and the welfare of working women. Students taking a course on Victorian literature have a notion that the period's prose writers tackled these problems but are surprised (and frequently delighted) to see them addressed in a long poem *not* set in a remote time and place, as are Tennyson's *The Idylls of the King* and Robert Browning's *The Ring and the Book*.

Before we consider some possible course templates, there are a few basic approaches, which should prove useful in any given scenario, whether the poem is taught as a whole in a course devoted entirely to Victorian literature or only in brief highlights in longer cultural and literary surveys. The following are some helpful ground rules:

Text and context

Aurora Leigh is a rich poem that opens up to numerous important contexts. Introductory lectures on Victorian art, religion, domesticity, authorship or politics might be given before reading the poem, but it is preferable to address these contexts as they emerge from the poem itself in the process of close readings. The instructor will most likely want to be selective in the choice of contexts on which to focus. Chapter 3 of this *Guide* recommends three contexts in which students might interpret *Aurora Leigh*: aesthetic ideas, women in society, and the 'condition of England'. To gain a broad historical sense of these contexts, the chapter entitled '1848' from Blackwell's *Companion to Victorian Literature and Culture* offers a concise, yet detailed, introduction. One might also assign students this chapter, and ask them to report on one of the primary documents included in Chapter 3. See below for more commentary on using these resources.

What is the poem's purpose?

Does *Aurora Leigh* have an overarching argument, as Milton's *Paradise Lost* does ('to justify the ways of God to men')? Or does it consist of many: to justify 'writing for my better self' (Book I, line 4), to prove that 'Art is much, but love is more' (Book IX, line 656), or to claim that England has grown 'too materialistic' (Book VIII, line 630)? The best way to begin addressing these questions is to set students core questions to consider:

- Who is the narrator, and does she change over the course of the poem?
- How does she portray other characters' lives and the places in which she lives? Does the narrator pass judgement on people and places?
- Does she judge her own actions?

These sorts of questions are important because they prompt students to become active readers and dispel the notion that *Aurora Leigh* is a straightforward romance in which the heroine finds a career and a soul-mate. The quicker the students get a sense of the narrator's (and other characters') misapprehensions, omissions, exaggerations and self-corrections, the more interested they will be in the poem as a group portrait of modern individuals living in an age as complex as their own.

Annotated editions

EBB's wide learning and multiple allusions can prove an obstacle for students coming to the poem for the first time. Many students skim the text, often not stopping to check the story behind a mythological or historical allusion or Biblical reference. Assigning a good annotated edition of the poem is therefore crucial. The Norton edition edited by Margaret Reynolds remains the definitive paperback edition and the one from which this *Guide* derives the text of *Aurora Leigh*. Other annotated, single-poem editions are listed in the bibliography.

Teaching the Poem In Full

Ideally, *Aurora Leigh* would always be read in its entirety, and including it in a seminar on Victorian poetry offers a rich context for teaching it. I first read the whole poem in a graduate seminar along with the other major Victorian poets and have taught it to advanced undergraduates in a course on women's lives in the nineteenth century. I do not think it is common to teach the whole poem in either context but have found that it is not only possible but also highly enjoyable.

One way to grapple with the poem's length is to assign students the 'Aurora Leigh at a Glance' section of this *Guide*, before they begin reading the text. If one does not wish to reveal specific (and perhaps surprising) plot developments to the new reader, a more skeletal outline might work, such as the one created by Helen Cooper.*

ENGLAND		ABROAD
1	Union	9
2	Romney and Aurora	8
3	Marian's story	7
4	Marian's story / the wedding	6
5	Art	

The outline draws attention to the symmetry of events that take place in England and abroad (France and Italy), and the way in which 'Art' stands in the centre of the narrative. 'Union' refers to Romney and Aurora's relationship (friends in Book I; lovers in Book IX) and frames everything that occurs within the narrative. 'Union' provides an outer ring to the internal rings of the debates between 'Romney and Aurora'

* Cooper, p. 155.

(Books II and VIII) and 'Marian's story' (Books III–IV and VI–VII). The pattern of concentric rings is a design typical of epic poems. Ask students to think about internal symmetries created within Cooper's schema and to focus on one of them as they read *Aurora Leigh* for the first time. Specific topics include: Aurora and Romney's debates about *either* women and art *or* society and art in Books II and VIII, Romney's two marriage proposals to Marian Erle in Books III and IX, Vincent Carrington's letters in Books III and VII, and the parallels in Marian's life story (and the difference in the way her story is recounted) in Books III and IV and Books VI and VII.

When reading the poem with students, you might ask them to focus on a recurring allusion (even if it appears just twice) and report on its function. The following exercise enumerates mythological or Biblical characters but historical figures would work as well, especially Charles Fourier, Michelangelo Buonarroti or Dante Alighieri.

Tracing a mythological or Biblical character

Aurora makes numerous allusions to specific figures from classical mythology and the Bible. Students might be assigned an allusion to trace and sent to web resources, such as the *Concise Oxford Companion to Classical Literature* (available online through a library subscription) or biblegateway.com (searching the King James Version). Ask them to report on their findings once they have finished the poem, and explain how the allusion (or set of allusions) works in specific passages. Some examples: Book I, lines 155–62, is dense with figures (for example, Psyche, Lamia and the Muse) that occur in other places in the poem. Jove appears first in Book III, lines 122, and elsewhere. 'Homer's heroes' are cited in Book V, lines 146–9. Moses and Miriam first appear in Book II, lines 171–2 and elsewhere. The Virgin Mary first appears in Book I, lines 75–85 and so on. Other Biblical figures include Lazarus, Adam and Christ.

Course Syllabus Suggestion

Aurora Leigh *and Women's Lives in Print and Portraiture*
Aurora Leigh is an excellent text on which to base a course on women's lives, demonstrating the poem's relationship to poetry, fiction, memoirs and biography of the nineteenth century. Sections of *Aurora Leigh* can be used to explore various topics outlined below. The twelve-week course schedule can be used to teach undergraduate or postgraduate

students and allows two weeks for essay revision or presentations. The course begins with an introduction to *Aurora Leigh* and, in subsequent weeks, sections of the poem are assigned for closer study. Students read these excerpts in concert with a canon of writing about women's lives by other poets and prose writers.

Week 1 begins with close focus on *Aurora Leigh*, Book I, and an overview of the poem's narrative, themes and plot. Assigning the outline in Chapter 1 of this *Guide* enables students to understand the trajectory of the poem and see where the assigned excerpts appear in its overall design. Weeks 2 to 4 examine two influential models of first-person narrative (Wordsworth and Brontë). In Week 5, women's portraiture will be considered as both EBB experienced it and as her husband Robert Browning dramatised it. In Week 7 discussion focuses on the way two nineteenth-century authors (Robinson and Oliphant) describe their writing lives, especially in relation to the demands of family; and Week 8 invites students to consider the theme of the woman artist as failure (Tennyson and Jameson). Weeks 9 and 10 focus on the intersection of fiction and documentary in accounts of working-class women (Gaskell and Engels). The course ends with the American Lucy Larcom's *An Idyl of Work* (1875), a poem greatly influenced by *Aurora Leigh* and set in the mill community of Lowell, Massachusetts, and Boston.

Outline

Note: the instructor should make short selections from *Aurora Leigh* to review each week alongside the following texts:

Week 1: Introduction
    Aurora Leigh at a Glance (Chapter 1)
Weeks 2–3: *Aurora Leigh*
Week 4: The Composing 'I', Part 1
    William Wordsworth, *The Prelude* (1850), Book I, lines 1–58
Weeks 5–6: The Composing 'I', Part 2
    Charlotte Brontë, *Jane Eyre* (1847)
Week 7: Portraiture
    Frontispiece portrait of EBB, *Aurora Leigh* (1859), 4th edition
    EBB to Benjamin Robert Haydon, 1 January 1844 (excerpt)
    Robert Browning, 'My Last Duchess' (1842)
Week 8: Authorship and Domesticity
    Mary Robinson, *Memoirs* (1801) (excerpt)
    Margaret Oliphant, *Autobiography* (1899) (excerpt)

Week 9: Women and Art
    Alfred, Lord Tennyson, 'The Lady of Shalott' (1832)
    Anna Jameson, 'Thoughts on Female Artists', from *Visits and Sketches* (1834)
Weeks 10–11: Working Women in Manchester
    Elizabeth Gaskell, *Mary Barton* (1848)
    Friedrich Engels, 'Factory Hands', *The Condition of the Working Class in England* (1845), pp. 147–9
Week 12: Transatlantic Influence
    Lucy Larcom, *An Idyl of Work* (1875)

Class Activities: Portraiture

Fig. 1 *Elizabeth Barrett Browning with Flush* by Matilda Carter. 1841. Miniature. Courtesy of the Browning Settlement.

Fig. 2 Engraved Frontispiece of Elizabeth Barrett Browning by Thomas
Oldham Barlow with Dante Gabriel Rossetti. *Aurora Leigh*. 4th edn.
London: Chapman & Hall, 1859. Print.

These two portraits of EBB offer good material for a discussion of portraiture in relation to the poem, particularly its opening lines and Vincent Carrington's picture of Kate Ward described in Book VII. The miniature and the engraving portray EBB at two moments in her literary career: pre- and post-*Aurora Leigh*. EBB's correspondence with the Royal Academy painter Robert Benjamin Haydon provides context for the miniature, particularly the conflict it created between the poet and her father. The frontispiece portrait was created in response to public demand for an authorised likeness of the woman who wrote the immensely popular *Aurora Leigh*.

Students should be asked to compare the portraits, taking into account the differences in composition, media and context (the miniature was a privately owned object; the frontispiece circulated with the printed book). It may be worth noting that the Barlow engraving was based on an ambrotype, an early form of the photograph. Questions to consider: What ideas about the sitter do the two portraits convey? What does the poem say about the conventions and uses of portraits? Why should Kate Ward in Book VII, lines 571–622, wish to fashion her portrait in the image of an author?

Asking students to read 'My Last Duchess' raises the question of a portrait's audience and reception. Although the poem is set in sixteenth-century Italy, the narrator's desire to control his dead wife's image taps into Victorian anxieties about the subjugation of wives, female sexuality and the fixity of identity. Questions to consider: What happens to women's portraits in *Aurora Leigh*? Why should the narrative begin with a portrait analogy? How should one interpret the death portrait of Aurora's mother in Book I? Does Kate Ward take possession of her likeness before the male artist can?

For the instructor who may want more background on gender and portraiture, see Shearer West's *Portraiture*, pp. 145–57, and Michele Martinez's 'Elizabeth Barrett Browning and the Perils of Portraiture'.

Class Activities: The Composing 'I', Part 1 and Part 2

Part I

Ask students to reread *Aurora Leigh*, lines 1–64, and the opening 54 lines of Wordsworth's *The Prelude* (1850), keeping in mind the following questions:

- What inspires these two poets to recount their life stories?
- What is the effect of the 'Friend' (line 46) in Wordsworth's poem?
- Why does Wordsworth never mention the act of writing in his opening stanza? What is his emphasis instead? Why should Aurora mention forms of the verb 'to write' five times in the first ten lines?
- How do verb tenses work in these two passages? What kind of relationship between past and present do these poets create?
- What does Aurora's description of her mother say about the poet's mind or imagination?
- What role does nature play in both texts?

Part 2

Jane Eyre is a narrative hybrid: part romance (an English governess inherits a fortune and finds a soul-mate in a rich landowner), part spiritual autobiography (a Christian woman undergoes a series of trials that bring her to a deeper faith and transcendent vision), part social satire (the narrator targets the cruelty of those entrusted to care for orphans and the frivolity of women seeking a wealthy suitor) and part imperial gothic (Rochester's secret marriage and subjugation of Bertha Mason originates in their Jamaican plantation past). The various plots are woven tightly and carefully throughout the narrative and resolve in a conclusion satisfying to the female protagonist and often troubling to the modern reader.

In Week 3, the class might take two of these plots, analysing the first-person narrator's roles as romance heroine, spiritual pilgrim / visionary, social satirist or gothic victim. Then, in Week 4, the instructor can assign the relevant passages from *Aurora Leigh*, asking:

- How does Aurora Leigh adapt these plots? Which identity seems to matter most: being a poet, a wage-earning writer, a woman or a foreign-born orphan?
- Are Romney and Rochester unconventional protagonists? What makes them normative? What makes them unusual? Why are they both blinded?
- Would Aurora view Jane Eyre as an artist? What function does Jane's art serve in the tale?
- Are Lady Waldemar and Marian Erle satirical, spiritual or gothic characters? How are their stories resolved?

Teaching the Poem Comparatively

In a survey course on Victorian poetry, *Aurora Leigh* shares diverse and important connections with much of the period's verse. It offers a conversational blank verse counterweight to Alfred Tennyson's lyric elegy, *In Memoriam* (1850), a poem that is often taught as a whole and has been frequently anthologised. As these were the two poets competing for the crown of Poet Laureate at mid-century, EBB and Tennyson's two masterpieces make sense in the same course.

Thematically, Tennyson's elegy and EBB's novel-epic might not seem to share much. To first-time readers, Tennyson's poem appears depressive, fragmented and sceptical. In comparison, *Aurora Leigh* seems to be quite the opposite: spirited, unified and expressly faithful. Choosing a theme on which both writers comment allows the poems to speak to each other, and what both poems share is a concern about being read. Ask students to analyse *Aurora Leigh*, Book II, lines 453–85 (excerpted in Chapter 2), and then compare Aurora's sense of her poetry's purpose to that of Tennyson's speaker in the following section:

> LXXVII
> What hope is here for modern rhyme
>   To him, who turns a musing eye
>   On songs, and deeds, and lives, that lie
> Foreshortened in the tract of time?
>
> These mortal lullabies of pain   5
>   May bind a book, may line a box,
>   May serve to curl a maiden's locks;
> Or when a thousand moons shall wane
>
> A man upon a stall may find,
>   And, passing, turn the page that tells   10
>   A grief, then changed to something else
> Sung by a long-forgotten mind.
>
> But what of that? My darkened ways
>   Shall ring with music all the same;
>   To breathe my loss is more than fame,   15
> To utter love more sweet than praise.

Comparative Exercise no. 1: Poetry and its Readers

After reading these selections carefully, ask students to answer the following questions, keeping in mind that Aurora is in a rather heated debate with her suitor Romney:

1. In what context(s) do the poets imagine their poems being read? Do they see their poems as useful?
2. What does each poet imagine the purpose of his / her poem to be?
3. Do the poets care about fame?
4. Discuss the way both poets use enjambment, alliteration and (in Tennyson's case) rhyme. What do these sonic elements add to the argument that the speakers make?

In a course where EBB's long poem might be taught with other verse forms, *Aurora Leigh* also possesses elements of the Victorian period's most famous product, the dramatic monologue. The invention of the dramatic monologue is attributed to Tennyson and Robert Browning, and *Aurora Leigh* incorporates the quasi-confessional form into its narrative. Dramatic monologues typically feature a speaker whose transgressions are confessed or uttered to a real or implied listener. Marian Erle's description of her abduction and rape in Book VI, lines 1182–274, is addressed to Aurora, who sympathetically listens. Augusta Webster's 630-line 'A Castaway' (1870) offers a boldly different treatment on the fallen woman monologue (http://rpo.library. utoronto.ca/poem/2563.html). The narrative begins with a woman reading diary entries written when she was an innocent girl. Her thoughts about whether she is the same person as the diary writer resemble *Aurora Leigh*'s opening lines about using a portrait to hold together one's identity (lines 1–8). But the more pointed comparison to Marian Erle arises when the speaker, who has become a fashionable courtesan, recounts her one-time job as a governess and the birth and death of an illegitimate child (lines 343–480). Although Webster's speaker was not physically forced into being a prostitute, she reflects on the circumstances that led to her becoming one. Both Marian and the 'Castaway' narrator express feelings of alienation and corruption in 'feed[ing] men's lusts' and in different ways try to make sense of their fallen condition ('A Castaway', line 395).

Comparative Exercise no. 2: Dramatic Monologue and Fallen Women

A unit on this topic might also include Dante Gabriel Rossetti's poem *Jenny* (1870), a dramatic monologue in which a male speaker talks to and about a sleeping prostitute in his room (http://www.rossettiarchive.org). The difference in male and female perspective is quite striking, and students should be asked to consider whether Rossetti's speaker recognises his role in the fallen woman's plight. Questions for discussing these poems might include:

1. What is the tone of each poem? Does the presence or absence of an audience in the poem affect the speaker's frankness or feeling?

2. How do EBB and Webster's speakers represent their 'fall'? What figurative language do they employ to describe their condition? Does the presence or absence of Biblical allusion affect your interpretation? Does Rossetti's speaker use similar language?

3. Do EBB and Webster's speakers feel alienated from society? How do they represent being stigmatised or stereotyped? Do you detect resistance to it? Does Rossetti's speaker think he can help Jenny?

Be sure that students attend to the rhythmic patterns and sonic effects in the blank verse poems and consider Rossetti's use of rhyming couplets.

Teaching the Poem Thematically

It is not always possible to read *Aurora Leigh* in its entirety, and many instructors teaching a survey of Victorian literature often find they have only one or two lectures to devote to the poem. Victorian literature textbooks, such as the individual volumes produced in the Longman and Norton anthologies, typically organise texts (and even images) into thematic units. In the case of *Aurora Leigh*, both anthologies draw on the same excerpt from Book II, which focuses on the 'Woman Question' and factory reform. The supplemental texts, however, differ in each anthology: Norton pairs the Book II excerpt with EBB's 'The Cry of the Children' (1844) in order to offset Romney's criticism of women's poetry and sympathy. The Longman includes selections from the English parliamentary 'Blue Books' (1833, 1842) on child workers and Henry Mayhew's *London Labour and the London Poor* (1849–50).

Below are suggestions for using the materials in Chapter 3 in concert with the excerpts in Chapter 2. For selections not included in this *Guide*, please consult the Norton *Aurora Leigh* or an online version of the text.

Materials for Thematic Units Using Excerpts from *Aurora Leigh*

Below are suggestions for units in a survey class on Victorian literature. The question prompts may be used for class discussion or a student might be assigned to report on either *Aurora Leigh* or one of the other recommended texts. Other materials might also be substituted at the instructor's discretion.

Women's Education

Aurora Leigh, Book I, 384–470 (not excerpted in this *Guide*), 1030–66; Chapter 1 of this *Guide* on EBB's education; Sarah Ellis's *The Women of England* (excerpt in Chapter 3); and Charlotte Brontë's *Jane Eyre* (1847).

QUESTIONS: What is recommended that middle-class women learn in the course of their education? Why should women not be overly educated? How do Aurora and Jane handle Mrs Ellis's advice that women be dutiful, selfless and subservient?

The Misery of Milliners

(That is, needlewomen, seamstresses and dressmakers)

Aurora Leigh, Book IV, lines 1–57, on the death of Lucy Gresham (not excerpted in this *Guide*); Anna Jameson's 'The Milliners' (excerpt in Chapter 3); and Thomas Hood's 'The Song of the Shirt' (1843) (http://www.victorianweb.org/authors/hood/shirt.html)

QUESTIONS: What is the effect of rendering the voices of seamstresses in these three texts? What common complaints do all three accounts share? Do the poems have the same purpose as Jameson's review essay? Or do Hood's narrator and the narrator Aurora add something more?

The London Poor and the Language of Contagion

Aurora Leigh, Book IV, lines 553–95, on the St Giles wedding guests; Thomas Carlyle's *Latter Day Pamphlets* (excerpt in Chapter 3); and Thomas Beames's 'St. Giles', from *The Rookeries of London* (1852), pp. 19–43 (http://www.victorianlondon.org/publications5/rookeries-03.htm).

QUESTIONS: Across the three texts, compare the language used to describe London's poorest denizens. How does Beames's documentary account differ from Carlyle and EBB's representations? What is the role of Biblical allusions in these texts? What is the effect of Aurora, including the middle- and upper-class responses to the poor?

English Socialism: Ideal and Reality

Aurora Leigh, Book VIII, lines 883–940 (not excerpted in this *Guide*); Robert Owen's *New Lanark* (excerpt in Chapter 3); and 'A

French Model Republic' from *Politics for the People*, p. 12, a journal edited by Charles Kingsley (accessible online through http://books. google.com).
QUESTIONS: What do the historical documents say constitute a successful working commune (or 'phalanstery' to use Romney's term)? On what basis is success measured? What happens in Romney's version of the commune? What seems to be the source of failure? Do these lines articulate a coherent critique of a utopian community? Would Owen's model have been possible on Romney's estate?

Students should be reminded to look up all allusions in the assigned lines and to relate any allusions or figurative language to the topic at hand.

For the advanced undergraduate or postgraduate student, assignments might move beyond the printed text to consider *Aurora Leigh*'s critical history and composition process. The poem's nineteenth-century reception and critical fortunes in subsequent centuries is a rich subject of enquiry. Chapter 5 of this *Guide* lists contemporary Anglo-American reviews of *Aurora Leigh* and a select bibliography of secondary criticism. An annotated bibliography assignment might require students to compare different approaches to a single issue in the text, such as authorship, domesticity, work or education. Alternatively, in a course that emphasises literary and critical theory, the annotated bibliography assignment can be assigned after the instructor (or advanced student) has chosen a school on which to focus. Feminist critics, who in the late 1970s restored the poem to its rightful place as a major Victorian text, have adopted ideas from cultural studies, new historicism, and deconstructionist theory to interpret *Aurora Leigh*, but other approaches that explore the poem's philosophical, linguistic, and psychological dimensions should be encouraged as well. Students might be asked to think about what areas of the poem benefit from a particular approach and whether the insights work elsewhere in the text.

Instructors interested in textual criticism can direct students to selected textual notes, which are included in the Norton edition and more extensively in the Ohio University Press edition. Authorial changes expose students to the process of composition and revision, allowing them to focus on how even slight alterations can affect interpretation. Graduate or advanced undergraduate students interested in archive sources can search for the location of manuscripts in *The Browning*

Collections: A Reconstruction (Wedgestone Press) or the updated website *The Brownings: A Research Guide* (www.browningguide.org).

In most cases of teaching *Aurora Leigh,* I have found that the text both surprises and challenges new readers; a student, who never liked poetry before, finds the blank verse fun to read. Or, the poem's allusions and metaphors divide the class (as it did EBB's reviewers), some arguing that they are excessive and others essential. Or the final book creates debates about Marian's future and whether Romney and Aurora still have a social mission. The poem's troubled characters, who inhabit scenes limned with beauty and fraught with hardship, and its vibrant, aspiring verse make *Aurora Leigh* a worthwhile and remarkable teaching text.

Chapter 5

Print and Internet Resources

Annotated Editions of *Aurora Leigh*

Sandra Donaldson (ed.), *Aurora Leigh*, vol. 3, in Sandra Donaldson (ed.), *The Works of Elizabeth Barrett Browning*, 5 vols, London: Pickering & Chatto, 2010.

The most recent annotated edition of the poem. Some new notes supplement those based on the Reynolds edition.

Kerry McSweeney (ed.), *Aurora Leigh*, Oxford World's Classics, Oxford: Oxford University Press, 2008.

A good teaching text but not updated since the first edition of 1993.

Margaret Reynolds (ed.), *Aurora Leigh*, New York: W. W. Norton, 1996.

Selections in this *Guide* come from this edition. The text of the poem comes from the 1859 4th edition, which was the last EBB oversaw.

—, *Aurora Leigh*, Athens, OH: Ohio University Press, 1992.

The edition on which the Norton is based. Contains extensive textual and critical commentary and annotations. Also includes important textual variations, such as authorial changes to the draft manuscript, as well as EBB's 1859 revisions to the 1856 text.

Select Contemporary British and American Reviews of *Aurora Leigh*

'Aurora Leigh Mrs. Elizabeth Barrett Browning's New Poem', *The New York Daily Times*, 9 December 1856, p. 2.

'Aurora Leigh by Elizabeth Barrett Browning', *The Atlas*, 13 December 1856, pp. 794–5.

'Aurora Leigh', *The National Magazine*, vol. 1, part 5, March 1857, pp. 314–15.

'*Aurora Leigh*', *Dublin University Magazine*, vol. 292, April 1857, pp. 460–70.

William Edmonstone Aytoun, 'Mrs. Barrett Browning – *Aurora Leigh*', *Blackwood's Edinburgh Magazine*, vol. 81, January 1857, pp. 23–41.

Henry Fothergill Chorley, *Athenaeum*, 22 November 1856, pp. 1425–7.

George Eliot, 'Belles Lettres', *Westminster Review*, vol. 67, January 1857, pp. 306–10.

C. C. Everett, 'Poems by Elizabeth Barrett Browning', *The North American Review*, October 1857, pp. 415–41.

John Nichol, '*Aurora Leigh*', *Westminster Review*, vol. 68, October 1857, pp. 399–415.

Coventry Patmore, 'Mrs. Browning's Poems and *Aurora Leigh*', *The North British Review*, vol. 26, no. 52, February 1857, pp. 443–62.

William Caldwell Roscoe, '*Aurora Leigh*', *National Review*, vol. 4, no. 8, April 1857, pp. 239–67.

R. A. Vaughan, *British Quarterly Review*, vol. 25, January 1857, pp. 263–7.

Primary Sources

Thomas Carlyle, *On Heroes, Hero-Worship and the Heroic in History: Six Lectures*, London: James Fraser, 1841.

E. T. Cook and Alexander Wedderburn (general eds), *The Letters of John Ruskin, 1827–1869*, vol. I, from *The Works of John Ruskin*, vol. 38, London: George Allen; New York: Longmans, Green, 1909.

Letters of Percy Bysshe Shelley, with an Introductory Essay by Robert Browning, London: Edward Moxon, 1852.

Maurice Buxton Forman (ed.), *The Letters of John Keats*, 3rd edn, Oxford: Oxford University Press, 1947.

Merritt Y. Hughes (ed.), *John Milton: Complete Poems and Major Prose*, New York: Macmillan, 1957.

Anna Jameson, *Sacred and Legendary Art*, 2 vols, London: Longman, Brown, Green & Longman's, 1848.

Philip Kelley and Ronald Hudson (eds), *Diary by EBB: The Unpublished Diary of Elizabeth Barrett Barrett, 1831–32*, Athens, OH: Ohio University Press, 1969.

Frederic G. Kenyon (ed.), *The Letters of Elizabeth Barrett Browning*, 2 vols, London: Smith, Elder, 1897.

Paul Landis (ed.) with Ronald E. Freeman, *Letters of the Brownings to George Barrett*, Urbana: University of Illinois Press, 1958.

John Stuart Mill, 'The Spirit of the Age', *The Examiner*, no. 1197, 9 January 1831, pp. 20–1.

Christopher B. Ricks (ed.), *Tennyson: A Selected Edition*, Berkeley: University of California Press, 1989.

John Ruskin, 'On the Moral of Landscape', from *Modern Painters*, vol. 3, part 4, in E. T. Cook and Alexander Wedderburn (eds), *The Works of John Ruskin*, vol. 5, London: George Allen, 1904, pp. 363–70.

—, *The Letters of John Ruskin*, 2 vols, London: George Allen; New York: Longmans, Green, 1909.

Jack Stillinger (ed.), *Selected Poems and Prefaces by William Wordsworth*, Boston: Houghton Mifflin, 1965.

To Unionists. Abstracts of the Proceedings of a Special Meeting of Trades' Unions Delegates, held in London on the 13th, 14th, 15th, 17th, 18th, and 19th of February, 1834 [. . .], 1834.

Mary Wollstonecraft, *A Vindication of the Rights of Woman, Past Masters*, Intelex: Charlottesville, 2004, Web.

Select Correspondence and Manuscript Sources

Philip Kelley and Betty A. Colley (eds), *The Browning Collections: A Reconstruction with Other Memorabilia*, Winfield: Wedgestone, 1984.

Philip Kelley and Ronald Hudson (eds), *The Brownings' Correspondence*, 16 vols, Winfield: Wedgestone, 1984–.

Scott Lewis (ed.), *The Letters of Elizabeth Barrett Browning to her Sister Arabella*, 2 vols, Waco: Wedgestone, 2002.

Biographical and Critical Studies of *Aurora Leigh*

Peggy Dunn Bailey, 'Hear the Voice of the [Female] Bard': *Aurora Leigh* as a Female Romantic Epic', *Approaches to the Anglo and American Female Epic, 1621–1982*, (ed. and intro.) Bernard Schweizer, Burlington, VT: Ashgate, 2006, pp. 117–37.

R. A. Barrett, *The Barretts of Jamaica: The Family of Elizabeth Barrett Browning*, Winfield: Wedgestone; London: Athlone, 2000.

Kathleen Blake, 'Elizabeth Barrett Browning and Wordsworth: The Romantic Poet as a Woman', *Victorian Poetry*, vol. 24, no. 4, 1986, pp. 387–98.

Nathan Camp, 'The Christian Poetics of *Aurora Leigh* (With Considerable Help from Emanuel Swedenborg)', *Studies in Browning and his Circle*, vol. 26, September 2005, pp. 62–72.

Mary Wilson Carpenter, 'Blinding the Hero', *Differences: A Journal of Feminist Cultural Studies*, vol. 17, no. 3, Fall 2006, pp. 52–68.

Alison Chapman, '"All I have dreamed and more": Elizabeth Barrett Browning's Florence', *Journal of Anglo-Italian Studies*, vol. 6, 2001, pp. 127–37.

Helen Cooper, *Elizabeth Barrett Browning, Woman and Artist*, Chapel Hill: University of North Carolina Press, 1988.

Corinne Davies, 'Aurora, the Morning Star: The Female Poet, Christology, and Revelation in *Aurora Leigh*', *Studies in Browning and his Circle*, vol. 26, September 2005, pp. 54–61.

Susan Stanford Friedman, 'Gender and Genre Anxiety: Elizabeth Barrett Browning and H. D. as Epic Poets', *Tulsa Studies in Women's Literature*, vol. 5, no. 2, 1986, pp. 203–28.

Barbara Charlesworth Gelpi, 'Aurora Leigh: The Vocation of the Woman Poet', *Victorian Poetry*, vol. 19, no. 1, Spring 1981, pp. 35–88.

Sandra M. Gilbert, 'From *Patria* to *Matria*: Elizabeth Barrett Browning's Risorgimento, *PMLA*, vol. 99, March 1984, pp. 194–211.

Gregory Giles, '"The Mystic Level of All Forms": Love and Language's Capacity for Meanings in *Aurora Leigh*', *Victorians Institute Journal*, vol. 36, 2008, pp. 123–36.

Alethea Hayter, *Mrs. Browning: A Poet's Work and its Setting*, London: Faber & Faber, 1962.

Cheri Larsen Hoeckley, 'Anomalous Ownership: Copyright, Coverture, and *Aurora Leigh*, *Victorian Poetry*, vol. 36, no. 2, Summer 1998, pp. 135–61.

Christine Kenyon Jones, '"Some World's Wonder in Chapel or Crypt": Elizabeth Barrett Browning and Disability, *Nineteenth Century Studies*, vol. 16, 2002, pp. 21–35.

Cora Kaplan, Introduction, *Aurora Leigh and Other Poems*, London: Women's Press, 1977.

Daniel Karlin, 'Victorian Poetry of the City: Elizabeth Barrett Browning's *Aurora Leigh*', in Valeria Tinkler-Villani (ed.), *Babylon or New Jerusalem? Perceptions of the City in Literature*, Amsterdam: Rodopi, 2005, pp. 113–23.

Holly Laird, '*Aurora Leigh*: An Epical *Ars Poetica*', in Suzanne W. Jones (ed.), *Writing the Woman Artist: Essays on Poetics, Politics, and Portraiture*, Philadelphia: University of Pennsylvania Press, 1991, pp. 353–70.

Mary Loeffelholz, 'Mapping the Cultural Field: *Aurora Leigh* in America', in Meredith L. McGill (ed.), *The Traffic in Poems:*

Nineteenth-Century Poetry and Transatlantic Exchange, New Brunswick, NJ: Rutgers University Press, 2008, pp. 139–59.

Deborah Logan, 'The Economics of Sexuality: Elizabeth Barrett Browning and the Victorian "bad conscience"', *Women's Studies*, vol. 24, 1995, pp. 293–305.

Michele Martinez, 'Elizabeth Barrett Browning and the Perils of Portraiture', *Victorian Review*, vol. 37, no. 1, 2011, forthcoming.

—. 'Sister Arts and Artists: Elizabeth Barrett Browning's *Aurora Leigh* and the Life of Harriet Hosmer', *Forum for Modern Language Studies*, vol. 39, no. 2, April 2003, pp. 214–26.

Dorothy Mermin, *Elizabeth Barrett Browning: The Origins of a New Poetry*, Chicago: University of Chicago Press, 1989.

—, 'Genre and Gender in *Aurora Leigh*', *Victorian Newsletter*, 69, Spring 1989, pp. 7–11.

Monique R. Morgan, *Narrative Means, Lyric Ends: Temporality in the Nineteenth-Century British Long Poem*, Columbus: Ohio State University Press, 2009.

Cynthia Scheinberg, 'Elizabeth Barrett Browning's Hebraic Conversions: Feminism and Christian Typology in *Aurora Leigh*', *Victorian Literature and Culture*, vol. 22, 1994, pp. 55–72.

Marjorie Stone, 'Elizabeth Barrett Browning and Victorian Versions of Byron and Wollstonecraft: Romantic Genealogies, Self-Defining Memories and the Genesis of *Aurora Leigh*', in Andrew D. Radford and Mark Sandy (eds), *Romantic Echoes in the Victorian Era*, Aldershot: Ashgate, 2008.

—, *Elizabeth Barrett Browning*, London: Macmillan, 1995.

—, 'Genre Subversion and Gender Inversion: *The Princess* and *Aurora Leigh*', *Victorian Poetry*, vol. 25, no. 2, Summer 1987, pp. 101–27.

Marjorie Stone and Beverly Taylor (intro. and eds), *Elizabeth Barrett Browning: Selected Poems*, Peterborough, Ontario: Broadview, 2009.

Gardner B. Taplin, Introduction, Elizabeth Barrett Browning's *Aurora Leigh: A Poem*, Chicago: Academy Chicago, 1979.

Beverly Taylor, '"School-Miss Alfred" and "Materfamilias": Female Sexuality and Poetic Voice in *The Princess* and *Aurora Leigh*', in Beverly Taylor and Antony H. Harrison (eds), *Gender and Discourse in Victorian Literature and Art*, DeKalb: Northern Illinois University Press, 1992, pp. 5–29.

—, 'Elizabeth Barrett Browning and Transnationalism: People Diplomacy in "A Fair-going World"', *Victorian Review*, 33.2, Fall 2007, pp. 59–83.

Herbert F. Tucker, '*Aurora Leigh*: Epic Solutions to Novel Ends', in

Alison Booth (ed.), *Famous Last Words: Changes in Gender and Narrative Closure*, Charlottesville: University Press of Virginia, 1993.

Chris R. Vanden Bossche and Laura E. Haigwood, 'Revising *The Prelude*: *Aurora Leigh* as Laureate, *Studies in Browning and his Circle*, vol. 22, May 1999, pp. 29–42.

Susan Walsh, '"Doing the Afra Behn": Barrett Browning's Portrait of the Artist', *Victorian Poetry*, vol. 36, no. 2, Summer 1998, pp. 163–86.

Eun-Jung Yook, 'Aurora Triumphans: Portraits and the Gaze in *Aurora Leigh*', *Feminist Studies in English Literature*, vol. 12, no. 2, Winter 2004, pp. 181–208.

Secondary Sources

Robert Altick, *The Shows of London*, Cambridge: Belknap, 1978.

Amanda Anderson, *Tainted Souls and Painted Faces: The Rhetoric of Fallenness in Victorian Culture*, Ithaca: Cornell University Press, 1993.

Simon Avery and Rebecca Stott, *Elizabeth Barrett Browning*, Harlow: Longman, 2003.

Paul Barlow, 'Facing the Past and Present: The National Portrait Gallery and the Search for "Authentic" Portraiture', in Joanna Woodall (ed.), *Portraiture: Facing the Subject*, Manchester: Manchester University Press, 1997, pp. 219–38.

Terry Castle, 'Phantasmagoria, Spectral Technology and the Metaphorics of Modern Reverie', *Critical Inquiry*, vol. 15, no. 1, Autumn 1988, pp. 26–61.

Carol Christ, 'Painting the Dead: Portraiture and Necrophilia in Victorian Art and Poetry', *Death and Representation*, in Sarah Webster Goodwin and Elizabeth Bronfen (eds), Baltimore: Johns Hopkins University Press, 1993, pp. 133–51.

Deirdre David, *Intellectual Women and Victorian Patriarchy: Harriet Martineau, Elizabeth Barrett Browning, and George Eliot*, Ithaca, NY: Cornell University Press, 1987.

Joseph Farrell, 'Walcott's *Omeros*: The Classical Epic in a Postmodern World, *South Atlantic Quarterly*, vol. 96, no. 2, March 1997, pp. 243–73.

Pauline Fletcher, 'Landscape and Cityscape', in Richard Cronin, Alison Chapman and Anthony H. Harrison (eds), *A Companion to Victorian Poetry*, London: Blackwell, 2002.

Kate Flint, *The Victorians and the Visual Imagination*, Cambridge: Cambridge University Press, 2000.

Elizabeth K. Helsinger, *Ruskin and the Art of the Beholder*, Cambridge, MA: Harvard University Press, 1982.

Lloyd N. Jeffrey, 'Homeric Echoes in Byron's *Don Juan*', *South Central Bulletin*, 31, 1971, pp. 188–92.

Linda S. Kauffman, *Discourses of Desire: Gender, Genre, and Epistolary Fictions*, Ithaca: Cornell University Press, 1986.

Christopher M. Keirstead, *Victorian Poetry, Europe, and the Challenge of Cosmopolitanism*, Columbus, OH: Ohio State University Press, 2011.

Jacqueline Labbé, *Romantic Visualities: Landscape, Gender, and Romanticism*, Basingstoke: Macmillan; New York: St Martin's, 1998.

Thaïs Morgan (ed.), *Victorian Sages and Cultural Discourse: Renegotiating Gender and Power*, New Brunswick, NJ: Rutgers University Press, 1990.

Ellen Moers, *Literary Women*, New York: Oxford University Press, 1985.

David Paroissien, 'Mrs. Browning's Influence on and Contribution to *A New Spirit of the Age* (1844)', *English Language Notes*, vol. 8, 1971, pp. 274–81.

Linda H. Peterson, *Traditions of Victorian Women's Autobiography: The Poetics and Politics of Life Writing*, Charlottesville: University of Virginia Press, 1999.

Julia Miele Rodas, 'Misappropriations: Hugh Stuart Boyd and the Blindness of Elizabeth Barrett Browning', *Victorian Review*, vol. 33, no. 2, pp. 103–18.

Carol Smart, 'Disruptive Bodies and Unruly Sex: the Regulation of Reproduction and Sexuality in the Nineteenth Century', in Carol Smart (ed.), *Regulating Womanhood: Historical Essays on Marriage, Motherhood, and Sexuality*, London: Routledge, 1992, pp. 7–32.

Glennis Stephenson, 'Letitia Landon and the Victorian Improvisatrice: The Construction of L. E. L.', *Victorian Poetry*, vol. 30, no. 1, Spring 1992, pp. 1–17.

Barbara Taylor, *Eve and the New Jerusalem: Socialism and Feminism in the Nineteenth Century*, New York: Pantheon, 1983.

Herbert F. Tucker, *Epic: Britain's Heroic Muse, 1790–1910*, Oxford: Oxford University Press, 2008.

Judith Walkowitz, *Prostitution and Victorian Society: Women, Class, and the State*, Cambridge: Cambridge University Press, 1980.

Shearer West, *Portraiture*, Oxford: Oxford University Press, 2004.

Susan J. Wolfson, '"Their She Condition": Cross-Dressing and the Politics of Gender in *Don Juan*', *ELH*, vol. 54, no. 3, Fall 1987, pp. 585–617.

D. A. B. Young, 'The Illnesses of Elizabeth Barrett Browning', *British Medical Journal*, vol. 298, 18 February 1989, pp. 439–43.

Bibliographical Studies

Warner Barnes, *A Bibliography of Elizabeth Barrett Browning*, Austin: University of Texas, 1967.

Sandra Donaldson, *Elizabeth Barrett Browning: An Annotated Bibliography of the Commentary and Criticism, 1826–1990*, New York: G. K. Hall, 1993.

Philip Kelley and Betty A. Coley, *The Browning Collections: A Reconstruction with Other Memorabilia*, Waco: Armstrong Browning Library; New York: Browning Institute; London: Mansell; Winfield: Wedgestone, 1984.

William S. Peterson, *Robert and Elizabeth Barrett Browning, An Annotated Bibliography: 1951–1970*, New York: Browning Institute, 1974.

Websites

A Celebration of Women Writers (full text of *Aurora Leigh*)
http://digital.library.upenn.edu/women/barrett/aurora/aurora.html
The 1864 edition published by J. Miller. There are no annotations to this text, but it is useful for word searches.

Elizabeth Barrett Browning Archive
http://ebbarchive.org
Teaching texts and resources edited by Beverly Taylor and Marjorie Stone to supplement their *Elizabeth Barrett Browning: Selected Poems* (Broadview). Additional scholarly, critical and media resources supplement, *The Works of Elizabeth Barrett Browning* (Pickering and Chatto).

The Elizabeth Barrett Browning Project
http://www.und.edu/instruct/sdonaldson
A website under construction devoted to a group of 'substantially revised poems'.

The Brownings: A Research Guide

http://www.browningguide.org

The website is part of the Armstrong Browning Library, Baylor University, Waco, Texas.

The Browning Society

http://www.browningsociety.org/index.html

The Browning Society was formed in 1969 to provide a focus for contemporary interest in Robert and Elizabeth Barrett Browning. The Society arranges an annual programme of lectures, visits and so on, in London and elsewhere, as well as publishing the *Journal of Browning Studies*. The aims of the Society are to widen the appreciation and understanding of the poetry of the Brownings, and of other Victorian writers and poets, and to collect items of literary and biographical interest.

Victorian Poetry Network

http://web.uvic.ca/~vicpoet

Scholarly blogs, a poem of the month with commentary, events and announcements relevant to the field.

Index